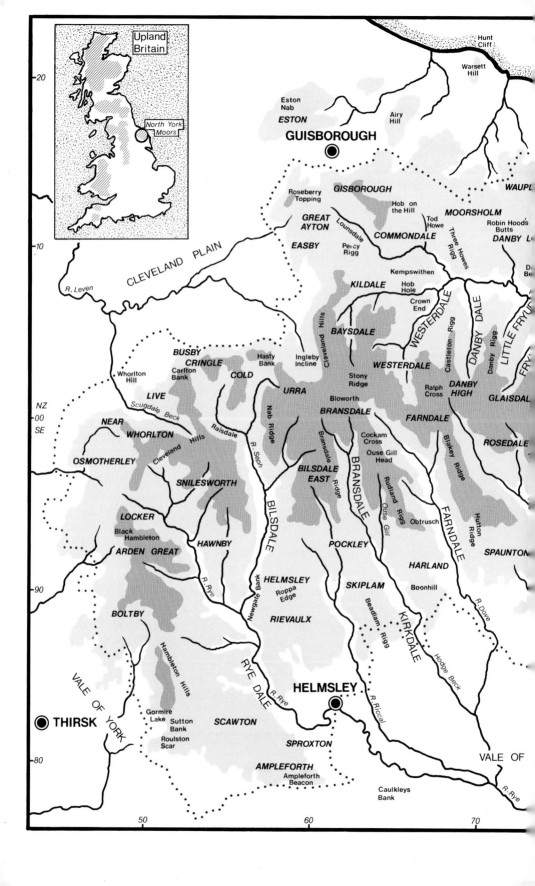

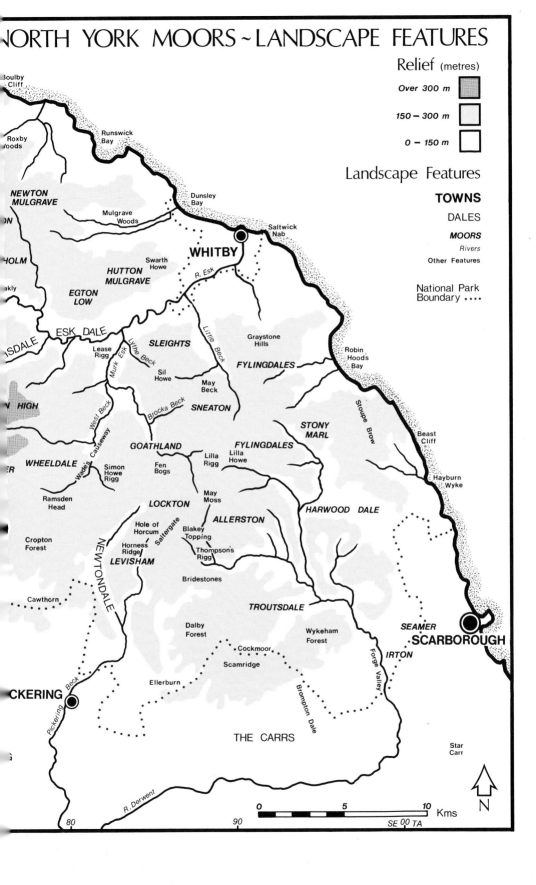

THE NORTH YORK MOORS
Landscape Heritage

THE NORTH YORK MOORS
Landscape Heritage

Edited by
D.A. Spratt & B.J.D. Harrison

Series Editor:
Allan Patmore

Illustrated by N. R. Staley

CONTRIBUTORS

M. A. Atherden
I. H. Goodall
B. J. D. Harrison
J. K. Harrison
B. R. Hartley
J. T. Lang
J. McDonnell
B. K. Roberts
I. G. Simmons
D. A. Spratt
D. C. Statham

North York Moors National Park

Acknowledgements

This book originated in discussions of the Archaeology Group of the North York Moors National Park under the chairmanship of Mike Webster. The National Park Authority has supported it generously, both financially and in provision of the services of the Cartographer (Nick Staley), the Publicity Officer (Alan Staniforth) who selected and provided photographs, and the Word Processor Operator (Mrs Lily Pickard). Several members of the Park Staff and Professor Allan Patmore (Series Editor) helped with ideas and advice. The Royal Commission on Historical Monuments in England gave support in several aspects of the work. Dr Anthony Harding, Dr Margaret Faull and Mr Colin Hempstead provided many helpful suggestions for Chapters 2, 4 and 9. All are warmly thanked for their efforts. A special word of thanks is due to John McDonnell for invaluable support to the editors.

Photographs
Front: Hawnby (*Ian Carstairs*)
Inset: Newtondale (*Alan Staniforth*)
Back: Bonfield Ghyll (*Alan Staniforth*)
Page 2: Kildale Moor (*Alan Staniforth*)

British Library Cataloguing in Publication Data
The North York Moors: landscape heritage.
1. North York Moors. (England) - History
1. Spratt, D.A. II. Harrison, B.J.D. III. North York Moors
942.8'46

First published in 1989 by David & Charles.
This edition published in 1996 by the North York Moors National Park

ISBN 0 907480 58 6

Phototypeset by ABM Typographics Limited, Hull
and printed in Great Britain
by Studio Print, Guisborough
for the North York Moors National Park
The Old Vicarage, Bondgate, Helmsley, York, YO6 5BP

CONTENTS

The aim and scope of the book   8

1 **The landscape** (M. A. Atherden, I. G. Simmons)   11
   The formation of the landscape   11
   Vegetation and use of the land   15
     The moors   16
     Woodlands   20
     Grasslands   23
     Arable fields   25
   History of the vegetation   26

2 **The prehistoric remains** (D. A. Spratt)   28
   The early hunters   29
   The long barrows   30
   The round barrows   31
   The cairnfields   33
   The Bronze Age territories   36
   The dykes   37
   The hillforts   42
   The landscape at the end of the prehistoric period   44

3 **The Romans** (B. R. Hartley)   45
   The effect of the Roman army   46
   The Romano-Britons   51
   The final years   53

4 **Anglo-Saxons and Vikings** (J. T. Lang)   55
   The Anglian settlement   55
     Place-names, archaeology and the landscape   55
     The coming of Christianity   62
   The Viking settlement   65
     Settlement and place-names   65
     Churches and sculpture   66
   People on the landscape   71

5 **The medieval landscape** (B. J. D. Harrison, B. K. Roberts)   72
   What the Domesday Book says   73
   Organising the medieval landscape   79
   The shapes of villages and hamlets   83
   The village fields   86
   The case of Snainton   88
   The moorlands   94
   Exploiting the landscape: land use after AD 1200   100
   Vaccaries and deer parks   104
   The monastic contribution   106
   Medieval churches   110

6 **After the Middle Ages: agriculture and settlement** (J. McDonnell)   113
   Enclosure of the common fields and pastures   113
   Reclaiming waste and felling woodland   119
   Agricultural improvement by landowners   121
   Settlement in and around the moors   133
   The people: landowners, workers and tourists   137

7 **Domestic buildings** (I. H. Goodall)   141
   Houses of the nobility and gentry   141
   Houses of the professional classes   147
   Farmhouses   150
   Cottages   154

8 **Landscapes of industry** (J. K. Harrison)   159
   Corn milling   159
   Mineral industries   164
      Whinstone   165
      Limestone   166
      Coal   167
      Alum   170
      Roman cement   174
      Jet   174
      Iron   175
   Conclusion   183

9 **Communications** (J. McDonnell, D. A. Spratt)   184
   Early travel   184
   Medieval and later communications   185
      Sea routes   185
      Long-distance land routes   186
      Local tracks   192

The nineteenth century roads and railways 193
The twentieth century 198

10 **Modern times** (D. C. Statham) 199
 The landscape in 1900 199
 The elements of change 201
  The use of the land 201
  People and work 207
  Visitors 210
  Modern industry and technology 215
 Controlling change 218
  Town and country planning 218
  The National Park 219
 The future 221

 Locations of old industrial sites 223

 Bibliography 226
 Index 228

THE AIM AND SCOPE
OF THE BOOK

T HE NORTH York Moors are one of the best loved landscapes in the north of England. This is partly due to their natural beauty, with the striking contrast between the Cotswold-like Tabular Hills along the southern fringe, and the wild, sweeping horizons of the moors, the delight of the streams in the dales, the light on the coast. Much of this is the work of nature, described by a famous Yorkshireman, Herbert Read – 'Mountains I have no love for; for they are accidents of nature, masses thrown up in volcanic agony. But moors and fells are moulded by gentle forces, by rain, water and wind and are human in their contours and proportions, inducing affection rather than awe.' A great deal of the character and charm of the landscape, however, is the work of man, the details of farms, fields, woods and tracks. One of John Constable's friends wrote of him 'The solitude of mountains oppressed his spirits . . . He could not be satisfied with scenery, however grand in itself, that did not abound in human associations. He required villages, churches, farmhouses and cottages.' Our book starts from this point: the look of the place, its essential features, natural and man-made, are our beginning. But then we go further, for our intention is to penetrate beyond what we now see, to explain how it came to be, to suggest what was there before, and to estimate how much is a survival from either the recent past or from long ago.

Living in an age of rapid development, we are accustomed to landscape change: fields become housing estates, a salt-marsh an oil refinery, spoil heaps from mines are reshaped and made into playing fields. Perhaps we are so used to this pace of alteration that we come to think of our times as being the only era of change, imposing its often brutal lines across a landscape which had hitherto been unchanging, almost eternal in its qualities. Yet that is not so. Almost every human community that has existed since the Ice Age has wrought some changes on its surroundings. The landscape is therefore like a parchment which has been re-used repeatedly, each successive writer only partly eliminating the work of his precursors. If we can read the different scripts we are able to interpret, though in a fragmentary way, the whole use of the parchment. Fortunately, the marks of each age on the landscape are usually quite distinctive, and one purpose of this book is to provide readers with a working knowledge of them. They can then decipher for themselves the record surviving across the moors and dales.

Indeed visitors can easily observe the outline of the whole story as they go on a day's journey through the moors. The great antiquity of man's occupation is most readily seen from the Bronze Age burial mounds, silhouetted along the skylines, dating to about 1500BC. Less obvious is the fact that the heather moorland itself is the result of the prehistoric people's removal of the ancient forest which once covered the whole terrain. The most striking evidence of the Roman occupation is the military road 'Wade's Causeway', exposed across Wheeldale Moor. The name Wade, an obscure saga-hero, dates from the dark ages; and most of the village and town names are either Saxon or Norse. The most interesting remains of these people are their crosses and memorials in the churches. The Normans likewise left splendid architecture and carvings in many village churches during the period of recovery after the Harrying of the North in 1069, the time which also saw the founding or re-founding of religious houses. The medieval period is the most spectacular of all because of the famous monasteries and castles, but it has also left much of its farming pattern imprinted on the landscape. After the fall of the monasteries, we see on the scene the later expansion of industries and towns. In the eighteenth century farms were re-organised and the characteristic stone farmhouses were built, displacing the earlier longhouses which often became cottages. The pace of change quickened in the nineteenth century with the coming of the railways and large-scale ironstone mining. In the present century, especially since 1945, the advent of motor car, tractor and electric power into the countryside has completely changed most aspects of life and work.

Thus there are three periods of great importance in forming the present landscape: the prehistoric whose remains are preserved very widely across the moors; the medieval which inherited and developed the farming methods of the Saxons and Norse; and the post-medieval which responded to the needs of the industrial age by improving its farming, expanding its mining, and providing for holiday visitors from the towns. In early times the moors were moulded by the forces of nature and by the men who lived upon them. As time passed, events outside the area mainly shaped their destiny and will doubtless do so into the future. We hope to show that an understanding of the landscape's history will both deepen our appreciation of what now exists, and help to guide its development into the future.

The area reviewed is not restricted to the formal boundaries of the National Park, for we include interesting features between the Vale of

Egton Bridge *(Tindale's)*

Pickering and the River Tees. We have been unable, however, to deal more than cursorily with the landscapes of the larger towns in the area, although these places have played important parts in the economy of the whole.

As this book will be read by holidaymakers and newcomers to North Yorkshire, as well as by established residents, the place-names quoted in the text are featured on the maps, the most commonly used on the end-plates. Most of the sites, houses and lands described in the book are private property. Visitors are urged to respect the privacy of their owners.

1
THE LANDSCAPE

THE North York Moors form a block of upland about 60km (37 miles) east–west and 35km (22 miles) north–south in the north–east corner of Yorkshire, bounded by the North Sea on the east, the Cleveland basin on the north, and the Vales of Mowbray and Pickering on the west and south. On the west and north are steep scarps about 300m (984ft) high which afford spectacular views to the distant Pennines and the Durham lowlands, and on the east the dramatic coastal scenery at Boulby includes the highest cliff in England (203m; 660ft). Only on the south do the hills slope gently to the Vale of Pickering. This clearly defined mass contains a landscape visibly different from that of the Pennines or the Yorkshire Wolds. Despite some superficial similarities, anyone who has travelled even occasionally in northern England would not mistake Farndale for one of the Pennine Dales, Egton High Moor for part of Nidderdale Moors, or the Hackness Hills for part of the Yorkshire Wolds. The fundamental reason is that they lie on a completely different geological base. The North York Moors belong entirely to the Jurassic period, composed of rocks laid down between 180 and 135 million years ago; the Pennines belong to the preceding Carboniferous and the Wolds to the subsequent Cretaceous periods.

THE FORMATION OF THE LANDSCAPE

The geological structure of the North York Moors is basically very simple and is often used as a training ground for beginners in geology (Fig 2). It consists of several layers of different rocks, laid down horizontally in varying conditions in the sea, then uplifted and tilted by earth movements toward the south. Later on, the wind and rain eroded away the upper layers, leaving flat surfaces dissected by streams and valleys. Because of the tilt, the erosion exposed the oldest rocks, bands of shales and ironstone, on the northern scarp; the middle layers form the sandstones of the moorlands; and the youngest layers, the limestones, are the Tabular Hills lying in a strip some 5–15km (3–9 miles) wide along the southern fringe. They can be seen in succession from north to south along the coastal cliffs, where the distinctive fossils such as the spiral ammonites,

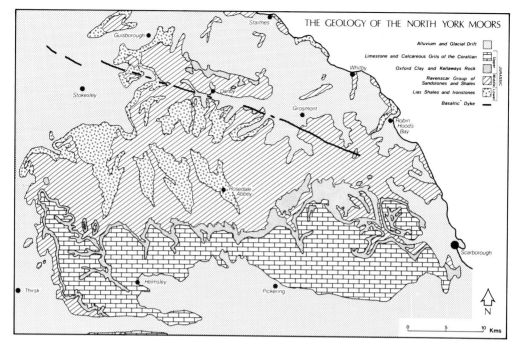

Fig 2 The rocks ultimately determine much of the scenery, vegetation, agriculture and pastoral farming, mining industry and local building materials

which feature on Whitby's town crest, can still be seen. The scenery of the coast has been created largely by marine erosion, but it has greatly altered where the alum shales and ironstones were extracted in recent centuries.

As we journey across the moors from north to south, we pass across the same succession, not as clearly displayed as on the coast, but nevertheless instantly recognisable. The main scarp on the north represents the edge of the sandstones which spread south as far as the limestone Tabular Hills. The northern scarp is steep because it is underlain by the soft shales, making it unstable. The same is true of the dales, where the rivers have cut down through the sandstone into the shales, giving steep-sided but wide and fertile valleys, whose sides are often littered with fallen sandstone blocks. Rosedale is a typical valley, where the river Seven has exposed the shales and ironstones below the sandstone. This was a major mining centre into the twentieth century, but has now reverted to farming and tourism, so that it is hard to imagine that the rural peace was ever disturbed. The sandstone terrain itself is largely covered with heather moorland, surpassingly beautiful in late summer, but dark and forbidding in winter, whence its old name of Blackamore.

Immediately south of the moorlands is a narrow belt of clay ('Oxford Clay') running along the foot of the spectacular limestone scarp which crosses the whole area from east to west. The landscape of the clay band can be distinguished easily from the moorland sandstone, for it sustains grassland. The limestone scarp rising to the south above the Oxford Clay is yet again steep and unstable, because, like the northern scarp, the hard rocks are underlain by softer layers. This scarp is one of the most important and obvious features of the National Park. Stand at Saltersgate Brow, above the Hole of Horcum, or on Rievaulx Moor above Newgate Bank. To the north lie the wide horizons of the heather moors; to the south are the Tabular Hills gently sloping down to the Vale of Pickering. Once on the Tabular Hills we are in a vastly different terrain.

This is limestone country with characteristic deep wooded dales, an upland spread of mixed arable and pastoral farms. It was cultivated since the first days of agriculture in prehistoric times (Chapter 2) and is now laid out much as it was in the reorganisation of the land around the time of the Enclosure Acts, just before 1800 (Chapter 6). The Tabular Hills are in fact alternate layers of calcareous grit and purer limestone, so they bear a rather varied pattern of forestry, pasture and agriculture, depending on their fertility. This landscape is reminiscent of the Yorkshire Wolds and the Cotswolds, and like them, the terrain lacks surface water. Most of the valleys are now dry, and the streams flow underground, to emerge in a series of springs where they meet the clays underlying the Vale of Pickering. Even if the valleys are dry today, they were clearly formed by running water in the past. To explain them, we must turn to the Ice Age, and its effects.

During the last two million years there have been numerous changes of climate and at least three periods when ice sheets spread on land. Because each of them tended to obliterate the evidence of the previous episodes, we know most about the last one. It is likely that in one of the early glaciations ice over-rode the whole of the North York Moors, smoothing off the outline of the hills and deepening the valleys, but few traces remain of this dramatic event. In the last glacial episode, ice pushed into the Esk Valley and the Vale of Pickering from the west, carrying with it pebbles of Shap granite from across the Pennines. Another ice sheet spread from Scandinavia right across the North Sea basin to reach the coast of the North York Moors. Here it pushed lobes into the Whitby and Robin Hood's Bay embayments and up the smaller coastal valleys. It also penetrated westwards into Eskdale and the Vale of Pickering.

The effects of this glaciation on the landscape were considerable. All along the coast, the ice dropped its boulder clay on top of the Jurassic rocks, and with it pebbles from Scandinavia, including attractive crystalline rocks which may be picked up on the beaches. The boulder clay is the basis of valuable farmland today but causes problems at the coast, where it is prone to slipping. As the ice sheets either retreated or melted on the spot, they deposited their load of debris to form hummocky terrain known by the aptly descriptive term of 'dead ice features'. Such features are seen well in Eskdale, and in the western part of the Vale of Pickering where they are interspersed with isolated hills formed by outcrops of the underlying clay. Between deposits of glacial debris, temporary lakes were sometimes formed: in central Eskdale the very flat valley floor provides a clue to this. In the eastern part of the Vale of Pickering, a series of small lakes formed which were not completely drained until recent times.

The ice sheets also had far-reaching effects on the rivers of the North York Moors. The central part of the area was not over-ridden by an actual ice sheet, but it would have been a tundra-like landscape, with snow accumulating and only a few arctic plants and animals able to survive. As the ice and snow melted, vast quantities of water laden with debris from the bare ground rushed down the river valleys, deepening them out of all proportion to the size of the streams which occupied them either before or after the Ice Age. With its sheer sides and great depth, Newton Dale is the most spectacular of these valleys, running from Fen Bogs near Fylingdales Moor south to Pickering. Water also flowed overland on the Tabular Hills, carving out the pattern of valleys which are dry today (as noted above) but would have been full of glacial meltwater at the end of the Ice Age. Sometimes the courses of existing streams were blocked by glacial debris, forcing them to cut new channels. These are seen today as deep wooded gorges, particularly well illustrated along part of the river Esk between Glaisdale and Sleights. The water flowing round the edge of the ice also cut channels, not related to the rivers, called 'glacial drainage channels'; conspicuous examples can be seen near Goathland, and on Fylingdales Moor. A remarkable example of a drainage diversion is afforded by the river Derwent, which used to flow out to the sea at the eastern end of the Vale of Pickering in pre-glacial times. When debris from the Scandinavian ice sheet blocked its course, it found a new route south and west across the Vale of Pickering and eventually flowed into the Ouse river system and out to the sea at the Humber.

After the Ice Age, the main alterations in the physical landscape were caused directly or indirectly by the global rise in sea level due to the melting of the ice sheets. This occurred rapidly around 7000BC, cutting the last land bridge with the continent. This was followed by erosion of the coastline, which in 8000BC stood in places several miles to the east of its present position; remnants of the submerged land can still be seen off the coast at Redcar. Moreover, the rivers then became less powerful because the drop between their headwaters and the sea decreased. As a result they deposited their loads of sand, gravel and boulders, creating relatively flat floors along the valleys, as in Bilsdale and Eskdale. The process was accelerated by human action on the moors from about 8000BC onward (Chapter 2), which destroyed some of the forest vegetation, enabling more rapid erosion to take place and eventually leaving the moors almost bare of trees. In the flat areas of the moors and dales, however, vegetation debris built up and did not rot away because the microbial decay action was stopped by stagnant acid conditions. We therefore find deep peat bogs both on the flat cols of the moors (eg Glaisdale Moor, Harwood Dale Bog) and in the dales (eg West House at Kildale, Fen Bogs and May Moss), where the peat can be more than 10m (32ft) deep. The widespread destruction of the hill forests in prehistoric times also led to a blanket of peat over much of the flat parts of the moors, which is still obvious along the hilltops traversed by the Lyke Wake Walk, a 67km (42 miles) trail from Osmotherley to Ravenscar. The soils were continually leached by the rain, which formed a layer of hard impervious iron compounds ('iron pan') in the coarse sand above the bedrock. This further accelerated the erosion of the soils and retarded regrowth of the forest.

The major features of the shape of the Moors were, it is clear, fixed during geological time by the emplacement of the rocks themselves. The events of the Ice Age, and subsequent adjustments of land, sea, rivers and climate, have all contributed to the shape of the land: a certain chiseling and chamfering, so to speak, of the main structures. But before written records exist, humans were beginning to alter the landscape, to help establish the processes of deposition in the valleys and the accumulation of peat. The results of these changes are still evident in today's scene and serve to remind us that on the Moors the man-made contribution to the landscape is very old indeed.

VEGETATION AND USE OF THE LAND

The present surface is a complicated patchwork of different vegetation types and land uses, all essentially the result of man's activities. Each element of this landscape has a story to tell and many signs of past ages are still there to be seen. The purpose of this section is to help the reader unravel some of these clues and to 'read' the record of the vegetated landscape. Much of the information for early times comes from pollen analysis, the study of fossil pollen grains preserved in the many peat deposits on the moors. From this it is possible to build a picture of how plant life first colonised the area after the Ice Age and gradually clothed the bare bones of the physical landscape with its green mantle. Much of the later history of the region has consisted of people altering the style of dress, sometimes by adding new clothes or modifying old ones, and sometimes by stripping the vegetation to leave the underlying soil bare and exposed.

The map of the present vegetation and land-use (Fig 3) summarises the situation after ten thousand years of such changes to the vegetation. Had the map been drawn eight thousand years ago, it would have shown the area covered with mixed woodland in which Scots pine was the most important tree, accompanied by birch, elm, oak, alder and hazel. A

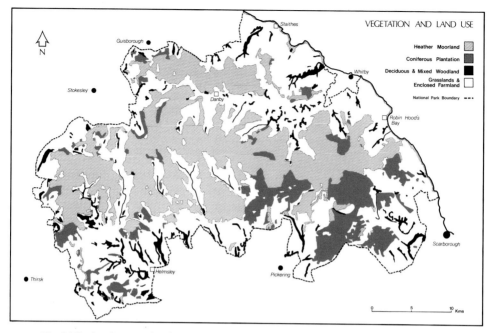

Heather Moorland
Coniferous Plantation
Deciduous & Mixed Woodland
Grasslands & Enclosed Farmland
National Park Boundary

Fig 3 The land use is clearly related to the geology as shown on Fig 2. The map refers only to the National Park *(NYMNP)*

similar map drawn six thousand years ago would have shown a different picture, in which virtually the whole area was covered in a tapestry of mixed oak forest. Two thousand years ago the map would have changed again, and parts of the woodland would have been replaced by grassland and heath on the higher ground and by cultivated fields in some of the dales and on the Tabular Hills to the south.

Sweeping though these and subsequent changes have been, they have left tell-tale signs here and there. High on the open moorland near Ousegill Head and on Bilsdale East Moor, tree trunks of oak, birch and pine may be found embedded in the peat; these are remnants of the former forest cover. Wood remains are also common in the peat at the bottom of many of the valleys. And the present structure and make-up of the moors, woods and fields themselves provide further clues to their past history and use.

The Moors

Writing about the Pennines, the poet Ted Hughes said that moors 'are a stage for the performance of heaven'; in our region this is even more true, for they occupy largely flat upland surfaces and the drama of the sky is played on and above them. They are the key element in the landscape: after all we speak of the North York *Moors*. In England, moorland is land generally above 300 metres, covered with low plants such as heather, bracken, cotton sedge, bog-moss, purple moor grass, rushes, fescues and

16

bents. Trees are by definition absent, though an occasional birch, rowan, or thorn may shelter in a valley or be found in more abundance towards the moorland fringes. The lower edge of the moorland abuts either woodland or enclosed grassland; in the latter case the boundary is often ill-defined since if the walls are not maintained and the enclosed pasture not effectively managed, then the moor begins to spill downwards.

If we look at the components of today's moorland, the predominance of heath-clad terrain is at once clear, giving the region some of its most characteristic views and colourings: wide, flat vistas of dark grey or black land which turn to purple in the late summer sun. Closer examination of a piece of heather moorland will show that there are few plants other than the heather itself: a couple of species of grass, perhaps, and some mosses where the stand is not so dense. A short walk will also establish that patches of different ages of heather may also be present: areas of low rather tender plants set in a lot of bare ground may be juxtaposed with patches of 'leggy' heather whose stalks are bent over under the weight of upper branches and leaves. Intermediate is the dense, bushy heather just below knee height which is so tiring to walk through. In many areas, the heather is the only plant to be seen. On the Moors, the heather may be growing on quite deep peat, up to 3 metres deep on the highest ridges. Outside these zones, it is characteristically found on a very shallow soil which has only a few centimetres' thickness before the rock surface is reached, or on a deeper soil whose surface layers consist of a grey sand. Beneath this, sections in road cuttings or ditches show the orange zone of the 'iron pan' where iron has been moved down the soil by acid water.

The heather plant likes wet conditions and very acid soils. The next most common moorland plant is less tolerant of both of these: it grows where the drainage is freer, the soil less acid, and there is no layer of iron pan. This plant is, of course, the bracken fern. It grows densely, perhaps up to chest height, and the fronds shade the ground, allowing the growth of only a few species of grass and moss beneath them. From core areas on rocky slopes, bracken has spread outwards in recent times at a very rapid rate for reasons that are not completely known. It is suspected that a slight warming of climate may have resulted in fewer late frosts higher on the slopes, allowing the plant to colonise grassland and heather land further up-slope, but it is also thought that some factors of moorland management may be involved. For example, the intensities of burning and grazing may affect the competition for root and air space between bracken and heather, and the reduction of cattle grazing may also have had an influence.

Where the rocks are less sandy, or where hill slope wash has created areas of relatively deep soil which are quite rich in mineral nutrients, then grasslands are found. These are commonly the Bent and Fescue types found throughout the British uplands and are especially good forage for sheep; under certain conditions they are, however, vulnerable to invasion by bracken and today are tending to diminish. (Below the moorlands are the enclosed grasslands: these are described below.) Also present in small quantities are single shrubs of birch, rowan or thorn, or possibly a cluster of these sheltering in a clough by a stream. Where a piece of moorland is no longer grazed by sheep and has not recently been burnt then a scrub of these species may develop, and we can imagine that if it were left to itself, it would become woodland in a few decades: the roads north from Hutton-le-Hole pass through some examples of this process at work.

The great sweep of the heather moors and their fringe mantles of bracken give them an air of permanence, and the Yorkshire archaeologist Frank Elgee mistakenly thought that they had formed after the Ice Age and remained thus because the climate was too severe for forest growth. But they are certainly not unchanging, for there are factors at work now bringing about alterations and we may imagine that some of these also influenced the vegetation in the past. In fact, the heather moors themselves provide a good example, for they are an essentially nineteenth century creation. Before the 1850s and 1860s, the land now occupied by the heather was indeed moorland, but areas in which a greater variety of vegetation existed: some heather, some grassland, cotton-sedge in wetter places along with bog-moss, and only a little bracken. In the mid-nineteenth century, it became popular for grouse to be shot by breech-loading guns after driving them over butts (frequently to be seen on the Moors) rather than shooting them from behind with muzzle-loaders after dogs had put the birds up. It was also discovered that grouse ate mostly heather and needed a territory in which there was very young heather suitable for the chicks to eat along with bushier heather to protect the nests. If there was more heather per unit area then there could be more grouse territories on the moor and more birds by 12 August. The achievement of this higher density came via the medium of fire: this weakened other plants, but since heather could regenerate quickly from below-ground rootstocks, it was able to oust grasses, sedges and rushes. Deep peat was drained to encourage heather at the expense of cotton-sedge. Grit was put out to aid the birds' digestion and keepers tried to eliminate any bird or mammal that might eat grouse, their chicks or their eggs. Travellers were also discouraged from leaving the main thoroughfares during the nesting and shooting seasons. In modified forms, these practices persist today (since letting the shooting of a well-stocked moor is a good source of income to the landowner) and so a crucial element of the so-called 'natural' beauty of the moors is kept up.

Grazing of animals is another economic process likely to produce change. Though only sheep are now pastured, historical evidence suggests that at various times cattle have also been grazed upon the open moorland commons. The relative numbers of sheep and cattle and the absolute numbers of both are likely to affect vegetation since they exert different pressures upon plants: sheep nibble close to the base of the stems, while cattle pull at a plant with their tongue. If tall leafy grasses are eliminated, only sheep can tackle shorter and bunchier species. Management of the moors was also attempted: shepherds would fire areas of heather or purple moor grass to get rid of dead leaves and stems and encourage an early 'bite' from the growth of, for example, cotton-sedge. When animals were housed in the winter, large quantities of bracken were cut for bedding. It has been argued that bracken spread is due largely to the cessation of this practice plus the withdrawal of cattle from the hills; cattle may sometimes eat young bracken fronds before they get poisonous and may inhibit their growth by trampling them while still tender. So given that grazing of domestic animals on open land in this region probably started in the Bronze Age (Chapter 2) and has continued without any documented interruption ever since, it is likely that the practice has had its effects upon the landscape.

Less obvious to the eye, but active nevertheless, is the process of erosion. This is a natural, continuous process in which frost and rain move soil and rock material downslope to be borne away by the rivers. But it is one which can be aided by human activity, as described earlier in this chapter. We do not know whether the 2–3 metre deep gulleys ('griffs') on Levisham Moor are entirely natural or partly man-made, but they seem to indicate that there have been a number of periods of soil erosion and deposition on the moor in historic times. We are more certain that whenever there is a fire, the bare soil loses silt, sand and mineral nutrients to the water courses (especially if the fire is soon followed by heavy rain), and some nutrients quite literally go up in smoke. Severe fires like those at the head of Rosedale and Glaisdale in 1976 reduce the moor to something resembling a desert, and under dry conditions the remnants of the soil and peat layers simply blow away. Aerial photographs show how vehicle tracks across heather moor may break through the peaty top of the soil and act as an initiating site for erosion of the 'ash-soil' layer of bleached sand. This process is analogous to the wear caused on certain footpaths (notably the Lyke Wake Walk) by thousands of walkers: erosion is an inevitable accompaniment of these recreational routes which, like the equivalent motorways for vehicles, inevitably get wider and wider.

If the vegetation and the animal communities are seen to be in a state of change even today, it is not surprising that they have changed just as much, or more so, in the past when they were a more integral part of the rural economy. As we have seen, some changes have been gradual, as when a shifting composition of plant species reflects the type, number and seasonality of grazing animals, whereas others are massive, as when a moor is enclosed and the land put to the plough or managed so as to produce improved grassland. So the soils and vegetation at any one place are the outcome of thousands of years of man-initiated processes like fire, grazing and enclosure as well as of natural features such as slope, altitude and drainage. The whole upland was covered in oak forest in about 8000BC except for some areas where bog growth had started and perhaps a few exposed hill-tops and ridges. It was the use of the forests for construction, fuel and grazing, coupled with the management of the open landscape to prevent tree regrowth (a process which started in 8000BC) which has produced the moors. They have had origins, therefore, in ways of making a living. Yet our generation has come to adopt the values put on the wild by the Romantics like Wordsworth and to want to preserve the working landscape of one era as the pleasure-ground of another. Herein may often lie the origins of the conflicts about land-use and landscape discussed in Chapter 10.

Woodlands
We must now take a closer look at the broadleaved woodlands, as these are derived from the natural vegetation of the area. The once continuous cover has been reduced to scattered remnants today, mostly on the valley sides or near the coasts. Many of them owe their survival to their inaccessibility, clinging to the steepest hillsides where the plough never reached. Some of the river diversions of the glacial period have provided deep gorges which are still wooded, such as the picturesque valley of the West Beck near Goathland and the spectacular incised meander of Crunkly Gill on the river Esk. Also wooded for most of its length is the dramatic glacial drainage channel of Newton Dale, but most of the broadleaved woodland here has been replaced by conifers in the last few decades.

Near the coast, some streams cut 'twin' valleys either side of lobes of ice projecting inland from the Scandinavian ice-sheet, and these are usually wooded. The best examples are probably the valleys either side of Ridge Lane, near Roxby, but smaller examples may be found near Ellerby, Dunsley and elsewhere. Further south along the coast, woodlands are found where the cliffs are interrupted by a structural bench or 'undercliff', as at Hayburn Wyke or the wild and remote Beast Cliff, south of Ravenscar.

Some of the broadleaved woods have survived through being deliberately preserved down the ages as sources of fuel wood and timber. This is especially true of many of the woods on the Tabular Hills, which were used by occupants of the springline villages along the northern edge of the Vale of Pickering. Some have personal names, suggesting their former ownership, such as Dawson's Wood, near Sinnington, or Garbutt Wood, near Sutton Bank. Others bear the name 'hagg', probably derived from an Old English word for an enclosure and often signifying a formerly coppiced wood. Another common name for a coppiced wood is 'spring wood', examples of which are scattered throughout the region.

20

There can be no doubt that most of the woods were extensively used in the past, as the evidence of names like 'hagg' and 'spring' is backed up by numerous documentary references, discussed further in Chapters 5 and 6. In medieval times woodland was an important resource, providing not only fuel but timbers for building houses and ships, and wood for dozens of everyday items, including fences, carts, wheels, furniture and utensils. Being heavy to transport, wood and timber were needed close to hand, and there are references from Domesday Book onwards to the woodlands which formed part of the lands of every village. Sometimes the timber belonged to the lord of the manor while the peasants had rights (all carefully laid down by law) to collect the smaller wood for specific purposes. Woe betide anyone who stole timber or wood: the court records are full of such cases and the resulting fines.

The commonest system of woodland management was that of coppice-with-standards. This ensured a steady supply of both larger timber for major constructional purposes and smaller wood for other uses. Standard trees were placed at regular intervals, so that each could develop without competition from the next and hence provide good straight timbers. Oak was the favourite standard tree but sometimes others, such as ash, were used. Between the standards, all other trees and shrubs were coppiced or cut down to near ground level every few years. The stumps would then sprout (or 'spring') again, providing a constant supply of small poles of varying diameter. Hazel was particularly good as a coppiced shrub, and was sometimes planted as such, but many other species were used as well, including any oaks which were not required as standard trees. A coppiced stool might live for a thousand years or more and the coppicing actually prolonged the tree's life and it provided a more or less unending supply of wood. Certainly the coppice-with-standards system did not run out of materials; rather, time ran out on the system, as substitutes were found for many wood products and the demand for timber declined. By the time of the Parliamentary Enclosures of the late eighteenth century, many coppices were already falling into disuse and on the North York Moors hardly any survive today under traditional management.

The signs of former coppicing are clearly visible in nearly every broad-leaved woodland in the area. Step inside any wood which has not been obviously recently planted and take a close look at the trees. Many of them will have multiple trunks arising from a common stool. These represent the last generation of coppiced poles, which grew up unchecked after the final cutting, competed with one another for light, and eventually produced perhaps three or four dominant stems. Each one of these stems may now be the size of a respectable tree trunk and the total circumference of the old coppiced stool may run to several metres. Magnificent specimens may be seen from the public footpaths through Cropton Banks Wood, north of Sinnington, but almost any other wood in the National

Park will have its own examples. Between the old coppiced stools will be seen the single-stemmed giants, which formed the old standard trees and have long since outgrown the normal size for house timbers.

Further clues about the history of the woodland may be gleaned from examining the ground flora. Under a natural broadleaved wood, plant life is severely restricted in the lower layers by the shading effect of the trees. Wild flowers occur in greatest profusion in clearings where a tree has fallen, beside streams or along the edge of the wood. However, the coppicing system allowed much more light to reach the woodland floor and each time the trees were cut back there was a sudden rush of colour as primroses, wood anemones, bluebells and the rest revelled in the unaccustomed light. As the coppice poles grew up, the shade gradually increased and wild flowers bloomed with less and less vigour until the coppice was cut again and the cycle was repeated. So formerly coppiced woodlands are likely to have a better developed and more varied ground flora than unmanaged woods. Indeed, the picture which many of us cherish from childhood of 'typical' English woods, full of primroses and bluebells, is not the picture of a natural wood but of an intensively managed one.

Some woodland flowers not only tell us about the former management of the woods but also hint at their antiquity. Most woodland ground flora are poor seed-producers and generally rely on the growth of roots and shoots to spread from one site to the next. This is one reason why the floors of many woods have large patches of single species rather than a mosaic of different ones. But it also presents the woodland flowers with a problem. At a time when much of the North York Moors was still wooded, plants could diffuse freely from one area to another, using hedgerows or strips of woodland as corridors. Once the woods became more scattered, it was very difficult for woodland plants to move out of their own particular woods. Only those species able to colonise easily by seed were able to 'escape'; the rest were effectively marooned where they were! There are many of these 'captives', which have poor powers of seed dispersal and which are therefore good indicators of sites which have been wooded for a long time. They include some of our most lovely and treasured woodland flowers, such as the early purple orchid, lily of the valley and herb Paris. Even the presence of plants such as primrose and wood sorrel probably indicates a long history of woodland on the site.

The formerly coppiced woodlands are perhaps the most beautiful, but they are not the only type of wood to survive on the North York Moors. Others, it will be noticed, have a more grassy ground flora, dominated often by the aptly named 'Yorkshire fog', or with taller undergrowth in which bracken is the main component. Both these latter types of wood are likely to have been grazed in the past, and the foraging habits of the animals resulted in the elimination of the original woodland flowers and their replacement with grasses or bracken. In fact, many of our woods were used as 'wood pasture' for domestic animals, once the young trees were tall enough not to succumb to the grazing themselves. This led to the elimination of the shrub layers and left mature trees with grasses below. Walking through such a wood, even today, is easy compared to walking through a former coppice or a natural wood, as there is hardly any obstruction. The 'feel' of old wood pasture is quite different from the 'feel' of old coppiced woodland and immediately gives away the former management system. A walk along the right of way through Birch Wood, 8 km (5 miles) south of Chop Gate in Bilsdale, is a good experience of this.

If a supply of small poles was still required, the trees could be cut at head height instead of ground level, producing 'pollards'. This was done commonly along woodland margins and for single trees outside the wood, such as those often used to mark parish boundaries. Once again, the practice has left its mark. The last generation of poles to grow up have competed to produce several trunks arising from head height, giving the old pollard a top-heavy look, with one trunk at the bottom but several higher up. There is a fine example of an old pollard on the main road at the foot of Sutton Bank but others are to be found dotted throughout the region.

The two systems, coppicing and wood pasture, were often used side by side. In several woods on the North York Moors adjacent blocks of woodland were managed differently, as at Spring Wood in Hawnby. The boundary between them is sometimes marked on the ground by a ditch and bank, on which a fence would have stood in the past to keep grazing animals out of the coppiced part. Although both methods of woodland management were at their height in the medieval period, they go back way beyond that, probably into the prehistoric period. It is most likely that Iron Age communities used coppicing to produce the wood for building houses and for charcoal to smelt iron. It is probable that wood pasture dates back even further, since in a generally forested landscape the only available pasturing for sheep and cattle would have been in the woods. From Bronze Age times or even before, domestic animals have been nibbling away at our woodland ground flora, causing modifications in the areas which remained as woodland but bringing about even more profound changes elsewhere. Without the deliberate preservation of the woods by fencing and/or pollarding, the animals would have eaten most of the young trees, thus preventing the woods from regenerating. Over the centuries, by this means, woodland turned to pasture in the form of grassland or heath, according to the nature of the soil and the intensity of the grazing pressure.

Grasslands
If our moorlands, at first sight, might be mistaken for natural vegetation, the same cannot be said of the enclosed farmland, which is obviously an

artificial part of the landscape, much of it reshaped in the eighteenth and nineteenth centuries. Even to the most casual observer, the neatly arranged fields in the dales, precisely marked out by stone walls or hedges, are attributable to the hand of man. The vegetation they contain, even where not actually planted, has been modified beyond all recognition from the original woodland cover. However, this does not mean that the wild plants have been entirely excluded. Some of the less intensive farming methods have allowed a rich flora and fauna to survive alongside the intended crop or pasture, and this partnership of man and nature has produced some of the most fascinating plant communities on the North York Moors.

The limestone grasslands of the Tabular Hills in the south of the region provide one example of a rich, interesting vegetation type produced by human activities. They would not exist at all without the continuous impact of grazing, mostly by sheep, which prevents the invasion of trees and shrubs. The grazing pressure also suppresses the growth of the coarser grasses, producing a sward in which no one species is dominant but where many co-exist to form a diverse mosaic of plants. But the richness of the vegetation is not the product of the grazing pressure alone; it is also a reflection of the soils of the Tabular Hills, developed over the limestones and calcareous grits. Sometimes the limestone grasslands are to be found on the steep upper valley sides or on the north-facing escarpment, as in the Arden–Hawnby area. Others are associated with the many old limestone quarries, whose abandoned surfaces support a thin layer of soil which gradually deepens with time.

The grasses which grow on these limestone pastures tend to be the more delicate and less invasive species, such as red fescue, sweet vernal grass and quaking grass. They are accompanied by a large number of flowers, which turn them into a carpet of many colours by mid-summer. There is the brilliant yellow of bird's-foot trefoil, the intense blue of germander speedwell, the pale pink of yarrow and the delicate purple of wild thyme. Here and there, more unusual flowers may be found such as wild columbine, bloody cranesbill and bee orchid.

The plants which thrive on the limestone grasslands all have one feature in common: they cannot withstand competition from taller vegetation. Wherever fertilisers have been used to promote a lush growth of pasture, the limestone flowers are ousted by more aggressive species, such as perennial rye-grass, clovers and docks. Once the pasture has been 'improved' for agriculture and the seed-bank has been lost, the limestone grassland community is gone for ever. So the survival of these grasslands is dependent on less intensive farming methods and their distribution shows us the areas which have escaped recent agricultural innovation. The greater the number of species found on a site, the more likely it is to have been grassland for many years, especially where rare plants are included. As with the woodlands and the moorlands, the plants have much to tell us about the past land use of the area.

To enjoy these grasslands at their best, visit them in June or July on a sunny day. The Yorkshire Wildlife Trust nature reserve at Ellerburn Bank is one such place. There are many others, such as those alongside the old road between Arden and Kepwick, from which the views are surely amongst the finest in England. It is worth reflecting that the beauty of this scenery is very largely man-made and that the view would almost certainly have been less appealing when the primeval forest covered the area: where every prospect pleases, man is not always vile.

Had this book been written forty or even twenty years earlier, a similar story of rich plant communities reflecting traditional farming methods might have been told for the hay meadows. Local people recall the colourful lowland fields of the Esk Valley and the dales in the Tabular Hills, where green-winged orchids and cowslips grew alongside frog orchid and ragged robin. They were produced by a farming system which dated back at least to the Anglo–Saxon period, in which stock were grazed on the fields in winter and early spring, after which the meadows were 'shut up' for hay until the crop was taken in June or July. Only farmyard manure was used on these fields by way of fertiliser and this allowed a great diversity of flowers to survive alongside the grasses, including the yellow rattle, meadow cranesbill and the ubiquitous butter-cups and daisies, without which no traditional hay meadow would be complete.

Practically all these meadows have disappeared over the past few decades, ploughed and reseeded with rye-grass, timothy and clover to provide the faster-maturing silage demanded by modern farming. Be-cause the crop is cut so early in the season, the traditional hay meadow flowers are unable to set seed for the following year. In any case, they would find it hard to compete with the aggressive grasses which thrive on the regular applications of nitrogenous fertiliser. Only a handful of old-fashioned hay meadows now exist on the North York Moors, invariably indicating a particularly conservative farmer making little profit from his land. As this generation of farmers dies out, it is inevitable that the last of the traditional hay meadows will go too, unless any can be saved as nature reserves. A recent survey found only four sites on the North York Moors worthy of conservation, so it may already be too late.

Arable fields
Similar processes affect most of the present-day arable land. The use of fertilisers and pesticides and ever more sophisticated machinery leaves little room for cornfield weeds or herb-rich hedge bottoms. However, if the insides of the fields are uninformative, the pattern made by their boun-daries in the landscape still holds clues to the past. Take, for instance,

the irregular pattern of small squarish fields at the southern end of Farndale or near Kilburn, derived from piecemeal enclosure of a mainly pastoral landscape. This contrasts markedly with the long narrow fields around Helmsley, Kirkbymoorside and Pickering, where the strips of the old open fields were enclosed directly, as reflected also in place-names such as 'Westfield Farm', near Hutton-le-Hole, 'Oldfield Lane', Spaunton, and 'Eastfield Lane', now part of the built-up area of Pickering. At the time of the Parliamentary Enclosures, some areas were divided up into large square fields, whose boundaries were obviously drawn with a pen and ruler (Chapter 6). Examples may be seen all along the Tabular Hills, for example at Cold Kirby and Old Byland, and in parts of Eskdale.

Not all former fields are still in use today. The North York Moors are littered with old enclosures ('intakes') high on the dalesides, as near Moor Gate north of Hawnby or in parts of Bilsdale, where the enthusiasm of one age was not sustained into harder times. Many of these old fields have now become infested with rushes or subsumed in a sea of bracken but their outlines survive as witnesses to the farming patterns of bygone ages. Perhaps most fascinating of all are the tantalising glimpses of prehistoric field systems ('cairnfields') showing up only from the air or by painstaking fieldwork after a moorland fire has cleared away the vegetation and peat overlying the foundations of the walls. Some may date from the Bronze Age, but their exact age is difficult to ascertain (Chapter 2). Many such field systems are marked on the Ordnance Survey maps, as, for example, on Locker Low Moor, on Hawnby Moor and on Danby Rigg. Slowly archaeologists are piecing together the evidence to suggest that large areas of land were divided up systematically in the late prehistoric period. The evidence is best preserved on areas which are uncultivated moorland today but other patterns may well underlie our present farmed landscape. We should heed Professor Hoskins' dictum that, in the English landscape, everything is older than we think.

HISTORY OF THE VEGETATION

As we have seen, the vegetation of the North York Moors has been altered over the centuries out of all recognition from the original forest cover, so that it is impossible to understand the present landscape without knowing something of its vegetation history. The impact of man began in the prehistoric period, the effects becoming more marked as time went on. Sometimes the changes were brought about by the deliberate felling of woodland to create fields or land for settlements, but many of them were the accidental side-effects of activities such as grazing or burning. Some were probably hardly noticed at the time, as the souring of the soil, the spread of bracken or changes in the composition of the woodland ground flora are long-term effects, often spanning more than a human lifetime.

However, although earlier generations have been responsible for widespread and fundamental modifications to the vegetation cover, the present century has seen the most dramatic changes of all. Modern practices on the enclosed farmland have been described above which have altered the character of many of the grasslands and hay meadows of the North York Moors. The moorlands have seen a continuation of rotational burning, leading in places to the ultimate run-down of the soil and vegetation, a symptom of which is soil erosion. But not all moorland has survived, since a surprisingly large proportion has been ploughed up and converted to reseeded pasture. The spread of bracken, too, is a largely twentieth century phenomenon, at least in its present proportions, and has prompted the drastic remedy of chemical spraying in recent years. Deciduous woodlands have been felled to make way for the more lucrative conifers. Evergreen plantations have spread out also across some areas of former moorland, so that a vast area in the south-east of the National Park is now dominated by softwoods, all planted since the 1920s. Other sizeable plantations occur in the northern part of the National Park near Guisborough and down the western and south-western fringes, while smaller areas may be found in Eskdale, Kirkdale, Riccaldale and elsewhere. We shall discuss these changes further in Chapter 10.

2
THE PREHISTORIC
REMAINS

W̲E have seen in the first chapter how man's activities affected the soil and vegetation of the hills, slowly destroying the natural forests. This took place even from the time of the hunting groups between about 8000 and 4500BC. As numbers of people grew after 4500BC and settled farming extended through the region, with both herding and cultivation, the effects on the landscape intensified, so that by Roman times the moors were in much their present barren condition. This is why there are so many prehistoric stone remains left on them: few people thought it worth the effort to clear them away; though from time to time they have been robbed to build walls and roads, and have sometimes been damaged by pursuits such as military training. In the more fertile areas on the Tabular Hills and in the dales, they have been quite extensively removed by farming operations throughout the historic centuries, and, more especially in the dales, covered by the soil washed down from the hills. In these areas only the major monuments survive, but the traces of those which have been ploughed away can sometimes be detected by air photography, and there are often prehistoric finds of flint and stone and even bronze.

The same people whose activities affected the ancient forests left their marks in very large monuments and earthworks which are conspicuous even today, and which in some ways reveal the same human story as the vegetation history. But to understand them we have to rid our minds of the ideas of prehistoric man which used to be taught. It was traditionally supposed that prehistoric people lived in sparse numbers, eking out their precarious lives in little settlements of round hovels surrounded by small square 'Celtic' fields. This is now known to be a caricature of the truth. By the time the Romans arrived, they were present in very large numbers, testified indeed by contemporary writers. Many scholars now believe that the population of England at this time was commensurate with that of the Domesday period. Hence the enormous effects of the prehistoric people on the vegetation, and their massive earthworks, described later in this chapter. They did not live in uncoordinated groups. They divided up and managed the whole landscape with elaborate boundaries, in a system not unlike the present township boundaries, and by the end of the prehistoric period they were organised into tribes occupying large areas. Their presence was therefore very widespread, and relics of them can be found nearly everywhere, either as surviving structures or isolated finds.

The features which they left and which survive today are mainly large earthworks built by the efforts of groups of people, which to some extent allow us to deduce the development of their social organisation. In addition, the pastoral use of the moorlands through the centuries has allowed the survival of about seventy areas of prehistoric fields ('cairnfields') which can be quite conspicuous to walkers passing near them. In this chapter we shall discuss these visible remains in chronological order. First the barrows (burial mounds) of 4500 to 1400BC which are widespread, often in prominent positions on the uplands, then the ancient fields probably dating from 1500BC onward. We then describe the dykes, long ditches and banks which run sometimes for miles across the terrain and originate from about 1000BC. They were boundary markers, and often still continue in use as township boundaries, especially on the limestone hills. They were probably a response to an increasing population which required formal divisions of the land. Finally we deal with the hillforts which usually seem to be contemporary with, or later than, the major earthworks. They indicate an even higher pressure of numbers, the inhabitants needing some form of defence of their territories. The prehistoric remains often relate to the darker aspects of life, signifying warfare and death.

THE EARLY HUNTERS

The first people who lived here after the retreat of the ice, the hunters of game, the fishers of river and sea and the gatherers of plant foods (the 'mesolithic' people), left no marks on the landscape which can be seen today. So we shall not linger over them, interesting though they are. They lived throughout the area, from the Vale of Pickering to the very top of the moors in the summer months, and on the banks of the Tees, exploiting the resources of the whole terrain. They had reached considerable numbers by the time they were gradually drawn into the settled farming lifestyle of the 'neolithic' peoples who came in from Continental Europe from about 4500BC onwards. The relics of the mesolithic people are obscure, being mainly scatters of flint tools and flakes lying on the moors below the layers of peat which formed as the forest was destroyed later in the prehistoric period. The flints only appear when the peat has been eroded, so it is not easy to find them, though the hill-walker might see them in passing across a bare moor top. The fishermen's flints by the Tees and the lowland camps, such as the famous Star Carr site just inland from Filey, have been found by those deliberately searching for flint tools in likely areas on the ploughed fields.

THE LONG BARROWS

There are rather more relics of the neolithic people, but not very many, for they generally chose to settle in the best farming areas, then as now on the lower ground around the moors, in the valleys and especially on the Tabular Hills. In these areas agriculture has often been virtually continuous ever since, so that the neolithic houses and many of their distinctive 'long barrows' (long mounds or cairns) have been destroyed by their successors. However, some dozen long barrows survive. The greatest concentration is a rather inaccessible group of three in the fields near Scamridge in Ebberston parish. The long barrow at Kepwick can be more easily seen just west of the Hambleton Street, about 300 metres north of Steeple Cross, and still shows the trenches made by a noted barrow-digger, Canon Greenwell of Durham, in the mid-nineteenth century. Perhaps the most interesting barrow to visit is the long cairn on Great Ayton Moor, excavated in the 1960s by a local team. The cairn is unusual, for it has a stone chamber (5 x 2m/16 x 6ft) which is rare in Yorkshire, and a long stone 'tail' comparable to a long barrow. The cairn continued in use in the Bronze Age when cremated human bones and pottery were buried in the adjacent stone circles. By far the most detailed investigation of a long barrow was made by Cleveland County Archaeology Section in 1979–81, at Street House Farm, Loftus, above the high coastal cliffs. It had a wooden wall at the east end of the mound with a courtyard beyond it. Beneath the long mound itself was a kerbed stone enclosure and a tomb structure of wood and stone. As at Great Ayton Moor, its use continued in the Bronze Age when a round barrow was built upon it, which for many years obscured its true nature. Unlike the Great Ayton cairn, however, nothing visible remains after the excavation.

The long barrows are, in essence, group ceremonial centres, and involved building impressive structures at which there were rituals such as feasting and commemorating the remains of the dead. There are some places, particularly the chalk downlands of southern England and some of the Scottish islands, where the distribution of long barrows near the arable land has suggested that they were built by farmers, one to each territorial group. In other words, the long barrow served as a social focus for a definite territory, and indeed their situations often in spectacular positions support this idea. So many of the barrows in north-east Yorkshire have disappeared that a definite pattern cannot be discerned in the survivors, but they do for the most part stand in prominent situations. It is therefore reasonable to think of long barrows as the signs of an emerging

Plate 1 Lilla Howe, a typical mutilated Bronze Age barrow, named after a Saxon hero; it contained a later Anglian burial and is surmounted by a medieval cross. A recent cairn is on the right *(NYMNP)*

social organisation among the prehistoric peoples, a structure wider than the simple hunting group.

THE ROUND BARROWS

The idea of territorial markers can be more fully developed with the large round barrows which are such a conspicuous feature of the area. They can be seen on the skyline nearly everywhere across the moors, some of them very obvious near the important roads, as on Three Howes Rigg, a mile north of Castleton, where the line of large barrows commands a panoramic view of the Esk valley. Many of the round barrows ('howes' or 'tumuli' on the Ordnance Survey maps) have traditional names, like Robin Hood's Butts, standing near the north end of the Danby to Waupley Moor road, Obstruch Rook above Farndale, and Hob-on-the-Hill above Commondale. The hobgoblins who are commemorated in the barrow names were believed in by the country people well into the nineteenth century. They reputedly lived in the barrows, and were said to come out at night to plague or help the farmers, according to their mood, as described in Canon Atkinson's 1891 book 'Forty Years in a Moorland Parish'.

About 200 barrows have been excavated and recorded, most of these by the rather unsophisticated digging methods of the nineteenth century. As a result many look rather mutilated, as Lilla Howe, shown in Plate 1. In his 1846 'History of Cleveland', John Walker Ord recounted a typical barrow-digging day on which he helped to dig two barrows, still to be

31

seen south of Eston Nab Hill Fort. He described the noble view across the Tees in ecstatic terms, taking the clear November morning as a sign of divine approval of the dig, and quoting Wordsworth as appropriate to the scene.

Glory beyond all glory seen
By wakening sense, or by the dreaming soul.

Of the 200 barrows, some four-fifths contained Bronze Age pottery and three-fifths had cremated human bones, but, usually, very little else. Not infrequently the barrows contain later cremations inserted into their structures as well as the early ones at their very centre. If the grave goods are an indication of the social standing of the family, then the Bronze Age people seem to be, as in most parts of England, a rather egalitarian society. Only on the Wessex chalklands do the barrows give indications of a wealthy and stratified society. Very occasionally on the North York Moors, however, we find barrows, placed at panoramic viewpoints, which contain more elaborate articles, sometimes of bronze; these barrows seem to be the memorials of high status families. There is one at Swarth Howe, standing on a conspicuous position opposite the car park 5½km (3½ miles) along the Guisborough road inland from Whitby, whence there is a magnificent view of the coastal area. The barrow named Loose Howe on the central watershed, overlooking Rosedale, only about 200m (656ft) north of the Rosedale–Ralphs Cross Road, is also in a superb position. It was excavated by Dr and Mrs Elgee in the 1930s and yielded two bronze daggers, a stone ceremonial axe, an oak coffin with a lid and an oak 'canoe'. Both these barrows are accessible by car and are well worth visiting on a clear day for their marvellous views, and for their archaeological interest. They probably signify the beginnings of a somewhat more hierarchical society in the area by about 1500BC. Many round barrows are in fact placed in conspicuous positions on the watersheds, often in long lines spaced out on the ridges (Fig 4) and are constantly in view to travellers. A complete survey of them has been made by Cleveland County Archaeology Section for the area north of the Esk Valley. It is very striking to see how they run along the watershed which forms the present Cleveland County boundary, and those of its constituent townships. This is in fact quite a common phenomenon in England, as for example along the centre of the Felixstowe peninsula in Suffolk, where there are twenty-nine barrows along the parish boundaries, and at Farway Hill in East Devon where there are twenty-five. The suspicion arises that the round barrows may have been boundary markers when they were first built, staking out as it were the ancestral lands. It is a practice known in other early societies, such as the Anglo–Saxon. Something similar is recorded in Genesis 31 v51, describing how Jacob and Laban marked the division of

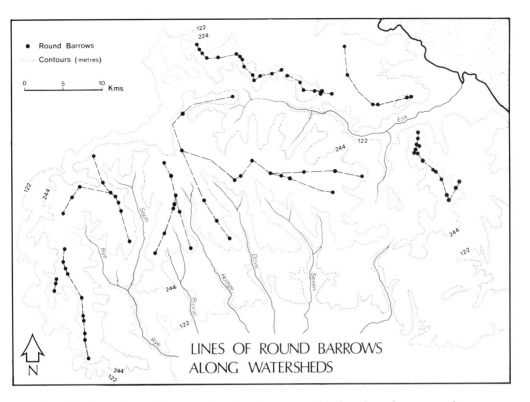

Fig 4 The lines of round barrows along the ridges are visible from long distances and probably formed land boundaries in the Bronze Age. Many are still used as township boundaries

grazing lands with a heap of stones and a stone pillar, and celebrated their agreement with a ritual meal. When we have studied the Bronze Age hill farms, we shall see further reasons for thinking of the North York Moors barrows in this way. It is clear, however, that not all the barrows were in positions suitable for boundary markers. Some for example were built in large groups as barrow cemeteries as on the Eston Hills and Ampleforth Moors, the former partly, the latter entirely, destroyed. And some round barrows were built on or near early dwelling sites, the traces of which were found when the barrows were excavated.

THE CAIRNFIELDS

The remains of the prehistoric farms are most easily seen on the spurs of land which project into the dales, particularly Upper Ryedale and Eskdale. There are also some good examples along the foot of the north scarp of the Tabular Hills, for example at Thompson's Rigg near Blakey Topping, now owned by the National Trust, and Harland Moor north of Gillamoor. There are about seventy in total on the moors: the majority

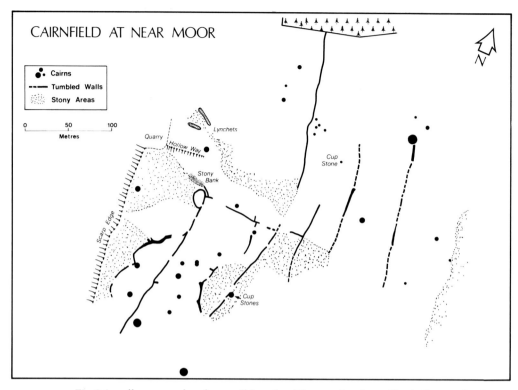

Cairns
Tumbled Walls
Stony Areas

0   50   100
Metres

Quarry
Lynchets
Hollow Way
Cup Stone
Stony Bank
Scarp Edge
Cup Stones

N

Fig 5 A well-preserved and accessible upland Bronze Age farm *(D. A. Spratt after R. Inman)*

are quite small, but some are several acres in extent and conspicuous to walkers. They consist of heaps of stone of 5m (16ft) or less in diameter, scattered in almost random formation, and are therefore called 'cairnfields'. Among the cairns are the remains of stone walls, which when mapped carefully can often be seen as the remains of ancient field boundaries. Occasionally the cairnfield is bounded by a ditch and bank, called a 'cross-ridge dyke', dividing it from the open moorland. When they are excavated, the cairns normally contain nothing but a few pieces of charcoal. Very occasionally a carved stone or a stone cist has been found, indicating a religious or burial connotation, and on a few occasions excavation of a large barrow on a cairnfield has yielded early Bronze Age pottery. The cairnfields are therefore thought to originate in the Bronze Age but some could be of later dates. They were believed by early antiquaries to have been cemeteries, and indeed Dr Elgee in his famous 'Early Man in North East Yorkshire' had elegiac thoughts among the cairns.

And at that solemn hour when night falls over Blackamore, when the darkness of heaven mingles with the darkness of earth, how often, whilst meditating among these stony tombs, do I ask what has become of the ancient moorlanders.

34

But the evidence now points to them being field clearance cairns, with funerary activity an infrequent event. Modern investigators consider that the Bronze Age was one of at least patchy soil deterioration on the moors, with the formation of infertile 'iron pan' soils as described in Chapter 1. As the fields eroded the stone had to be cleared into walls and cairns, and the cairns are often piled against large earthfast boulders. Sometimes, as on a site on Near Moor near Swainby (Fig 5), one can see some areas cleared of stone, which has been built into walls and cairns or even thrown into earlier fields. It is hard to believe that they were ever working farms, for often the terrain is so inhospitable and stony. We see them, however, at their point of failure as the early farmers abandoned them, to be followed by two or three thousand years of erosion, so that their appearance is now infertile indeed. Originally they were farms, possibly mainly pastoral, to judge from the deep tracks ('hollow-ways') which almost invariably lead up the hillsides to the cairnfields. (It is a fairly good archaeological rule to follow 'hollow-ways' on to the moor, for often they lead to these prehistoric remains.) The cairnfields also seem to have had some agricultural element to judge from the small field banks (lynchets) which are sometimes found upon them. It is a curious fact, however, that human settlements have seldom been found upon the cairnfields, just very occasionally the stone wall of a round prehistoric

Plate 2 Iron Howe prehistoric farm in its setting on a ridge. Notice the hollow-way leading into the valley *(A. L. Pacitto)*

house. Either the houses were of wood, and therefore now very difficult to find, or, as seems quite likely, the cairnfields were worked by people living in more sheltered situations in the valleys. But the answer is uncertain for, at present, no houses have yet been certainly identified as belonging to the Bronze Age in the whole area.

Nearly all cairnfields lie on grouse moors, and should only be visited out of the breeding and shooting seasons. The Near Moor cairnfield (Fig 5) is readily accessible from the car park at Sheepwash on the Osmotherley–Swainby road, and is one of the clearest and least disturbed. There is a stone enclosure for stock, and walls marking out fields kept free of stone. Much of this south-facing slope is covered by prehistoric remains, apparently of the Bronze Age, to judge from the stone carvings called 'cupstones'. Iron Howe (Plate 2) has a large number of cairns and walls, the shapes of the fields being very well preserved. There are the foundations of two circular houses, but no other indication of its date. A very marked hollow-way runs southwards from the cairnfield toward the Rye Valley. Danby Rigg has another spectacular cairnfield, situated on a spur, bounded on the south by linear banks and ditches across the neck of the spur. It contains one or two large round barrows, and six ring-cairns (rings of tumbled stone) which have yielded Bronze Age pottery during excavations. Danby Rigg also has marked hollow-ways leading to and from the cairnfield, but some recent accurate surveys even show the remnants of the early fields. Most of the cairnfields, including these three, command views of the valleys below them.

THE BRONZE AGE TERRITORIES

Thus far, two kinds of conspicuous Bronze Age remains on the moors have been described. The first are the large round barrows which were family monuments and often placed in positions where they would form suitable boundary markers for pastoral territories, and the second the cairnfields which appear to have been mainly pastoral farms. The question naturally arises whether the boundaries were those of the herdsmen who worked the cairnfield farms. Fortunately on one area of the moors, the Snilesworth and Hawnby area of Upper Ryedale, the Bronze Age remains have been extremely well preserved, and it is even possible to see them in the heads of the dales. Fig 6 shows the organisation of the Bronze Age landscape in this area, showing that the curved line of barrows around the watershed and the streams in the valleys divide the terrain into viable farms or 'estates'. Each 'estate' has a cairnfield, a stretch of grazing land on the hills, meadows in the dales or lowlands, and access to water supplies. These proposed Bronze Age estates are strikingly similar to the present-day townships and their medieval predecessors, which had similar requirements for their mixed farms. In fact where the modern

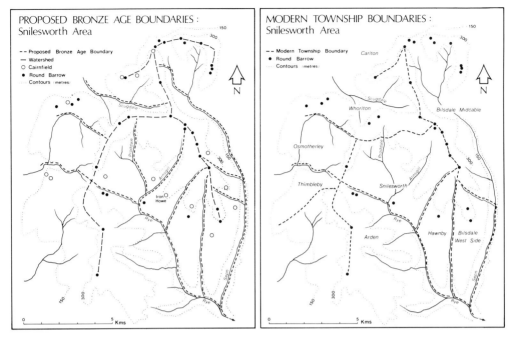

Fig 6 (Left hand map) Boundaries deduced from the positions of Bronze Age round barrows and cairnfields
(Right hand map) The present day township boundaries. Changes from the prehistoric pattern were made in medieval times *(D. A. Spratt)*

boundaries differ from the proposed prehistoric ones, it may be shown from documents that changes took place between the thirteenth and seventeenth centuries. The question arises therefore whether our township boundaries had their roots in the prehistoric period, a question which will be discussed again in the next section and in later chapters.

THE DYKES

The term dyke is used in northern England for a hedge, a stone wall, a bank or a ditch-and-bank. In North Yorkshire it usually means a ditch-and-bank, of which there are several kinds. In this chapter we describe the prehistoric dykes which are earthworks up to 10km (6 miles) long, mostly a single ditch-and-bank but sometimes a spectacular multiple dyke. They are related to the natural features of the land such as scarps and valleys, and usually survive on unploughed lands.

There are also several sorts of medieval dyke – the 'acredykes' which separated arable fields from pastures, the park dykes around the deer parks, moor dykes marking off the moorland, and wood banks surrounding woodland. They are all related to areas of land use and although some survive, many were destroyed in the past two centuries when there were

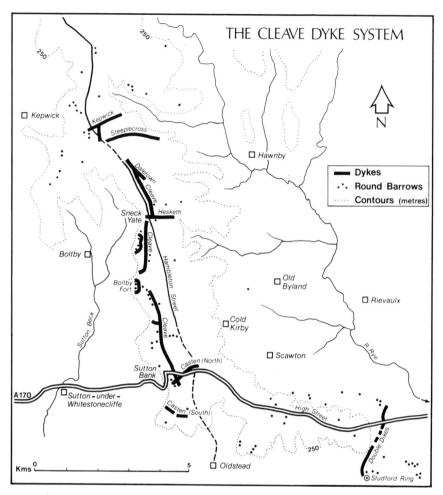

Fig 7 The dykes are prehistoric boundary marks. Many are still in use as township boundaries *(Yorkshire Archaeological Society after B. G. Drummond)*

changes in farming methods. There are also the dykes which drain the Vale of Pickering, some dating from monastic times or even before, and still in use. An example is the Friar Dyke at Wilton Carr.

The first class, the prehistoric dykes, is a very important part of the prehistoric scene, for dykes such as these are almost unknown in Continental Europe. In Britain there are larger concentrations only on the Wessex downs and the Yorkshire Wolds and these are, on the whole, not as well-preserved as ours. The Yorkshire dykes seem to date from about 1000BC onward, and always post-date the round barrows when the two are found together.

The Cleave Dyke (Fig 7) and those associated with it on the western scarp of the Hambleton Hills are the most important in respect of dating and explanation, though they are not the most extensive or spectacular.

Indeed, much of the Cleave Dyke has been ploughed out, though its associated Steeple Cross, Hesketh and Casten Dykes are major earthworks, easily accessible. Perhaps of all the dykes, these run through the most beautiful countryside, with fine views east and west across the Vales of Pickering and York.

The Cleave Dyke and its associates form a system of territorial boundaries, similar to those made by the lines of Bronze Age barrows in the Snilesworth area to the north. Together with the river valleys they outline 'estates' containing all the needs of mixed farming. There are upland grazing, arable land on the lower hills, meadows in the dales and access to the river water. These are the requirements for traditional farming at all periods, and it is perhaps no surprise that the dykes still continue in use as township boundaries. Their use is recorded in medieval times, for example Hesketh Dyke was the northern boundary of the original Byland estate (now Old Byland) in 1142. But we have no documents to show whether the dykes were used in the dark ages, though some Wessex dykes certainly were.

The main prehistoric dykes lie eastward from Newton Dale, where they form boundary lines across the Tabular Hills. Their pattern is more complex than that of the Cleave Dyke system since they lie on more irregular terrain, but it is clearly discernible owing to their excellent survival. Like the Steeple Cross, Hesketh and Casten Dykes, they mainly run from the scarp edge down to the river valleys, completing boundaries across the terrain. This arrangement is seen from the dykes on Levisham Moor, eastward through Dalby Forest, to the multiple Oxmoor, Scamridge and Cockmoor Dykes which lie in the fields above Ebberston and Snainton villages. It also extends eastward to the East Ayton–Seamer plateau. All these dykes are readily accessible to walkers, and parts of the spectacular Oxmoor, Scamridge and Cockmoor Dykes can be reached by car (Fig 8 and Plate 3). The sizes of these multiple dykes are indeed impressive, and captured the imagination of the early antiquaries, who thought that they were fortifications, probably Roman in origin. Today they are seen as boundary earthworks essentially the same as, but much larger than, the single Cleave Dyke. Sir Mortimer Wheeler studied these large dykes in 1931 and commented that 'the frontiers omitted by nature have been supplied by the handiwork of man', an opinion shared by modern archaeologists. Why then their replication and enormous size? The answer seems to be that they marked out the territories of large and powerful groups of people, a practice known also in Roman and Saxon times. However, the splendid Scamridge Dykes (Plate 3), six abreast, sweeping a huge arc from the scarp near Cockmoor to the head of Kirkdale, Ebberston, might well have originated not as a local demarcation, but as a major tribal boundary. It was only later converted to a more typical local boundary by the interposition of the Netherby Dale Dyke.

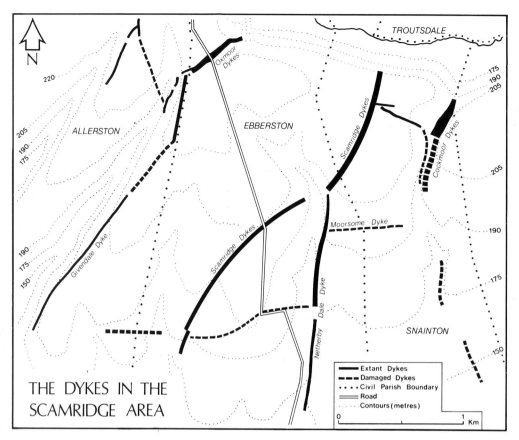

Fig 8 This is the most spectacular group of dykes surviving in Yorkshire, and perhaps in England *(D. A. Spratt after B. G. Drummond)*

When there is a huge earthwork which does not seem to make sense, in terms of equitable division of farm land, then it probably had a political significance to large numbers of people. The great Double Dykes on Sproxton Moor, apparently unconnected with the neighbouring Cleave Dyke system, is the other local example of such a political boundary. Others occur in Wessex and on the Yorkshire Wolds. The dykes seem to show the development of the organisation of prehistoric people from the more egalitarian communities denoted by the Bronze Age barrows, to larger and more highly organised groups.

There is another recognisable series of prehistoric dykes which occurs both on the Tabular Hills and on the moors. These are the 'cross-ridge dykes', which run across the necks of spurs between the valleys, subdividing the terrain into even smaller areas. They can be seen clearly on Levisham and Lockton moors, and on the hills above Harwood Dale. There are also several on the sandstone moorlands, particularly at the cairnfield sites such as Danby Rigg in Eskdale. Where they have been

40

Plate 3 Scamridge Dykes run in a great arc from the scarp above Troutsdale into Kirkdale at Ebberston *(Cambridge University Collection: copyright reserved)*

dated, as at Levisham and Horness Ridge, they appear to originate in the late Iron Age or Roman periods, though they are not necessarily all of the same period. Recent Carbon-14 dates at Danby Rigg suggest that the dyke was in use in the Dark Ages.

To summarise, there are two main series of prehistoric dykes, as well as the large tribal boundary earthworks. The major dykes, of about 1000BC onward, run off the scarps toward the valleys, defining farming 'estates', and the cross-ridge dykes probably built later to sub-divide the 'estates' into smaller areas. Many continue in use as township boundaries and were recorded as such in medieval documents. Little is known of what happened in the Dark Ages, though the Green Dyke near Ravenscar is thought to be the southern boundary of St Hilda's Whitby Abbey land. The later medieval dykes and their purposes can be identified by their positions in the landscape, particularly with the help of the first edition Ordnance Survey maps of 1854. A good example is the Meredyke at Middleton (Fig 27). All the dykes signify population pressures on the land, and the consequent necessity of marking boundaries.

THE HILLFORTS

Prehistoric hillforts are recognisable by their large earthen ramparts which enclose, or partly enclose, defensive hill-top sites, with the ditch invariably outside the rampart wall. They occur in very large numbers in the south of England and in Scotland and the borders, but are more rare in Yorkshire. There are few on the Yorkshire Wolds or on the eastern end of the Tabular Hills. Oliver's Mount overlooking Scarborough may have been a promontory fort, but this is uncertain as its rampart is now destroyed. The Thieves Dyke on the crest of the limestone scarp above Silpho has very large dykes still well preserved and accessible. They are in a defensive configuration and could have been an effective fort. There are four hillforts of various sizes, strategically placed at intervals around the northern and western edge of the hills. The most rewarding to visit is on the crest of Eston Nab (Plate 4), an impressive D-shaped rampart some 400m (1312ft) long surrounding the modern Nab Tower. It is a stiff climb up the hill-face from Eston village, but at the top one is rewarded by the splendid view which enchanted the 1840 barrow diggers, though it has now lost a little of its charm. The fort started life as a small palisade in the late Bronze Age about 1000BC; the rampart was built later with its ditch cut deeply into the rock, some time in the Iron Age, and evidently was abandoned when the Romans arrived. None of the three excavations of this century has discovered substantial settlement within it, and the large population needed to build and maintain the fort must have lived within a radius of about 20–30km (12–18 miles).

One can still see very clearly some of the settlements of these Iron Age people in Cleveland, particularly by visiting the circular stone house foundations adjacent to the road which runs along Percy Rigg from Kildale to Guisborough. On nearby Great Ayton Moor is a square pastoral enclosure with a bank and internal ditch, which also belongs to the Iron Age. These two sites can be visited on an afternoon's walk in one of the most interesting prehistoric areas close to Teesside. A site at Crown End, Westerdale also has a stone enclosure which appears to be of Iron Age date; both here and on Great Ayton Moor the Iron Age pastoral enclosures seem to be the successors to the Bronze Age cairnfields.

The small fort at Live Moor above Swainby was noticed only a few years ago, in spite of the fact that the Lyke Wake Walk cuts through the

Plate 4 Eston Nab Iron Age Hillfort surveys the River Tees to the north and the Cleveland Hills to the south. It fell into disuse before the Roman period (*Cambridge University Collection: copyright reserved*)

eastern end of the rampart! It also has no obvious traces of settlement, but it has not been excavated and its date is not known. It is worth a visit, because one can see an old trackway connecting the fort entrance to the Live Moor cairnfield at the top of the scarp, indicating a likely Bronze Age date. As all hill forts, it commands magnificent views. The Boltby Hill fort, at the gap in the Cleave Dyke at Boltby Nab, has a sad history (Fig 7). It was, until 1961, a small D-shaped fort with two barrows within it. In that year the farmer destroyed it to cultivate the scrap of land on which it stood. Fortunately there had been an excavation in 1938 which revealed some early Bronze Age gold earrings of about 2200BC and a pottery rim of about 1000BC beneath the rampart. So, as with Eston Nab and Live Moor, there is probably a Bronze Age origin at Boltby. It is well worth the walk from Sneck Yat southward down the Cleveland Way for the splendour of the views, and there is still a fragment of the rampart on the scarp top alongside the path.

There was more reason for the destruction of the rampart of the Roulston Scar Hillfort, for it lay across the long landing strip of the Yorkshire Gliding Club. It was studied by archaeologists during its removal in 1969 and shown to be a timber-reinforced rampart of a type in vogue about 500BC. It enclosed the much greater area of 20 hectares (50 acres) of the Roulston Scar. One can still see today the ends of the rampart from the Cleveland Way on the west and the road to the clubhouse on the east; a faint trace of the rampart can also just be discerned across the glider strip near the clubhouse.

An earthwork which is sometimes mistaken for a fort on account of its large bank and prominent position is the enclosure called Studfold Ring on Sproxton Moor, a few hundred metres east of the Double Dykes. It is not a fort, because the ditch lies within the bank similar to the smaller enclosure at Great Ayton Moor. Studfold Ring, however, has not been dated by excavation.

THE LANDSCAPE AT THE END OF THE PREHISTORIC PERIOD

Until about 4500BC the prehistoric people had lived a life entirely reliant on hunting, fishing and gathering plant food, making some little effect on the forest which almost completely covered the landscape. From that time onward they became steadily more dependent on cultivation of crops and herding of animals. By 71AD, when the Romans arrived, the native people had a mixed farming economy with sophisticated ancillary skills in wood and metal working, a basic lifestyle which continued until the nineteenth century. They had developed from hunting bands to highly organised major tribes. In the course of their evolution, however, they had over-exploited the hills by herding, so that the young trees did not survive and the moors had largely degenerated to much their present condition by the Roman period, leaving the relics of their despoilers. The Tabular Hills, however, and especially the limestone areas, could be maintained as good farm land indefinitely, for their fertility can be restored by fallowing. The Romans must have found prosperous farms and settlements along them, using for land boundaries the dykes which still dominate parts of the landscape. There are enough prehistoric objects from the dales to show that they too were inhabited, and in a few parts at least they were laid out in fields, not dissimilar from the present pattern. The Iron Age people had spread on to the boulder clay terrain of Cleveland and the Vales of Mowbray and York, which they could cultivate in areas where there was adequate natural drainage. In the western end of the Vale of Pickering probably every small hill had a thriving farm and there was even some settlement in the less well-drained central and eastern parts. The general state of the present landscape had been formed by the prehistoric people: their successors had, for better or worse, to cope with the consequences.

3
THE ROMANS

INTRODUCTION

IN most areas of our country clear traces of the results of the Roman occupation may be seen on or above ground. Often these traces may be very obvious, as for instance with the defensive walls around fortresses such as York, or towns like Colchester or Verulamium. Sometimes it is only possible to see the eroded banks and nearly-filled ditches which mark the sites of forts or towns, or possibly the romanised farms usually known as villas. The lines of Roman roads, too, are often traceable, either because the roads went out of use after Roman times and still show as slightly raised ridges, often coinciding with parish boundaries, or because modern roads have been built on them and reflect their straight alignments.

However, there were other areas of Britain where Rome's impact was diluted for one reason or another and few obvious traces are to be seen in the present landscape. Just as the nineteenth century railway system tends to radiate from London, so did the Roman network of roads. In the North two roads aimed for Scotland, using relatively easy eastern and western routes on each side of the Pennines. There were also a few major links between the two main routes, as well as some spurs to the east and west of them, aiming for the coasts. However, those places lying east of the eastern route were usually even more cut off from the life of the Roman province than those same areas were in Victorian England. An inevitable result was a considerable lessening of Rome's influence. The other parts of Roman Britain where romanisation was much diluted were the uplands of the Highland Zone, particularly in the North, in North Wales and in the Devon–Cornwall peninsula. Since the Moors of north–east Yorkshire also fall in that category, it is inevitable that the general level of romanisation was low, and that no towns or romanised farms developed, except on the very fringes. Usually any particular region of Roman Britain first went through a phase of military occupation, followed by the removal of army units, if the area was judged capable of self-government, and if there was a need for troops elsewhere. Our area undoubtedly followed that pattern though, as we shall see, the raids on the coasts which were becoming a

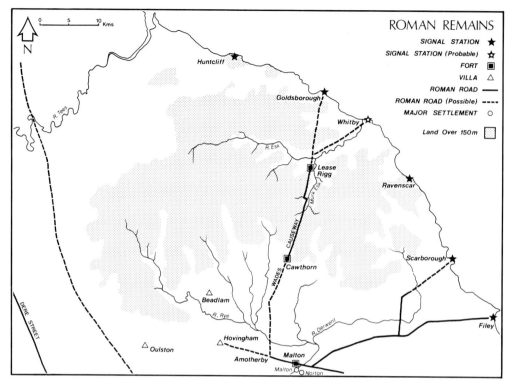

Fig 9 This was not an area of major Roman activity. The forts and roads were made at the beginning of the occupation, the villas and signal stations toward the end.

major worry in the later Roman period led to the need for army units to return. In the military phase the roads were constructed to aid rapid communication, as well as the transport of military supplies. Gradually the civilian use of the roads grew, especially with the increase in long-range trade which was a notable aspect of the life of the Roman province. But the ordinary Romano–Briton would not be slow to take advantage of the new roads in his own daily transactions, and of course he would continue to do so long after the initial purpose of the roads had been forgotten.

THE EFFECT OF THE ROMAN ARMY

Much of East Yorkshire was taken over by the Roman army during the campaigns in the early 70s of the first century AD which resulted in the crushing of the anti-Roman faction of the Brigantes, the main tribe of northern Britain. The fortress at York was then built to house the 9th Legion, or perhaps only part of it initially. Roman troops first appeared in the Vale of Pickering at this time, as some of the finds from Malton show. We know little about the earliest fort there, though it was probably bigger than the slightly later one, whose ramparts are still visible as grassy

46

slopes on the eastern outskirts of the town south of the road to Old Malton. Soon exploratory expeditions would be probing north and east, testing both the nature of the country and the reactions of its inhabitants to Rome. We have no evidence that any opposition was encountered, and it is quite likely that no further action was taken by the army, which would have been preoccupied at the time with the main struggle against the Brigantes further north. In all probability, as so often with later armies, the intelligence reports on the reconnaissances would be filed 'pending further action'. Meanwhile a programme of road works would be started to link Malton with York and with the south, and it is likely that a route to the west giving a link with the main road north would also have been built (Fig 9). All these roads are reasonably attested by indirect evidence. For that rarity, a Roman road which is visible today, we have to turn to the north and the occupation of the Moors.

A decision was probably taken in the middle or late 80s to advance forts to the Moors area, perhaps for no better reason than that troops had to be stationed somewhere after the evacuation of much of Scotland. The recent work at the site at High Burrows on Lease Rigg, south-west of Whitby, and lying between the Esk and Murk Esk, has shown that it was a permanent fort of the first century. That now makes sense of the road known as Wade's Causeway (Plate 5) on Wheeldale Moor which falls into

Plate 5 This is the foundation of the Roman Road at Wheeldale Moor, not its finished surface *(North Yorkshire County Library)*

place as part of the initial army system. It is one of the very few Roman roads in the country which is exposed to view, and so is well worth seeing, though the visitor needs to know that what is uncovered is the foundation of the road, and not its surface. While Roman roads would be exceedingly uncomfortable to use in the springless carriages and carts available, they would never be quite as bumpy as the Wheeldale remains might suggest!

The road may not have been linked direct to Malton, but rather, as Fig 9 suggests, have left the Malton–Hovingham road at Amotherby, even though no certain trace now survives. Its line only becomes certain at Cawthorn. There, Thomas Strangways Robinson, a notable eccentric of the early eighteenth century, lord of the manor of Cropton and many other manors in the Pickering area, caused the well-known camps to be surveyed, and the line of the road on the Moors to be traced by a servant mounted on a horse. There was no difficulty across Wheeldale Moor but the descent to the Esk caused problems, and north of the Esk no certain traces were recorded, though Robinson thought that the road was aiming for Dunsley Bay. His view may not be out of the question, particularly as there is the hint of some occupation at Goldsborough before the building of the fourth century signal station. The same problem persists today: there are a few traces of what could be the continuation of the road beyond Lease Rigg to Goldsborough, but there is nothing absolutely certain as yet. Similarly, the possible route down the Esk valley to Whitby has produced remarkably little that may be regarded as its trace, though Whitby has evidence of early Roman occupation. The probability is that both routes were used. Whether other such roads crossed the northern parts of our area is unknown; there would be considerably larger numbers of native tracks in use but they are impossible to pin down (see Chapter 9).

So much for the roads, but what of the army sites they were built to serve? Until recently there was only one hint of military building activity north of Malton, namely at Cawthorn, but the excellent survey of Wade's Causeway published by Rutter and Hayes in 1964 focused attention once more on an earthwork recorded in the last century. It is still visible to the keen eye on the crest of Lease Rigg, where it is cut by the road to the ford at Grosmont. At the time of the survey it was thought that it might possibly be a temporary camp, like those at Cawthorn, but the recent excavations showed that it was a permanent fort, defended by a turf rampart and with timber internal buildings, as was normal in the first century in this country (Fig 10). The fort was unusually long and narrow, because it was designed to fit neatly the space available on the narrow ridge on which it was built, to take the greatest advantage of the position and allow clear views towards the coast at Whitby. As is shown by the presence of a central headquarters building or principia (Fig 10, A), the administrative staff of the unit was stationed there, and it is highly likely that the building behind it (B) was the commander's house or praetorium.

48

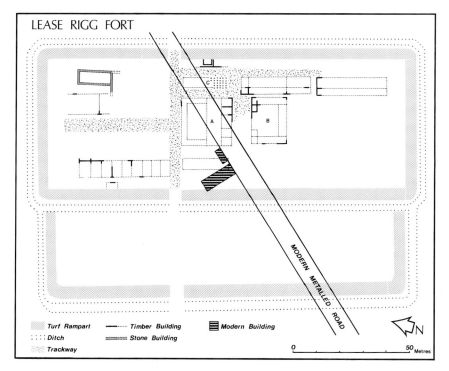

LEASE RIGG FORT

Turf Rampart	Timber Building	Modern Building
Ditch	Stone Building	
Trackway		

MODERN METALLED ROAD

0 ———————————— 50 Metres

N

Fig 10 Lease Rigg fort is discernible on both sides of the road east of High Burrows Farm *(after B. R. Hartley)*

Only one small granary was located (C), though there would have been room for another one on the opposite side of the principia. Even so, the provision would have been inadequate for a full auxiliary unit and particularly for one with some mounted troops which seems the likely kind to judge from several hints. In fact the interior of the fort was scarcely large enough for even the smallest size of infantry unit some 500 strong, and it seems clear that parts of the fort, such as the south-west corner, were never used for buildings.

The stationing of part of a unit at Lease Rigg would imply another part or parts elsewhere, and inevitably Whitby or Goldsborough, or both of them, are among the most likely candidates. But only future work can settle the question. More pressing is the problem of the relationship of Lease Rigg to Cawthorn, and of the nature of the latter. The earthworks there have long been regarded as special, in that the excavations done in the 1920s presented us with a classic picture of the Roman army building practice works during two training exercises.

The earthworks at Cawthorn, which can now be seen much more easily than in their former badly overgrown state, are among the best examples of Roman military construction south of Hadrian's Wall. But they still hold problems. If we assume that all are practice works, we have to face

49

the fact that the fort at Lease Rigg would be further away from the nearest fort at Malton than the conventional day's march. In fact it would be almost twice that distance. However, one of the works at Cawthorn (D on Plate 6) is very different from the others and it looks like a fort rather than a camp. Presumably, it could have been a practice fort, and there is the curious fact that it follows closely the plan used for Claudian forts of the invasion period in Britain. It is almost as if the officer who ordered its construction had gone into the filing room in the headquarters at York, pulled out a plan from one of the dead files and said 'There you are, go and build that'.

What are we to make of the evidence? As so often with archaeology, more than one interpretation is possible. Perhaps the traditional story is right and troops from York first constructed Camp C (Plate 6) as their base for the more leisurely building of Camp A. Then in the course of a second exercise, they enlarged A to the east and set about building the more elaborate and fort-like D. However, as has already been said, the position of Lease Rigg surely requires a fort intermediate between it and Malton. Cawthorn is the obvious site, and it may be suggested that D was the fort, whether its builders lived in A in its enlarged version or not.

On balance the second alternative seems more probable, but clearly the

Plate 6 Cawthorn Roman Camps are thought to have been army practice camps. But it may be that camp D was a more permanent fort. 1945 photograph (*Cambridge University Collection: copyright reserved*)

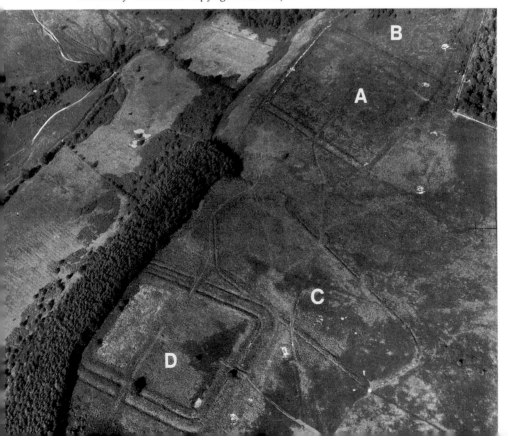

spade will have to be the final arbiter. At least one fact is sure: neither Cawthorn nor Lease Rigg has produced finds later than the early second century. Lease Rigg was certainly not held much after AD120, and it is almost certain that the troops were removed when Hadrian was building his frontier wall in the 120s. Garrisons over much of eastern Brigantia were then removed and many went from the Pennine forts, too. Hadrian evidently felt that many of the Brigantes were now on the way to becoming good Romans who could do without close supervision.

THE ROMANO–BRITONS

The Brigantian town at Aldborough began to grow at this time, and the countryside in general must have been pacific. Around the fringes of the Moors the peasant farmers would have continued to exist in much the same way as their pre-Roman grandfathers, and they would not have been a cause for military anxiety. What traces have their activities left in the present landscape? Here and there on the Tabular Hills there are some small square earthworks which presumably enclosed farmsteads and it seems likely that they were added in the Roman period. They may well have been associated with the field systems which aerial photography has been adding to the record for the areas around Cawthorn, Kirkbymoorside and Snainton, but neither the new enclosures nor the fields have left any major legacy. Still less the field systems in the flat carrs of the Vale of Pickering, for they may be seen from the air only under good conditions. However, here and there, the Vale did also develop romanised farms of the kind for which we generally use the Latin term villa, that is to say a farming estate equipped with at least some romanised buildings. We expect them to have houses in Roman architectural style with rooms set aside for particular purposes, some floored with mosaics and, or, under-floor heating. The implications of such sites are clearly that the owners thought of themselves as Roman, and while no doubt some were incomers, it seems from all the evidence which has accumulated over the last few decades from excavations, that most such owners were natives of Britain, probably descendants of the Iron Age tribal notables. The site at Beadlam is a villa which probably developed from an unromanised farm, but by the third century it had been given some quite elaborate buildings, including two houses, one of which was a conversion of a former barn – a process not confined to the twentieth century. At Hovingham and Oulston were similar, though more elaborate, sites. In addition some other villas, not as yet published, have been photographed from the air, and there is some, less conclusive, evidence for yet more nearby. This area, then, was gentleman farmer's land, which is not surprising in view of the good soils.

In contrast, the Cleveland Plain has much the same record as the Tabular Hills. The discovery of a villa there would not be astonishing, though recent meticulous fieldwork by Roger Inman has yet to produce one, and the native farmsteads obviously predominated there, as in the dales further south. These were not grouped in villages, but scattered across Cleveland, each farm having about 25 ha (62 acres) of land.

None of the farming we have been considering had any contemporary impact on the Moors proper, where low level pastoralism would have been the rule just as it is today. Except near Wade's Causeway there are few Roman finds from the moorlands. Very few visible traces are left elsewhere, apart from the excavated houses at Beadlam. The Department of the Environment once intended to consolidate the site and open it to the public, but unfortunately the idea seems to have been dropped.

However, there were certainly activities other than farming being carried out in the Roman period which at the time have left some considerable traces. The natural resources were not neglected, and the mining, and smelting, of iron ore is likely to have been common. Slag has been found at many of the Cleveland sites and the ores of the Esk valley are likely to have been worked, too. But mines of the Roman era have usually been obliterated by later intensive workings and that no doubt applies in our area. The winning of jet from the coastal cliffs of the Whitby region must have been a major enterprise and will have left its scars, though not ones comparable to the later working of the alum shales. Some of the jet was certainly worked locally, but it was also exported to other places, notably York, for working into more elaborate articles than the locals were making. It was in demand not merely as a decorative material, but because it was regarded as having semi-magical properties (not unconnected with static electricity). We need to visualise trains of mules with panniers making use of Wade's Causeway as they ambled to York with their raw material. The same route is likely to have been used in another even more important trade, which usually only leaves its trace at the consumer's end, namely the supply of fish, especially the shell-fish which were in constant and enormous demand in the Roman province. But by no means all the exports from the region would go to York. In the south of Britain, market towns were common: they were less so in the north, and their functions were often performed by the civil settlements outside the forts. Malton would have served the southern part of the region and Piercebridge was its equivalent for the northern moors and Cleveland. There the primary products, such as animals, grain, vegetables, wool, hides and minerals, could have been sold, and many manufactured goods bought. At Malton the vicus, as such settlements were called, grew greatly in the late second and third centuries and had an extension on the other side of the Derwent at Norton, where there was even a goldsmith's shop. There, also, were some of the kilns which supplied the area of the Moors with pots, though others working in more rustic traditions were active in Cleveland, as Roger Inman has shown.

52

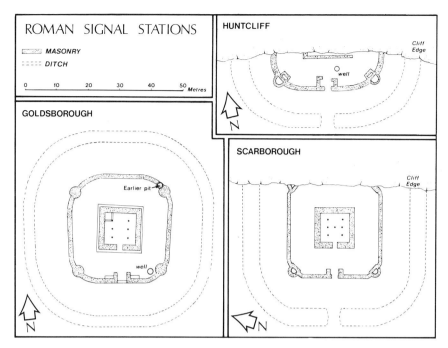

Fig 11 The signal stations were spaced along the coast.

THE FINAL YEARS

On the whole, life went on with little external threat for most of the Roman period. Though a garrison came back to Malton about AD160, it was probably a matter of finding a convenient posting for a unit no longer needed in the north, once Scotland had been evacuated for the second time. The practical effect would, of course, have been a large added market among the troops and their families. It is clear that Cawthorn and Lease Rigg were not reoccupied, so there is no question of local disaffection. But the clouds were slowly gathering nevertheless. From the late second or early third century onwards sporadic raiding of the coasts of Britain by groups from the Continent was on the increase. New forts were built around the south-east coast in response, usually, it may be suspected, to cover areas already successfully attacked. The east coast of Yorkshire was left unguarded for a long time, but eventually in the later fourth century, probably as the result of concerted barbarian action against Britain in AD367, signal towers in strongly defended fortlets were added (Fig 11). The function was probably the observation of potential attackers and the signalling of information about them to the fleet, whose job it was to intercept them – not always, one imagines, an easy task in coastal gales or mists.

The signal stations give us the last glimpse of Rome which we can still trace in Yorkshire. The station at Goldsborough is now little more than

Plate 7 The signal station at Scarborough is the best and most accessible for a visit (*Cambridge University Collection: copyright reserved*)

grass-grown mounds, but the one at Scarborough (within the circuit of the medieval castle, Plate 7), has been uncovered. They also remind us of the fate which overtook some Romano–Britons at least. At both Huntcliff and Goldsborough skeletons were found under the ruins of the structures. As they included women and old men as well as men of military age, it is likely that they were Romano–Britons who had taken refuge there once the fortlets had gone out of use after the withdrawal of Roman forces from Britain in the early fifth century. The raiders were becoming more persistent: soon they were to arrive and not return home.

The evidence discussed in this chapter shows clearly that the Roman episode brought little change to the countryside, which, if we could travel back in time, would immediately be recognisable to us. In the centre were the barren moorlands, with some settlement in the dales, especially Eskdale, and many prosperous farms lay on the Tabular Hills. The western part of the Vale of Pickering had some fully romanised farms, but both the Cleveland Plain and the western fringes of the hills had small, unromanised farms, evenly spread, quite similar to those of the prehistoric predecessors. The Romans brought few innovations in farming, and simply intensified existing methods.

4
ANGLO-SAXONS
AND VIKINGS

IT is easy to suppose, once Roman civilisation had disappeared, that the light went out. The phrase 'Dark Ages' implies barbarians, even anarchy, with roads and signal stations decaying, and an end to the villas with their economic order. The time between the departure of the legions and the arrival of the Normans in 1066, however, left a most enduring imprint on the area. We have only to read a map or look at a signpost and there it is: it was the great naming period and a time of widespread settlement. Many of the names, often much altered, are with us still. Others are unrecognisable or even completely altered; Whitby, for example, was *Strenaeshalc*.

THE ANGLIAN SETTLEMENT

Place-names, archaeology and the landscape
There are two basic types of place-name. Some names usually have a person's name tacked on to an element meaning something like 'farm': Lockton (Loca's farm) and Levisham (Lêofgeat's homestead), for example. Sometimes the name simply tells us the position of the farm, like Middleton. The other type offers hints about the nature of the land in the Anglian period. An element such as *mos* points to peat-bogs which were there then if not now. Even the wildlife can appear, in Ellermire (swan pool) and Brocka Beck (badger-hole stream). Trees too are there in Alder Carr (alder marsh) and Selley Bridge (bridge by the willows).

Reading the landscape through the names can, however, be a perilous business, often because the modern form obscures the earlier ones. Moreover, for most places the earliest recorded names are in Domesday Book of 1086, written centuries after the name was given. There have been further changes of spelling and speech up to our own times. Let us look at an example of the problem. The earliest version of Alder Carr, just mentioned, was *Ellerker*. The first element looks identical with that in Ellermire. But 'Eller' in Ellermire, means swan, and in Ellerker alder.

Then you notice that the first written version of Ellerker was recorded in 1537. The same applies to Troutsdale which had nothing to do with fish: Trutr was a Viking. Only the reference book (*The Place-Names of the North Riding of Yorkshire*) provides the evidence to interpret properly.

The significance of place-names of the Anglian settlements is in fact an area of much debate. Everyone is agreed that *-ham*, *-ton* and *-ing* are Anglian, but it is doubtful which came first. What is true for one part of the country does not always apply to another. Place-names are not such reliable evidence as archaeology or identification of preserved pollen grains. However, when they describe the surroundings, they do give us a hint of the landscape in the 500 years before 1066. This selected list of names with their original forms and meanings gives a flavour of this early landscape, if not an exact vegetation map.

SOME PLACE-NAMES WHICH REFER TO THE LANDSCAPE

Modern name	First recorded name	Meaning
Sleightholme	Sletholme	Flat ground near water
Farndale	Farnedale	Fern valley
Keldholme	Keldholm	Water-meadow near spring
Harome	Harum	Among stones
Cleveland	Cliveland	Steep district
Lease Rigg	Lecerigge	Pasture ridge
Lealholm	Lelum	Among the twigs
Cawthorn	Caltorn	Cold thorn
Elliker	Halaghter	Marsh near high forest clearing
Selley Bridge	Selibrigg	Bridge by willows
Sawdon	Salden	Willow valley
Thornbrough	Thornebergh	Thorn hill
Hambleton	Hameldine	Scarred hill
Wydale	Wyddale	Wood valley

Farming

Swinton	Swintun	Pig farm
Swinacle	Swenekelis	Place where pigs are few
Skiplam	Skipenum	Cowshed
Baysdale	Basdale	Cowshed valley
Stockland	Stokelund	Felled wood leaving stumps

Settlement

Douthwaite	Duvanesthwat	Duvan's clearing

(*opposite*) Cold Moor from the Wainstones. (*over page*) Roppa Bank, looking east (A. Stainiforth, NYMNP)

Modern name Settlement	First recorded name	Meaning
Smiddales	Smidliesdala	Smith's valley
Pockley	Pochelag	Poca's forest clearing
Thirley Coates	Tornelai	Thorntree clearing
Airy Hill	Ergum	Summer pasture
Mickledales	Mikeldailes	Large shares of common field
Seaton	Scetune	Farm by the sea
Ayton	Atun	Farm by a river

Thus, the place-names are a useful glimpse of the settled landscape, even if through a glass darkly. We can understand them because, almost literally, they speak our language. Both Angles and Vikings spoke varieties of the Germanic language, which we speak today in yet another form. According to Bede, the Angles came from Angeln in the Jutland peninsula of Denmark, though their burial urns show close links with the Low Countries and Germany. Archaeological evidence is sparse for the earliest phase of their settlement in this area and much of it open to interpretation. There are early cemeteries at Saltburn and possibly at Robin Hood's Bay. The larger one, at Saltburn, had sixteen cremations in a group of urns, in which beads of amber, crystal, jet and glass were found. Near them were twenty-four graves in two rows running north and south, with the urns more numerous at the southern end and inhumations at the north. A brooch lay nearby, carrying sixth century animal decoration, and an iron axe-head of a type found on the Continent in the fifth and sixth centuries was discovered. The Saltburn cemetery was on a promontory overlooking the sea, a fairly heroic spot for these Germanic incomers. It reminds one of the end of *Beowulf* where they build a mound 'at the edge of the headland, visible far and wide to seafarers'. The two cemeteries lie near Roman signal stations, and indeed the three early Anglian settlements known in the area (Wykeham, Seamer and Roxby) are all on the sites of Romano-British dwellings. However, we need much more archaeological evidence before we can generalise about the pattern of settlements and their continuity from earlier times.

It is also difficult to make any correlation between archaeological finds and the early place-names. The names are as scarce as the finds. Only Fyling, Pickering and Gilling East represent the early *-ingas* names. Lastingham was originally *Laestinga eu* (island). The most recent studies

(opposite above) Great Fryup Dale from Glaisdale Rigg. In the foreground is a typical dales farm with field patterns dating from the Middle Ages. *(opposite)* The North Yorkshire Moors Railway *(NYMNP)*

suggest that names with *ham* and *ingas* represent quite extensive settled areas rather than tight particular villages or farms. The precise meaning of -*ton* (*tun*) also presents difficulties. It probably means 'settlement' and its distribution therefore steers clear of the high moor. Often it is linked with adjectives which help to locate its position, such as Sutton and Middleton; Sutton under Whitestonecliffe is at the southern tip of the township area. This has led some place-name scholars to the view that -*tons* are components of large estates. Indeed, those linked with elements suggesting particular crops (Appleton) or livestock (Swinton) might point to precise units of the estate with specialised functions within the land-holding.

After the Angles were converted to Christianity, they left more substantial evidence. In Whitby a comb was found with a runic inscription of the seventh century which testifies to both their Germanic roots and their new-found faith. (Runes are the old Germanic alphabet, its letters angular to suit carved inscriptions.) It reads: 'May God look on us. May Almighty God help our race.' That is the prayer of a civilised Angle with rather more than a mere coastal foothold. There is slight evidence at Hawnby, in the shape of a burial with a hanging bowl, that the hinterland of the Moors was being penetrated before the conversion in the 620s. But it was at that time that the River Derwent witnessed the heroic sacrifice of Lilla, who threw himself between King Edwin and an assassin's knife in 626. A later rich Anglian burial in a Bronze Age tumulus, *Lilla Howe*, bears his name. A year later the king was converted and baptised.

The coming of Christianity

Christianity came to the region, as Yorkshiremen will understand, not through the 'establishment' version working from Rome via Canterbury, but from the north and, ultimately, from the west. Despite the famous conversion of Edwin by Paulinus at Goodmanham in the East Riding, when a thane compared life with a sparrow passing for a moment through a firelit hall before returning to the stormy night, that mission retreated quickly after a spate of river baptisms. Edwin was baptised in York in 627 but the evidence of an established church in north-east Yorkshire comes only after his death, and its imprint is significantly related to the local landscape. The first remote monasteries were founded.

Anglian war-lords were habitually occupied in dynastic feuding which often resulted in the defeated kings fleeing into exile, usually westwards. Iona was a favoured refuge, for not only was it remote enough from Deira and Bernicia, the two provinces of the turbulent kingdom, but it was a powerhouse of ideas and a haven of what we could call 'culture'. It became natural for a talented Northumbrian leader like Oswald to learn enough Old Irish to invite Aidan of Iona to found a monastery on Lindisfarne, under the shadow of his fortress at Bamburgh on the

Northumberland coast. It is easy to mistake Lindisfarne, only accessible at low tide, as a site chosen by monks opting out of the world. Far from it: the hermit-like aspect of the Celtic church was modelled on Christ's forty days in the wilderness as a preparation for ministry in society at large. St Cuthbert was as much an influential bishop as a recluse. Yet the ascetic preparation was deemed essential, and remote and inhospitable landscapes such as the Desert Fathers chose, were integral with such a life.

In the absence of tidal islands in our area, it comes as no surprise that the early monasteries were established on sites resembling Lindisfarne which offered similar opposing qualities of remoteness on the one hand and ready access to settlements on the other. They are found on the outer edges of the moors, rather than in the remote dales at their heart. Whitby was founded by Aidan himself and Hilda was its most famous abbess. It was there in 664 that the famous synod was held which, thanks to Wilfrid's political deftness, led to the church adopting links with Rome and severing the Celtic tradition. But grass roots were so firmly implanted that the monks must have operated for long enough in the style of their Irish and Ionan mentors. And that was mainly due to their situation in the landscape.

Whitby had its Anglian monastery on the cliff top in the same area as the present abbey, which is the third on the site. It was excavated in the 1930s and a number of small rectangular buildings emerged within a ditch. That pattern of monastic lay-out differs from the cloister arrangement familiar to us from the later Middle Ages but is more like the oratories and hermit cells of the establishments in the Celtic west. The Whitby site is symbolically isolated when viewed from the harbour, but a drive to it from the eastern approach shows that it is easy of access. It was as much a settlement site as a devotional one. Spindle whorls and evidence of fine metalwork point to industry related to the community. Weaving suggests sheep rearing in the locality and it is likely that the mineral deposits of Cleveland were being exploited. The houses were primitive: wattle and daub, of which considerable quantities remain, upon stone footings.

Quarrying of stone was apparently confined to producing monumental crosses. A fine series of these in the site museum speaks of a literate society, as do the styli which were found. The stylus implies literacy and learning, but it also spells cattle for the vellum, and that in turn pasture.

A cell, dependent on Whitby, was established at Hackness, in Forge Valley west of Scarborough. The principal abbess there was Oedilburga. In the present village church a memorial Anglian cross stands to her memory, the inscription in Latin, English, runes and enigmatic characters. Recent discoveries of stone carving at Hackness show that, while her memorial was cut from local quarries, other monuments are made from stone in the vicinity of Whitby, not in Hackness. We must imagine some heavy gravestones being transported, ready-made, across the moor or by sea via Scarborough. It is interesting that Scarborough's headland, rich in Roman and Norman remains, has so far no sign of Anglian occupation.

Hackness' remoteness depends upon its being crammed up in the narrow end of a winding valley: not good land. High ground and inhospitable moor provide the wilderness sought by the monastic community, but the seaways are only four miles away. That access allowed fashionable sculptural styles to arrive at Hackness for Oedilburga's cenotaph to be embellished.

The founding of the early monastery at Lastingham is vividly described by Bede. In 659 Edwin's son, King Ethelwald, gave land there to Cedd to set up a monastery where he could come to pray and eventually be buried. Today Lastingham is well heeled and trim, where even the local sheep seem civilised. Bede, however, calls this homely spot 'a site among some high and remote hills, which seemed more suitable for the dens of robbers and haunts of wild beasts than for human habitation'. His purpose in this was to fulfil the prophecy of Isaiah: 'in the haunts where dragons once dwelt shall be pasture, with reeds and rushes', and he wished the fruit of good works to spring up where formerly lived only wild beasts, or men who lived like the beasts. Perhaps the 'island' (eu) of the early form of the place-name refers to the function of the place rather than its topography. The monastic site has never been firmly identified though it probably lay close to the beautiful Norman church there. But what did Cedd's monastery look like? Originally it was a very humble affair. Bede tells us that Cedd purified the place by fasting there for Lent, living on a diet of 'a morsel of bread, an egg, and a little watered milk'. (Where were the quern, the hen and the cow, one ponders). The first buildings were no more than a couple of huts: one an oratory, the other a cell. By Bede's time in the early eighth century, they had been replaced in stone, still small separate structures, like Whitby's and Lindisfarne's. A few fragments of their decorative details still lie in the crypt of the church. Stone building was an innovation in Northumbria but little of the earliest Anglian churches still stands; they were mostly rebuilt, as we shall see, nearer the Conquest.

Recent study of these monasteries points to their having clusters of offshoot cells in the neighbourhood. The surviving early stone carving provides a hint of where they were, though the total pattern remains elusive. For example, we know from an eighth century letter to the Pope that monks at Stonegrave were complaining about their estate being given away over their heads. All the sculpture at Stonegrave, including the giant cross, is from the tenth century, however, and it is at Hovingham, the next village, that the Anglian carving is found. The two sites may have been connected, like Hackness and Whitby. A carved pinnacle from the gable of an oratory at Lythe suggests that Whitby also had a cell there.

The little church at Kirkdale presents an intriguing problem. Its setting is secluded to this day, with the old church lying across the narrow valley. Two grave slabs at Kirkdale are the kind of monument to be associated with an important ecclesiastical centre, rather than a secular settlement, yet there is no written evidence or remains of an Anglian religious house. One slab carries a large cross surrounded by a beautiful vinescroll. The design is an echo of one of the great full page decorations of a gospel book. At the centre of the cross is a setting for a precious stone or crystal. The other slab has delicate interlace pattern, and along its edges representations of tiny tassels and fringes. When the stone was painted, as they all were, it would have looked like a pall lying over the tomb, rich and embroidered for an important person. Was Kirkdale another Lastingham? Or was it an outlier of a greater monastery?

The early monastic churches were probably not parish churches as we know them today. They declined by the early ninth century, to be refounded as medieval parish churches, or as at Whitby and Lastingham, as religious houses. Along the southern edge of the Moors there is a string of villages with pre-Conquest stone carvings, but only Kirkbymoorside has anything suggestive of an Anglian church: the architectural fragment is at the Ryedale Folk Museum at Hutton-le-Hole. Only one of the churches has fabric of a pre-Viking building: the west wall of Middleton. The majority of stone crosses in that area belong to the tenth century, the hey-day of the Viking colony.

THE VIKING SETTLEMENT

Settlement and place-names

This part of Yorkshire saw two Viking settlements, both of them fairly peaceful. There is no evidence of a conquest of arms, except for the taking of York, which was the political centre and the market of the colony. In 867 York fell to the Danes but it was nine years later that *The Anglo-Saxon Chronicle* recorded: 'And in this year Halfdan shared out the lands of Northumbria, and they engaged in ploughing and in making a living for themselves.' The extent of that settlement is undetermined, both in geographical range and density of population. Assuming that as Danes they were speaking the eastern dialect of Old Norse, some place-names may have originated in that phase.

In the early tenth century a second wave of Scandinavian speakers, this time with Norwegian tongues, infiltrated the northern parts of Yorkshire from Cumberland, *via* the Eden Valley and Teesdale. Their dialect is also apparent in some of the place-names. But the Viking supremacy was short-lived. In 954 the last Scandinavian King of York, Eric Bloodaxe, was killed on Stainmoor, yet in that century the settlers established many of the names we see today in our area. Perhaps their language persisted after Eric's demise; perhaps at grass roots families remained, continuing to give names to places well into the eleventh century. We cannot be sure, but can only rely on the Domeday Book. And Viking words persist in today's Yorkshire dialects, a living link over 1000 years. Hundreds of examples can be given – slape (slippery), smout-hole (a sheep hole in a stone wall), roke (a sea mist).

In the North Riding as a whole there are 649 settlement names recorded in the Domesday Book, and 223 (34%) of those are of Scandinavian origin. Recent scholars have recognised three kinds which may stand for separate phases of settlement (in a tidy world). First, mixed names which are part English and part Scandinavian may represent older English settlements adapted by the new arrivals. Then the many names ending in -by may signify Scandinavian occupation of the most promising available land. Finally, the less attractive land or marginal areas were the -thorpes. Of course, they might not have bothered to change the name in many instances. All this is necessarily speculative to a degree because of the paucity of the evidence.

At first sight names like Danby and Normanby appear to tell us just exactly where Danes and Norwegians were ruling the roost. But when you reflect, the people who give the name to a place are not the folk who actually live in it. Fred does not call his home 'Fred's place', but his neighbours do. That means that the Danes of Danby were distinctive and very probably a minority. On the evidence of personal names and Old West Scandinavian elements, it has been thought that Norwegian speakers predominated in the Whitby area. Ryedale and Cleveland also have the same traits. However, it would be wrong to imagine the settlements as ethnically distinctive, with Dane not talking to Norwegian. In the Viking century in Yorkshire there must have been considerable inter-marriage with the English populace. This is reflected in those mixed place-names to some extent. But the situation was even more complicated, for the 'Norwegians' most likely came from the west, not from Norway directly. They were second generation colonials of mingled parentage and are sometimes even referred to as 'Norse-Irish'. Here and there an Irish element or name will occur in the place-name: Commondale was originally Colman's valley, an Irish name. Oswaldkirk, in some early forms, is recorded as Kirkoswald in the Celtic arrangement of its two elements, as it is in Cumbria.

Churches and sculpture

That same Celtic connection is seen in the many Viking sculptured crosses. Nearly all of them had wheel-heads, in which the arms of the cross are joined by a circle. They look like miniature Irish high crosses. Where the cross is a crucifix, the figure of Christ is on the cross-head, not the shaft, and that is an Irish rather than Anglian feature. Sinnington church has its walls crammed with interesting fragments and the crosses

Plate 8 Middleton church has several crosses commemorating Viking Christians. This is a famous example *(Photograph T. Middlemass, Copyright Durham University)*

at Middleton are complete monuments. One shows a Viking on his gift-stool surrounded by his weapons, and a lumpy dragon adorns the reverse (Plate 8). He was evidently a Christian Viking, despite his weaponry, for a large wheel-head cross surmounts his portrait. Only at Kildale is there any record of pagan Viking burials. Beneath the church floor graves were found containing a sword, an axe, a whetstone and buckles, as well as the balance of a set of scales, which reminds us that more Vikings were merchants than pirates. One may wonder why pagan burials with grave-goods should lie in a church site. Just as today many an agnostic finds a neighbourly grave next to a Christian, so it was then, though by far the majority of settlers were baptised or at least observing Christian burial rites. Some monastic sites continued to be used in the Viking period for burial, like Lastingham, which may point to continued settlement or, to be more cautious, a situation like that in the Scottish Highlands or Ireland today where old chapel sites are current cemeteries. Many English place-name sites have Viking Age sculpture but it should be remembered that tombstones tell us where the dead are, not where the living were. Secondly, we cannot be sure of the parish structure at this period or the location of churches other than monastic ones. Hackness has no Anglo-Scandinavian tombstones and Whitby only one, despite its new Viking name. The chief cemetery for the area round Whitby Strand seems to have been at the top of Lythe Bank where the church has a large collection of Viking monuments.

These Christian Vikings, who may have acquired their Christianity in the Celtic West, produced the greater part of the stone carvings of the pre-Conquest period. Eighty per cent is Anglo-Scandinavian, of the era of Viking dominance in the area, and only twenty per cent Anglian, chiefly confined to monastic centres. So much for the iconoclastic image of the Viking. The shift from monastic patronage of the monuments to secular commissions for tombstones commemorating landholders helps to explain the *floreat*. At Middleton not only do we find a picture of the local lordling, sitting amongst his weapons, but also a vigorous hunt scene. The pursued stag stands with a proud chest and branching antlers as two hounds and a spearman close in. Another like it at Stonegrave shows the hunter with a bow and arrow. It is interesting to find this theme in an area which, in the Middle Ages, was a royal hunting ground based on Pickering Castle: *plus ça change*. Other carvings to the north and west at Kirklevington and in Allertonshire similarly concentrate on the warrior cult, but through it all runs the cross and sometimes the Crucifixion. At Kirkdale, built into the south wall of the church, is a large cross carrying a bearded, clothed Christ who is bound to the cross, not nailed to it. This is a convention found in Scandinavia at a rather later date.

There must have been trade connections from the Yorkshire coast to the Scandinavian homelands, despite the colonial origins of the settlers. A lost trefoil brooch from near Ellerburn could well have been imported from Denmark or Norway. Conversely many Viking graves in Scandinavia contain ornaments made of jet, where it does not occur naturally. Cleveland and the Whitby area were the source, at least of the raw material. It has been argued in Norway that the Viking expansion is directly related to the exploitation of iron and their sophisticated smithing techniques: witness the subtle sword blades of the Scandinavian world, with pattern welding and hardened edges. The ironstones of Cleveland would therefore have been an important resource though as yet no tenth century mining has been identified in the landscape. Elsewhere in Yorkshire there are carvings of smiths on prestigious monuments, suggesting such activity.

The distribution of Anglo–Scandinavian stone monuments (Fig 12) is naturally closely associated with the place-name evidence and with the landscape. It lies chiefly on the three hundred foot contour on the escarpments, by spring lines and close to roads; no surprise. The many sculpture sites on the southern edge of the hills are due in large measure to the limestones which are readily available, with the sandstones also in very easy reach. Most of the colonial Viking crosses are carved from local stone, unlike the earlier Anglian ones which may have been transported, as we have seen. There is no evidence of stone buildings either for churches or houses, so stone quarrying was possibly confined to this single purpose. The sites with sculpture stand cheek by jowl with each other: Oswaldkirk, Helmsley, Kirkbymoorside, Sinnington, Middleton, Pickering and Ellerburn. Looking at the map it becomes apparent that they match the existing parishes, and indeed the carvings are usually found built into the existing church as medieval patching. Many of those parishes and townships* are long, thin strips of land running north and south. Each has a fair division of moorland, spring-line, road and marsh. In fact they make ideal land holdings. (Compare the territories deduced in Chapter 2

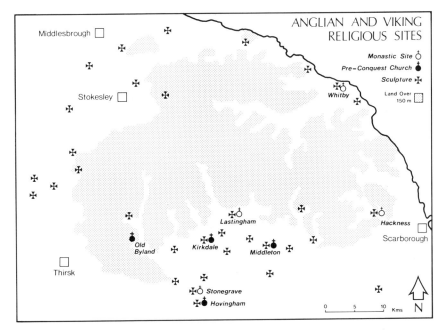

Fig 12 Notice the spread of religious monuments across the parishes along the Tabular Hills. The parish system was in place before the Norman Conquest

from the prehistoric evidence along the Tabular Hills.)

The distribution of the Anglo-Scandinavian sculpture in this corner of Yorkshire hints that the settlement was really quite dense along the slopes of the hills, especially the south-facing ones. The proximity of the sites and their correspondence with later parish boundaries suggest that we may be looking at estate burial grounds which form the basis for the forthcoming churches. That pattern of burial in early settlement can be seen today in the United States where family graveyards lie within sight of the big house. How far this is all part of a Viking takeover of existing Anglian estates we can never be sure in the absence of any substantial documentary evidence.

The carvings also assert strong links with York in the Rydale region but more far-reaching connections with Ireland in the Cleveland settlements. That kind of judgement, however, only applies to the craftsmen who made the crosses and does not necessarily apply to the indigenous population. The Celtic elements certainly suggest that the patrons, ie the rich landholders, were Norse-Irish and not Danish. That would imply that the land-taking in Cleveland was between 920 and 954 during the second Viking settlement. What happened after the English recovery of York we

---

*A *parish*, strictly speaking, is an ecclesiastical territory, supporting a church from its tithes. A *township* (or civil parish) is a territory with settlement, an economic unit. In the north of England, it frequently happens that a parish is composed of several townships, all supporting the one church.

cannot tell, but certainly the folk stopped raising imposing tombstones which symbolised their economic and political standing.

But the Viking period here ends with a bang, not a whimper. At the southern end of the Park in the eleventh century there was a great revival of church building. The church at Middleton had its width increased and a smart new tower added to the west end. The builders re-used the Anglian cross-slab of the early church, placing it over the west door. Very significantly, they also uprooted several Anglo–Scandinavian cross-shafts, barely a century old, and used them as the huge quoins to bond the corners of their new tower. That means that either tastes or local families had changed radically. What happened in the churchyard at Middleton about 1050 was simply a harbinger of our own habits of making paths out of Victorian tombstones. Generations slip quickly out of mind.

A few miles south, Stonegrave, Hovingham and Great Edstone all gained rebuilt churches. At Hovingham one can see architectural stones of the previous church built upside down in the tower, and at Great Edstone there is an Anglo–Danish sundial with an inscription, 'Othan has made me'. Oddly the coastal region and the northern and western fringes did not enjoy the same revival but in Ryedale even quite remote settlements saw their churches remodelled (Fig 12). Sometimes it is difficult to date these buildings for they are very local in style. Two of them, at Ellerburn and Levisham (the derelict church in the valley), seem to have been built by the same masons, who also re-used Viking shafts in the fabric, some of which can be seen at the Rydale Folk Museum.

By far the most spectacular of these churches is Kirkdale (Plate 15). Not only is it highly interesting historically; it is very beautiful because of its setting in the valley. We have seen how it may have originally been a monastic site, certainly an important Anglian burial place, and also a Viking cemetery. Over the south door of the church is a great monolithic sundial with a long inscription. It is in Old English but has Old Norse echoes. Around the half-moon dial it reads: *And Haward made me and Brand the priest*, and *This is the day's sun-marker at every hour*. At either side it runs: *Orm Gamalson bought St Gregory's minster when it was all broken down and fallen, and he had it built anew from ground-level to Christ and St Gregory, in the days of Edward the King and Tostig the Earl.*

It could not be better dated, and it is the only dated object from the period in the area. The king is Edward The Confessor (1042–1066) and Tostig was earl between 1055 and 1065. As for Orm Gamalson, with his Scandinavian name, he was rich enough to buy the ruin or pious enough to rebuild. He may be the Orm who held twelve Yorkshire manors, including Kirkdale, mentioned in Domesday Book. The inscription records the ruin and the new-found prosperity of that strip of the moors. Within months of the erection of that dedication stone, as Larkin put it

> The air would change to soundless damage,
> Turn the old tenantry away

Orm Gamalson's origins may have been incoming Norse but he is playing the English patron better than the English, perhaps trying to keep up with what he saw happening in York under rich archbishops. He was a different creature from his earlier cousins who climbed Roseberry Topping to name it 'Odin's berg'.

When you enter Kirkdale church, look about under the tower. From the nave you see a massive arch, tall and narrow, yet from what was the outside you see shafts and capitals, as you do at Hovingham, that remind you of Norman buildings. This corner of Yorkshire was very up-to-date in its architecture and there is no doubt, looking at Kirkdale, that the Romanesque style would have entered northern England without the help of the Norman Conquest. What such building needs is wealthy patronage and Orm Gamalson was a local lord who must have lived off a prosperous, developed clutch of estates. He provides a pin-hole for us to guess at a view of well-ordered estates with successful farming.

PEOPLE ON THE LANDSCAPE

Thus our vision of the pre-Norman countryside is at the same time blurred yet familiar. The place-names provide glimpses of pastures, valleys, marshes, farms. The profusion of sculpture and churches in the tenth and eleventh centuries hints at a growth of population around the edges of the moorland and on the lowlands and the coast. This was the pattern of settlement from early prehistoric times onward, and, later, of the medieval villages, simply because of the nature of the landscape itself. So we can think of a continuity of this pattern through the first millennium. Moreover, the distribution of the prestigious monuments points to a framework of parishes along the Tabular Hills stretching into the low ground. We do not know when these parishes were established, but we can guess that they may have been based on much earlier estates because of the fairness of land divisions between moor, spring-line and marsh. These divisions might have their origins before the arrival of the Anglo–Saxons, as discussed in Chapter 2. But there is no proof of this, partly because we have no Anglo–Saxon charters (legal documents). So we glimpse in dimly perceived patterns the landscape between the Roman and Norman periods. Its appearance was probably not very different from that of Roman and Norman times.

5
THE MEDIEVAL
LANDSCAPE

THIS chapter is a keystone of the book, vital to our understanding of the present landscape. Although the main features of the *vegetated* landscape had taken shape by the Roman period, the *constructed* landscape, the organised settlements and fields, was given its main outlines in the Middle Ages. The villages and farmland which we now see were largely set out after 1066, though they were affected by earlier layouts, and many township boundaries are much older. There are many medieval documents which give clues to the founding and later development of the settlements and fields, so many in fact that they reveal the complexity of the landscape history. To add to these complications, there are several kinds of terrain in the area which have diverse settlement histories and appear very different today – witness the contrast between the organised villages on the Tabular Hills and the isolated farmsteads of the dales. The medieval organisation depended also to a great extent on the ownership of the land, whether it belonged to the king, or feudal landlords, or the monasteries. And each settlement had its own pattern and history; the dates and reasons for setting out the fields and buildings and for their later reorganisation or desertion, vary from place to place.

This picture is difficult to present, without drifting into impossible complexity on the one hand or meaningless oversimplification on the other. We have therefore started with a discussion of the Domesday Book statements, which give in a kind of coded language some clues to the landscape as it had been developed by 1086. It confirms a well-ordered pattern. Then, in succession, we describe the general development through the Middle Ages on different kinds of terrain. Thus a picture emerges of the whole landscape as it was organised at this time and which is recognisable today, modified in ways which will be described in later chapters. To show how this picture is derived from the documents, an example of a highly organised village, Snainton, is given, in which the written evidence is compared with its present appearance.

WHAT THE DOMESDAY BOOK SAYS

The foundation for all English medieval landscape studies is Domesday Book. This great survey, compiled in 1085–6 on the orders of William the Conqueror, presents a remarkable picture. For over thirteen thousand places throughout England it gives some details of land ownership, of rateable value, of the men and other resources, the plough teams for tilling the arable, the meadows and the woodlands. It also provides a measure of the general condition of each estate, giving the value in the year 1066, before the Norman Conquest, as well as in 1085/6. However, when using this source, the terse Latin text must be translated and expanded, and even when this has been done it is necessary to 'read between the lines'. Domesday Book does not yield its secrets easily. Because it covers the whole country the quality of the evidence varies. Areas with much detail contrast with others where the information is sketchy: Yorkshire falls into the latter category. The entries do indeed name and describe hundreds of specific places, but the coded information given must be related to the likely circumstances of the settlement and fields through careful analysis. We are not even told if the inhabitants of each place live in scattered farmsteads or clustered in hamlets or villages.

Fig 13 shows all the settlements named in Domesday Book in northeast Yorkshire. It is the product of several generations of scholars. The original place-names, reported to Norman clerks by Anglo–Scandinavians using their regional dialect, were often hopelessly mangled, while others – *Cherchebi, Torp, Torentone, Sudtone* (Kirkby, Thorp, Thornton and Sutton) – are applied to widely separated places. The text contains chains of villages close to each other, perhaps reflecting journeys made by the clerks – distant echoes of hoof beats and cold east winds. Using this observation some places have been identified where there was uncertainty. Whatever the problems, it is clear that there are some correspondences between the places in Domesday Book and the modern pattern of villages, hamlets and farmsteads, which sweep like a giant tide through the fertile lowlands, and flood into hill margins and dales of the uplands. The names of 1086 are essentially those on the modern map. These settlements, like those of the preceding periods, are on the fertile edges of the uplands because the life of all early communities was closely linked to the plough and the harvest.

What were these medieval landscapes really like? How far are they still visible in the everyday scene? What changes were taking place during the medieval period? These questions are a long way from the cold symbols. In simple terms, of the settlements shown in Fig 13, almost fifty per cent recorded in 1086 appear as villages or hamlets on nineteenth century maps; twenty-five per cent relate to places which can be described as 'depopulated', ie where there has been post-1086 decline of a settlement;

73

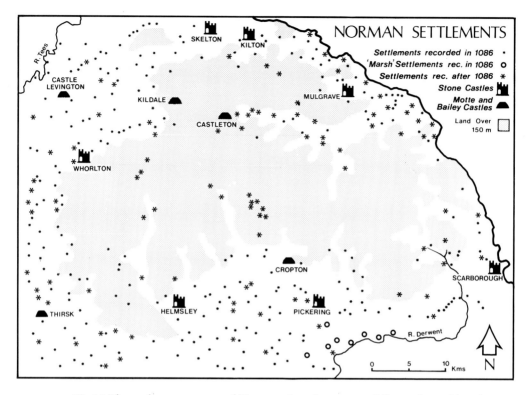

NORMAN SETTLEMENTS

Settlements recorded in 1086 ·
'Marsh' Settlements rec. in 1086 ○
Settlements rec. after 1086 ✳
Stone Castles 🏰
Motte and Bailey Castles ▲
Land Over 150 m ☐

SKELTON · KILTON · CASTLE LEVINGTON · KILDALE · MULGRAVE · CASTLETON · WHORLTON · CROPTON · SCARBOROUGH · THIRSK · HELMSLEY · PICKERING · R. Derwent · R. Tees

0   5   10 Kms

N

Fig 13 The settlement pattern of Norman times is not very different from either the prehistoric or the modern pattern. All were determined mainly by the availability of good farm land. In the succeeding two centuries settlements spread into the heart of the moorland *(after B. K. Roberts)*

the final twenty-five per cent relate to places which had become single farmsteads by the nineteenth century, together with some problem cases. There are also places first recorded *after* 1086: for every hundred rural places which are in Domesday Book and appear in 1850 as villages or hamlets, there are another fifty not documented in 1086 and which are either omitted or are post-1086 foundations. These figures can be interpreted in two ways: first, thinking about the year 1086, they raise questions concerning the variety of settlement types *already present by that date*. Can we really assume that Domesday Book is describing that mixture of villages, hamlets and single farmsteads *now* seen in North Yorkshire (Fig 16)? Indeed, can we ever be certain *what* a single entry is describing? Secondly, the depopulated sites, where village or hamlet once existed, and the new settlements documented for the first time after 1086 speak of changes through time. These changes have varied in intensity throughout the region. For example, proportionately more 'new' hamlets and villages have appeared in the inner moors than in the lowlands (Fig 16). And post-1086 depopulation was at its most intense in Cleveland to the north west. We have here a sharp reminder of the impact

74

of the nine centuries *after* 1086. As a result of colonisation and the extension of farming, new settlements appeared. On the other hand, population decline, linked with plagues or climatic and economic changes, led to settlement retreat. At this point it will help to examine some entries from King William's survey, for these will bring us face to face with real landscapes.

The Yorkshire account begins with a description of the city of York, already ancient by 1086, but this is preceded by a list of the great barons who 'hold' their land of the king, having sworn faithfully to be his men in peace and war. The order of this list structures the rest of the volume. Thus, the holdings of the king himself are followed by those of the Archbishop of York, Earl Hugh, Count Robert of Mortain, Count Alan of Brittany . . ., and many others, and here we glimpse armoured warriors and robed churchmen, figures upon the political chessboard of late eleventh century Normandy and England. Squadrons of mailed knights leap from castle to castle and secure their grip on the newly conquered land. The bishops and abbots move, deviously and diagonally of course, to establish an even tighter hold. Let us begin, however, with the entry for a great royal estate, or 'manor', at Pickering, held by the king himself, in 'demesne', so that its rents and revenues went directly to his coffers: words containing echoes of the account of the manor given before the king's commissioners amid the woodsmoke in the great timbered hall of the new royal castle at York . . .

Land of the King in Yorkshire

> In PICKERINGA, there are 37 carucates of taxable land which 20 ploughs can plough. Morcar held it for 1 manor, with its berewicks, BARTUNE (Barton le Street), NEWETUNE (Newton on Rawcliffe), BLANDEBI (High Blansby) and ESTORP (Easthorpe House). Now the king has (it).

'Carucates' (about 120 acres, but variable) and 'ploughs' are ways of assessing land for taxation. The estate, or manor, extended beyond Pickering itself, and four other outlying settlements – 'berewicks' or 'barley farms' (an Anglo-Saxon word) – were closely linked to the main estate centre. Formerly held by Morcar, Earl of Northumbria and York, the property was taken into the hands of King William after 1066. The account continues:

> There is one plough, and 20 villagers there, with six ploughs. Meadow half a league in length and as much in breadth. But all the wood(land) which belongs to this manor has sixteen leagues in length and 4 in breadth. The manor was worth T.R.E. (in the time of King Edward, ie 1066) £88, now (it is worth) 20s. 4d.

A plough team is a measure of agricultural capacity based upon the ideal unit of eight oxen which could work a single plough throughout the year, with each villager normally contributing one or two oxen to a team. A league in 1086 was probably one and a half miles. But the startling part of this entry is the vast decline in value between 1066 and 1086, which requires further explanation. However, the record continues:

> To this manor belongs the soc (jurisdiction) of these lands: BRUNTON (Brompton) 3 carucates, ODULFESMARE (in Pickering Marishes), ELDBRIZTUNE (Ebberston), ALUESTUNE (Allerston), WILTUNE (Wilton), FARMANBY (Farmanby), ROZEBI (Roxby Hill), CHINETORP (Kingthorpe House), CHILUESMARES (in Pickering township), ASCHILESMARES (?Foulbridge), MAXUDESMARES (Pickering Marishes), SNECHINTUNE (Snainton), CHIGOMERS (Thornton Dale Marishes), ELRESBURN (Ellerburn), TORENTUNE (Thornton le Dale), LEUECEN (Levisham), MIDDLETUN (Middleton) and BARTUNE (Barton le Street). Among the whole there are 50 carucates taxable, of which 27 ploughs can plough. There are now only 10 villagers there, having 2 ploughs. The rest (is) waste; however, there are 20 acres of meadow. In all there are 16 leagues of length and four of breadth.

The estate clearly involved control over a wide area in the Vale of Pickering and on the Tabular Hills, and from these settlements men went to Pickering for justice and to pay rent. While some members of the list, Thornton, Ebberston and Newton, are vigorous villages to this day, others, notably the names incorporating the elements *mares* or *marishes*, have disappeared from the modern map. They may have comprised no more than groups of booths, sod and thatch huts, in the *marshes* of the vale floor, housing herdsmen, fishermen, reed cutters and fowlers.

One thing is, however, chillingly clear; in 1086 the estate was producing only a fraction of the revenue it had generated in 1066, and the phrase 'The rest (is) waste' provides a clear explanation: *waste* was land which had been devastated. York was a primary local base, and in the autumn of the year 1069 its Norman garrison was massacred by an army of Yorkshire men, Northumbrians, and a mixed bag of Danes and warriors from Friesia, Poland and Saxony. The foreigners were driven out by the Normans, and this exposed the north to the full fury of William's anger. In the winter of 1069–70 the king's armies were allowed to devastate the countryside. There was military logic in this. Not only did William need to punish and establish his hold, he needed to deny any future rebels or Scandinavian invaders a secure base in the north. Thus, the lands to the east of the Pennines, from the Humber to the Tyne were despoiled and many new castles created (Fig 13). The impact of this devastation was tremendous, and here we have the reason for the decline in the value of

Plate 9 Helmsley Castle. The two large towers and the curtain wall are Norman. The domestic range by the square tower is sixteenth century, when the latter was altered (*Aerofilms*)

Pickering between 1066 and 1086 and a context for understanding much of the evolution of Yorkshire settlement in later centuries.

Nevertheless, this is not the whole story, as the case of Coxwold reveals:

Land of Hugh son of Baldric
Gerlestre Wapentac (Birdforth Wapentake)
M(anor) CUCUALT (Coxwold), Kofsi had 10 curacates of taxable land, in IRESTONE (?Thornton on the Hill) 3 carucates, EUERESLAGE (Yearsley) 3 carucates, AMPREFORD (Ampleforth) 1 carucate, ANSGOTBI (Osgodby Hall) 3 caracates, TURCHILBI (Thirkleby) 8 carucates, BASCHEBI (Baxby) 15 bovates. Together 20 carucates of taxable land, less one bovate (eight bovates make one carucate). There is land for 15 ploughs. Hugh son of Baldric has now there 4 ploughs, and 54 villagers having 29 ploughs. Wood(land) 8 leagues in length and 3 furlongs in breadth. The whole manor (has) 9 leagues in length and 4 leagues in breadth. T.R.E. (in the time of King Edward) it was worth £6; now (it is worth) £12.

This estate has not only doubled in value between 1066 and 1086, it has

77

more than doubled the number of plough teams working the land. If it ever had been devastated it had recovered. Once again we see a central place described, to which are attached dependencies assessed in carucates, each divisible into eight bovates of approximately fifteen acres of productive arable land. A glance at the map will show that many of the places named in Coxwold manor are settlements to this day, the royal centre itself having been a small market town since the early twelfth century. Coxwold and Ampleforth are now villages, others, Osgodby, Baxby and Thorpe le Willows, are no more than farmsteads, while *Irestone* is not on the modern map. This simple statement again forces us to ask questions concerning the real character of the settlements present in 1086. Can we assume that the villages of today were indeed nucleated villages, tight clusters of farmsteads, in 1086? The terse entries could just as well refer to scatters of dispersed farmsteads or hamlets within a named territory. This name, fossilised in documents from 1086 onwards, might then become attached to the village which developed at a later stage. Without doubt this is a possibility, and shows the caution which is needed with this eleventh century source.

Physical evidence for the initial Norman take-over is primarily found in the few 'motte and bailey' castles which ring the moorlands. These are conical mounds of earth (mottes), originally surmounted by wooden palisades, each surrounded by a banked enclosure (bailey). These were the residences of trusted lieutenants, bases controlling key routes from which mail-clad knights could operate, amid rusting northern damp. The sites of the early settlements at Thirsk, Helmsley and Pickering subsequently became integrated into small market towns, and indeed the castles probably helped start their growth. Pickering, in spite of later stone walls, remains a vivid evocation of what an early earth and timber castle must have been like. The site at Mulgrave is now a mere mound. It was presumably not reconstituted and restored once the Scandinavian threat evaporated and after Scarborough had become the main royal coastal castle. None of these are, of course, documented in 1086, but all are considered to date from the century between 1086 and 1189. The most interesting in many ways is Whorlton. On a high moorland edge ridge, where the Vale of Mowbray meets Cleveland, a massive motte and bailey is sited in a strong position in the entrance to Scugdale, with its high pass to upper Bilsdale, and commanding much of the scarp of the Cleveland Hills. To the east of the castle, on a flat spur and partly surrounded on the north by a rampart, are a series of low earthworks. This is often interpreted as a deserted village, and may indeed be so, but there is also a splendid ruined Norman church, some distance from the castle. This, as Pevsner says, is 'an eerie place, with a church in ruins, a castle in ruins and hardly anything else'. The most reasonable explanation is that here, on this bare hill-top, was an attempt to found a small town. If the place seems unlikely, and indeed quickly proved unsuitable, this argument can be countered by pointing out that Durham, Pickering (between castle and church) and many other Norman towns occupy such high ridges. A slightly different relationship can be seen at Cropton, where a castle mound, strategically placed to control east-west routes along the northern edge of the Tabular Hills, has nearby a planned village (or was it a town?), and – to jump ahead in our story – planted towns and planned villages are one of the most visible and lasting Norman contributions to northern England. That not all Norman attempts to plant towns were successful is also shown by Coxwold, which had market rights by 1086, yet failed to develop as a centre of more than the most minor local importance.

ORGANISING THE MEDIEVAL LANDSCAPE

The present National Park occupies the eastern portion of the former North 'Riding'. The term *riding*, 'a third part', is Scandinavian, suggesting that these large land units were organised during the period of Danish influence which began in 876. The ridings were in turn subdivided into *wapentakes*, also a Danish term, linked with the idea of a local assembly. The various settlements described in Domesday Book are allocated to Wapentakes, and from this evidence it is possible to create a map. Of course, like all administrative divisions these could, indeed did, alter. Wapentakes were divided into parishes, and parishes into townships, local communities, giving a picture of an ordered hierarchy, which seems to suggest that the Scandinavians imposed a unified system of land divisions upon the region. However, reality is more complex. It is likely that the basic building blocks of the system were the lands attached to individual settlements, ie the *townships*, and these were combined to create parishes. Thus, the parish of Lythe contains nine townships, including that which is the parish focus (Fig 14). In turn townships and parishes were linked to create wapentakes, a process of building up rather than dividing downwards, but of course the latter cannot be entirely excluded. Such maps are an essential framework for all studies of the medieval landscape.

The more one thinks about the overall pattern of administrative units, the more one becomes aware of an underlying logic in the pattern. Of course, the boundaries shown on the maps are late nineteenth century in date, but the exercise of plotting all the locations in medieval sources noted as 'lying within' particular township shows the medieval age of much of the system. In fact some townships may be even older, perhaps even prehistoric, but this is not the whole story, for other townships are clearly late creations, carved from older, larger units. However, we appear to have a layout of strip territories, each containing land of variable

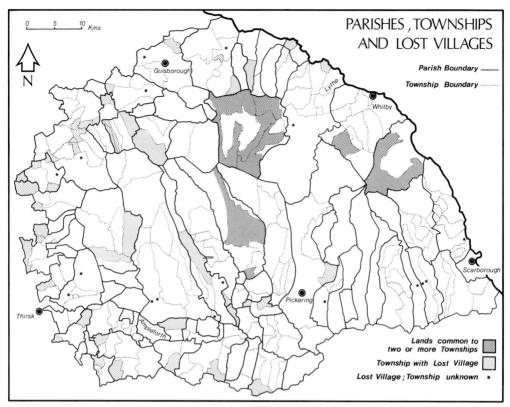

Fig 14 The parishes, some of which are based on ancient estates, often contain several townships which support the one parish church and its priest. The pattern of both townships and parishes was almost complete by about 1150, but may be of much greater antiquity *(after B. K. Roberts)*

quality, from lowland arable to rough grazing on the hills.

The irregularities tell of a long period of adjustment, with many peculiarities resulting from decisions we can no longer reconstruct. Some fifty of the villages contain churches part of whose fabric is Norman (Fig 15). They date from before 1200, sufficient to argue that the pattern of the parishes on the map must pre-date these buildings. Furthermore, the number of Norman survivals, in spite of centuries of later reconstruction, demonstrates a vigorous and far-reaching building campaign *in the twelfth century*, a point to be set against the devastation in Domesday Book.

The scale of Figs 14 and 15 conceals the great complexities found where parishes and townships intermix. There is need for further careful work here, for the nineteenth century maps may preserve a record of ancient divisions: thus Ampleforth was made up of three intermixed townships. They spread across the former arable strips and have fossilised the

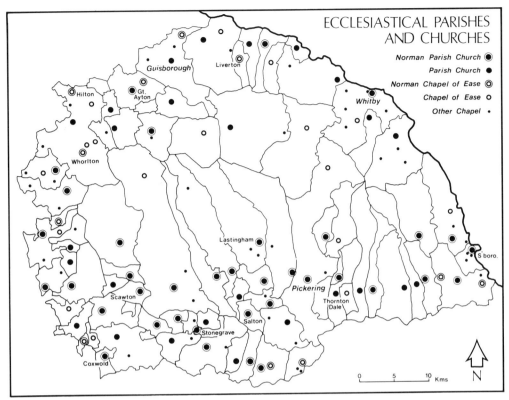

Fig 15 The parish system was in full force by the Norman period. Note the very large number of Norman churches. It was difficult to create new parishes later on, so most churches in the heart of the moors were merely chapels (*after B. K. Roberts)*

evidence for these on the mid-nineteenth century maps. There is a strong presumption that the division into three townships is ancient, surely reflecting the three separate manors present by 1086. Traces of such divisions survive because of their later administrative functions and because they are also related to one other factor underlying all discussion of Domesday Book – landownership. The landowners were the men at whose orders castles and churches were built and for whom the villagers toiled. It was their policies which created local landscapes. By 1086 we are clearly dealing with a landscape which was well-settled, and already divided into an organised system of territories. At the base of this lay the township, a community of peasant farmers, whose labour and rents supported, before 1066, an Anglo–Scandinavian aristocracy, and, after 1066, the new Norman lords and their followers. Nevertheless, it is clear that the Norman conquest of the North was a serious dislocation of all that went before, and society, economy and landscape were altered by the devastation. Global figures are difficult to give, but it appears that about

81

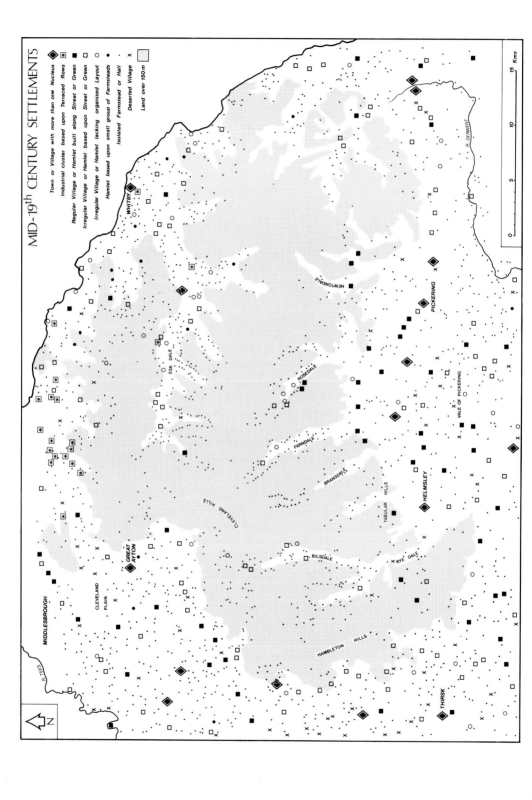

MID-19th CENTURY SETTLEMENTS

Town or Village with more than one Nucleus

Industrial cluster based upon Terraced Rows

Regular Village or Hamlet built along Street or Green

Irregular Village or Hamlet based upon Street or Green

Irregular Village or Hamlet lacking organised Layout

Hamlet based upon small group of Farmsteads

Isolated Farmstead or Hall

Deserted Village

Land over 150m

R. TEES

MIDDLESBROUGH

CLEVELAND
PLAIN

WHITBY

ESK DALE

ROSEDALE

FARNDALE

NEWTONDALE

PICKERING

VALE OF PICKERING

BRANSDALE

TABULAR HILLS

HELMSLEY

CLEVELAND HILLS

GREAT
AYTON

BILSDALE

RYE DALE

HAMBLETON HILLS

THIRSK

R. DERWENT

0   5   10   15 Kms

N

one half of all the recorded settlements in the North Riding suffered a degree of wasting. On any scale this was quite exceptional. Contemporary accounts record refugees as far afield as Worcester, and the monk Symeon of Durham claimed that not a village was inhabited between York and Durham. In the early 1070s hardship and starvation were the lot of most of the region's peasants.

THE SHAPES OF VILLAGES AND HAMLETS

Fig 16 shows a complete map of settlements on and around the moors in the mid-nineteenth century. They are classified into simple types denoted by the different symbols. Villages and hamlets can be divided into two types of plan, those built from rows, lines of buildings, or those based upon close clusters. Both types may be regular or irregular in their layout and may, or may not, possess a grassy green. The distribution shows the repeated regularity in the region's settlements. Larger composite villages, made up of more than one type of plan, are recorded by a diamond shape. For the pattern of dispersed settlements, the small dots show single farmsteads and the crosses are deserted or shrunken villages and hamlets. We must again ask the question: how many of the individual forms and how much of the pattern are truly 'medieval'? Our discussion from now on must focus on the villages and hamlets on the outer fringe. Later we shall describe the settlements in the heart of the moors.

The villages and hamlets fall into two quite clear groups, those whose layouts show deliberate planning and those which are so irregular that it seems they were not planned. Many plans can be interpreted by breaking them down into sections. The basic building blocks of all the region's settlements are *tofts*, ie more or less rectangular plots of land, which carried the farmhouse and its outbuildings, and fronted a public street. These belonged to one tenant farmer, who held his land from the lord of the manor. The tofts were set in a row as in the villages in Fig 17. Today such large plots may be subdivided, and fronted by a continuous line of cottages or houses, the results of post-medieval change. Medieval farmhouses can be pictured as long, rather low, but reasonably roomy thatched structures ('longhouses'), with timber roof beams and low side walls of local stone or even earth (see Chapter 7). The houses were home, storage area, the source of labour and manure for the land and symbol of the social status of the inhabitants. They were normally linked with a peasant holding of between 6 and 12 ha (15 and 30 acres) of land, more or less (i.e. one or two bovates). Associated with them were the vital rights to

Fig 16 Notice that most of the planned villages, probably laid out in Norman times, lie outside the moors. In the moors, villages developed slowly and irregularly over the centuries; in Cleveland many were built for the nineteenth century ironstone miners *(after B. K. Roberts)*

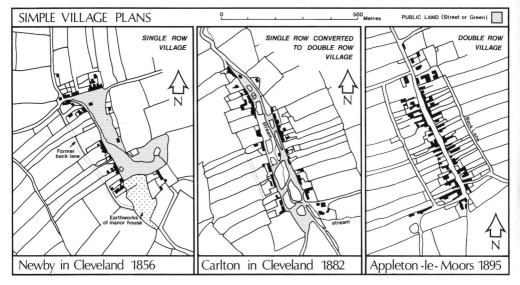

0 ————————————————— 500 Metres

PUBLIC LAND (Street or Green) ☐

SINGLE ROW VILLAGE

N

SINGLE ROW CONVERTED TO DOUBLE ROW VILLAGE

N

DOUBLE ROW VILLAGE

N

Former back lane

Earthworks of manor house

stream

stream

Back Lane

Newby in Cleveland 1856 | Carlton in Cleveland 1882 | Appleton-le-Moors 1895

Fig 17 These maps show common village plans, mostly Norman in origin. It is interesting to walk around them to see how the old patterns have persisted

take hay when the meadows were mown, to use the commons to graze animals, to cut fuel, timber or turves, to take building materials, fodder, and even quarrystone. Of course, there were obligations to pay rents and to work on the lord's own lands. Most villages answered to a landlord, either living in the manor house or a distant figure for whom the rents were collected by a bailiff. If a group of such tofts are placed side by side, as shown in the three villages of Fig 17, they form what can be called a *compartment*, and these are the building blocks of the planned villages of north Yorkshire. Compartments can occur singly, in a single row plan; face each other across a street or broad green, in a two row plan; be combined in varied ways to create a multiple row or composite plan, which is in effect two or more simple plans placed side by side. Finally, they may appear in a different guise where a settlement possessed both market rights and a community of craftsmen and traders, ie in the small market towns of the region, where the density of buildings is normally much greater and outbuildings and cottages pack into the tail of the 'toft'. Subtleties of the plans may have important stories to tell: Appleton le Moors (Plate 11) is very regular, showing clear signs of planning in the parallel back lanes on each side of the main street. It was surely laid out as a whole. In contrast, the back lane of Carlton is now only a slight hollow at the end of the tofts to the west of the village. There are no visible traces of a back lane on the east: the village began as a single row with a back lane, and was then doubled in size by adding a second row, leaving an open green in-between which has later been enclosed. A careful study of Hutton-le-Hole (Fig 26) shows the same pattern. This suggests that compartments with back lanes can pre-date those without. But here we face

Plate 10 Middleton, near Pickering. The fields were enclosed by local agreement, confirmed by Act of Parliament 1765. The enclosed fields retain the form of the consolidated medieval strips *(Crown copyright)*

Plate 11 Appleton-le-Moors. Like Middleton, this is a classic two-row village with back lanes behind both rows of tofts *(Crown copyright)*

the critical question: how can such plans be securely dated? This is very difficult. Fig 16 shows the very large number of such regular planned villages there are within the region. On balance we believe that the regularity of many Yorkshire plans originates in the medieval period, probably before 1200. The weight of opinion is that these regular plans represent post-Conquest re-ordering of earlier settlements, possibly in the wake of the devastation. Many regular villages must have come into being in the century or so after that date, perhaps by concentrating at a single place on the population of former scattered hamlets. Thus in Kirby Misperton thirteenth century charters use the settlement names *Westhorpe* and *Southorpe* as field names, showing that these scattered hamlets had been abandoned.

The Norman devastation of Yorkshire was followed by a phase of much village replanning linked with economic revival, but this conclusion begs many questions. These plans must have often been influenced by the settlement features, field boundaries and trackways already existing in the landscape. A clear example of these is to be found where rows are laid out over earlier ploughing as at Snainton. We have no specific evidence about the processes of planning. Who took the decision? The local lord or his steward? European examples suggest that sites were prepared before colonists arrived, but in Yorkshire a mixture of surviving tenants, local refugees and new colonists must have been involved. Ropes, measuring rods or even pacing were all good enough to make the measurements. Above all else, we must make the mental jump, that beneath many of the modern regular and part-regular villages of north Yorkshire lie planned medieval antecedents. If this is surprising, one can in fact argue that the whole process of measuring was linked with a precise sharing of limited resources, and included not only the formalised village plan but the arable strips of the fields and ultimately the rights to pasture, building materials, turves and other land resources. We may conclude that after the Norman devastation the lowlands around the North York Moors saw a major recovery, involving the renewal of wasted settlements and farmlands. In a later section the repercussions of these events upon the moorland core must be assessed, but to continue the discussion of the lowland fringe we must now turn to the question of field systems, for these tend to reinforce the tenuous evidence for a widespread process of deliberate planning.

THE VILLAGE FIELDS

Most medieval villages and hamlets were supported by arable townfields. These were usually shared among the farmers by subdividing the holdings into a series of long strips, about 5-10 yards wide. These can often be seen surviving as 'rigg and furrow' strips fossilised in grassland, the strips

Plate 12 Rigg-and-furrow at Wilton, near Thornton Dale. Note the inverted S of the plough-lines *(Photograph A. Staniforth, NYMNP)*

being one or two feet higher than furrows between them (Plate 12). True medieval strips are shaped like an inverted S, preserving the old ox-plough line. Their shape can sometimes be preserved in present-day field walls and hedges, most spectacularly at Middleton (Fig 27) and Pickering. (Straight, narrow, horse-worked strips date after the eighteenth century.) Each arable field (and a settlement might have two, three or even more) would be divided into convenient blocks of strips, called 'furlongs' – not to be confused with the furlong unit of length of 220 yards. Each furlong comprised several dozen strips. Hedges and walls were found only in the village itself, and as the occasional field boundary. The furlong and the individual holdings of strips lay open to each other, to allow communal work and pasturing of the fallows. Thus a village had ten, twelve or more furlongs and the strips of each farmer would be scattered through them – a fair but highly inconvenient arrangement. The scattering was normally not random; in fact, the order of strips in each furlong could follow the order of the houses in the village. A good example is at Morton, now Morton Grange near East Harsley. Here Rievaulx Abbey was granted in about 1173 'half of the vill of Morton . . . the carucate to consist of eight perches (one perch equals about 20ft) lying together towards the sun and the tofts and crofts likewise'. This description exactly places the strips making up the 49 ha (120 acres) in a carucate. 'Towards the sun' means the south or east half of the village. The clearest evidence for these regular arrangements comes from post-medieval records. A survey of 1685 describes the two groups of communal townfields in Thornton Dale, each containing three fields. Every group has exactly 84 bovates each of 16 acres. The groups were divided into furlongs (nineteen in the western and

87

twenty-five in the eastern field groups), which were of widely different sizes, but each furlong was planned to take the full sequence of strips appropriate to the 84 bovates. The basic holding in Thornton was 2 bovates (about 30 acres) which entitled the owner to a single broad strip in every furlong. These broad strips were all of a standard 2 perch width (40ft) in all the furlongs, but the strip length in each furlong was different. The holders of single bovates were provided with narrow strips only one perch wide, found scattered among the broad strips. In practice the length of each strip was controlled either by the limitations of available space or by the distance an ox-team could draw a plough without needing a rest, ie a linear furlong of 220 yards or 200 metres. In Thornton Dale intermixed broad and narrow strips can still be seen, just to the south of the village, beside the footpath leading to the earthworks of the old manor house on Roxby Hill.

The intricate arrangements at Thornton Dale were part of a process called 'regulation'. It is possible that, in their time, villages were regulated and re-regulated repeatedly, depending perhaps upon their economic fortunes. To add further complexity, each village differed from this simple model in response to local circumstances. Thus the following description of Snainton fields can only be a sample of the variety found within this large and diverse region.

THE CASE OF SNAINTON

Snainton (Fig 18) is typical of many townships along the northern edge of the Vale of Pickering. Its territory forms a strip of irregular width extending 13km (8 miles) from the inner recesses of the moorlands to the banks of the River Derwent. South of the village all the land lay in 'carrs' — seasonally waterlogged common grazings — but the settlement itself lies on slightly higher, dryer land. The medieval arable fields lay on the limestone slopes north of the village up to a height of about 170m (560ft). Beyond these lay open moorland extending northwards for several miles. The land north of the village is dissected by a series of dry valleys long known from west to east as Welldale, Nettledale ('Little Dale' in the Middle Ages), Wydale and Brompton Dale.

In the thirteenth century a suite of three open arable fields lay on the ridges between the valleys: *West Field* lay between Welldale and Nettledale; *Middle Field* between Nettledale and Wydale, and *Heydon Field* (with its northern extension of 'Moresum') between Wydale and Brompton Dale. These formed an apparently regular three-field system but there were other open fields nearer the village about which we know very little. We shall argue below that the fields near the village were regularly-cropped 'Infields' and those to the north 'Outfields' which were sown less frequently. Practically all the documentary evidence related to

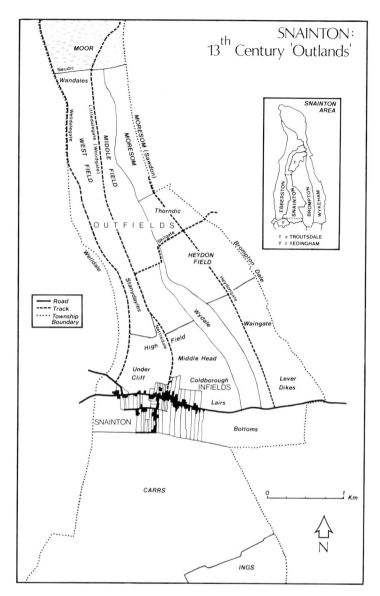

Fig 18 Layout of Snainton village, which was developed in the early Middle Ages on existing strip fields. It was then farmed on a complex infield/outfield system. Moorsome dyke is the medieval Neudic *(after B. J. D. Harrison)*

the 'Outfields'. Here the strips in each field were ordered into numerous furlongs in all of which the strips ran across the entire width of the field from east to west (ie from valley to valley). These furlongs were given simple names derived from local features such as roads or tracks (*Scotgate, Skilgate*), boundary ditches (*Thorndic, Neudic*) or soil quality (*Stanydales, Gretes*). In the thirteenth century Malton Priory received 24 grants of land in Snainton, almost all of it in the three fields mentioned above. A typical example is as follows:

> In *West Field* at Langedyle, between Welldalegate and Littledalegate, as much land as belongs to two bovates; at Gretes, between the same roads, as much land as belongs to two bovates; at Neudich a *wandale* belonging to two bovates. (A *wandale* is a measured share of land).
>
> In *Middle Field* at Halfhundryths at the end of Scotgate, as much land as belongs to two bovates; on the north side of the sheepcote belonging to the nuns of Yedingham as much land as belongs to two bovates.
>
> In *Heydun (Field)* at Skilgates, between Brompton Dale and Wydale, as much land as belongs to two bovates; beyond Thorndic as much land as belongs to two bovates.

This grant amounted to 10 acres of land in all, a good deal less than the two bovates which are constantly referred to in the text and which would probably have amounted to 25-30 acres. It is thus clear that it was *not* the two bovates which were being granted, but land which in some way belonged to or was attached to such a holding. The bovates themselves probably lay in the older open fields near to the village (the 'Infields'), while strips in the newer 'Outfields' were gradually attached to them as cultivation extended northwards across the higher land. In another charter a grant is described as comprising '. . . . . all the land belonging to him (ie the grantor) for two bovates at Houtlands towards the moor'. The Houtlands ('Outlands' or 'Outfields') are then described as lying in a number of furlongs which other charters locate in West Field, Middle Field and Heydun Field.

Some of the grants show that these 'Outfields' bear all the marks of a planned layout. Within the individual furlongs, holdings are not usually described in terms of acres but as 'rod-widths' or strips of one rod in width. The statute rod, pole or perch was 16½ft, but locally 18 or 20ft were more common lengths. It is quite clear that everyone who held a bovate of land in the 'Infields' of Snainton had the right to one 'rod-width' in each of the furlongs of the 'Outfields'. Since the standard peasant holding in this village was one or two bovates, strips of two 'rod-widths' (36-40ft) were the norm. A great many wide riggs measuring some 12-13 yards from furrow to furrow can still be found in the area. This relationship between 'Infield' and 'Outfield' holdings is very clearly demonstrated in the following grant to Malton Priory of 10 acres in the 'Outfield' area of Snainton:

> '. . . . . in Netherdun 4 rod-widths extending from Wydale to Haydungate; on the south side of Carles 4 rod-widths extending from

Littledalegate to Welldalegate . . . . . that is to say as much land as belongs to half a carucate (ie 4 bovates) in the said places'

We have not yet explained why 'Outfields' should exist at all on excellent
arable land which could easily have been integrated with the 'Infields' in a
single field-system such as one finds in many other parts of lowland
Yorkshire. The answer almost certainly lies in the sheep-corn husbandry
practised in this area by the late twelfth century. The land on the higher
limestone was just too valuable as sheep-pasture to be given over entirely
to corn crops. Furthermore the regularly-sown 'Infields' required the
manure of the sheep to maintain fertility. The system is nicely explained
for us in a twelfth century deed relating to the nearby village of Allerston.
A man called Torfin of Allerston granted to Rievaulx Abbey land in his
Outlands (ie 'Outfields') for constructing a sheepcote. The monks under-
took to provide Torfin with 'one half of the folding and manure of the
sheepcote', while Torfin agreed to provide straw for the manure.

In this area of light, free-draining soils the 'Infields' were probably
already cultivated by the time of Domesday Book, if not long before,
while the 'Outfields' were probably developed in the period c1150 to
1250. The frequent use of the term '-dales' (ie 'doles' or shares) to describe
outfield strips seems to indicate a systematic division of land among the
numerous peasantry. Near the limits of cultivation clusters of sheepcotes
were established by most of the larger landowners. At Snainton the nuns
of Yedingham and of Wykeham owned adjacent sheepcotes. Fig 19 shows
Malton Cote which survived until very recently in Ebberston. It was
strategically placed on the Snainton boundary in order to service Malton
Priory's wool-growing operation in both townships, and it was clearly
built within a furlong of arable strips. It comprised the remains of a very
regular enclosure, once walled or hedged, within which lay a sheep-house
and probably the shepherd's dwelling. It was granted to the Priory in the
early thirteenth century along with 21 acres of arable and pasture for 300
sheep. Unfortunately this historic site was ploughed out in 1987. The
sheep from this and other sheepcotes no doubt grazed on the remaining
grasslands to the north, but also over the 'Outfields' to the south large
tracts of which would have been left fallow in any one year. The
droppings of the sheep would have fertilised these lands. But the accumulated manure from the sheep-house, where the sheep were kept during the
winter, was no doubt applied to the regularly-cropped and therefore
much more demanding 'Infields' around the village.

How much of these complex arrangements can be seen in Snainton
today? The short answer is – a very great deal. Pay a visit to Snainton on a
fine day and walk around the village. Start at the west end of the village,
on the A170 road near that hospitable coaching inn, The Coachman. On
the hill to the north are the rigg-and-furrow strips of the infield, running

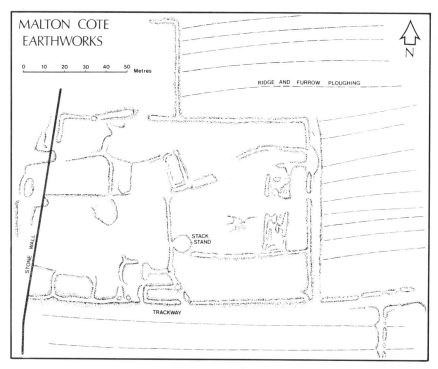

Fig 19 These earthworks were surveyed in 1985, destroyed in 1987 *(after B. K. Roberts)*

in a north-south direction, and not all of the same width. Walk to the village centre, turn up Nettledale, and after a hundred yards turn right along Garth Head Lane; you are now on the northern back lane of the village whence you can walk right around the village on both the northern and southern back lanes. Garth Head Lane, like Nettledale Lane, is a very deeply sunken track – evidence of the great age of both. From here you can see the many curving hedgerows of the tofts and paddocks, clearly showing that the village was laid out on a pre-existing strip field. If you follow Garth Head Lane to its northern stretch, you are then following the boundary between the infield and the outfield. Stop at the eastern end of the lane, and look at the field boundaries. The infield/outfield boundary continues eastward, on a marked lynchet (field-bank) indicating that the outland to the north had been ploughed east-west. Running south from this down to the High Street is a curved lynchet following the old plough line, showing that the infield had been ploughed north-south. Then follow Lairs Lane down to the southern back lane. Along the lane can be seen the excellent curved hedge lines and ridge-and-furrow of the pre-village fields (Plate 13). Finish the walk around the village lanes to the west, and see how many curved hedge lines you can spot.

Finally, take the car and motor north along Nettledale and Snainton Lane. Away from the village, in the area of the outfield, all the hedges are exactly straight, laid out east-west at the time of the Snainton Enclosure Acts (about 1770). There is no sign of rigg-and-furrow strips, which had little chance to form under the medieval alternate arable-pastoral regime. You will pass the medieval sheep farms Wydale Cote and Malton Cote on the right and left respectively. About six hundred yards before reaching Cockmoor Hall, you see on your left the ditch and bank of Neudic, part of the field layout of Malton Cote. In the woods behind Cockmoor Hall is another medieval dyke, originally separating the fields from the forest beyond. The great prehistoric earthworks, Scamridge and Cockmoor Dykes, are in this area, running north-south, marking out prehistoric territories, similar but not identical to the medieval ones. The medieval Thorn Dike cannot be seen from the ground, but shows up from the air as a crop mark running eastward from Wydale Cote. In this area are also the cropmarks of a Roman field system, laid out on a north-south axis, another reminder of the Hoskins warning 'Everything in the English landscape is earlier than we think'. Snainton thus presents a marvellous medieval landscape, and one we can understand from the surviving documents. But it is not the only one, and you can repeat this landscape study by walking around many villages.

It is likely that the arrangements described here are characteristic, with variations, of many of the townships between Helmsley and Scarborough. An important point is the way in which the strip division of the land found at parish level, then at township level, is also seen at the *field* level. In Snainton the furlong divisions run crossways, taking account of minor landscape features. This was also the pattern in Hutton

Plate 13 The curved hedges on the south of Snainton village, marking the medieval strip field on which the village was developed. The outlands can be seen on the crest of the hill (NYMNP)

Buscel, but field evidence from Pickering and Middleton (Fig 27) suggests that the individual strip holdings could run parallel to the township and parish boundaries. Of course, outland, or outfield, cultivation was not limited to this area. Similar arrangements are known in the parishes and townships of the coastlands, from Cloughton, north of Scarborough, to Saltburn, and cases are also found on the Cleveland Plain. Nevertheless, on the poorer soils of the eastern and northern flanks of the moors it is unlikely that the outlands were as extensive or as organised as on the good land of the Tabular Hills.

In summary, the pattern of villages and hamlets around the moorlands has a complex history. At root, there are prehistoric and Roman antecedents, followed by Anglo-Saxon and Scandinavian successors. The two latter are only sharply visible in place-names, but in the future we may be able to detect more surviving features from these periods. This shadowy settlement landscape experienced extensive devastation both before and during the Norman Conquest, followed by a revival, perhaps between about 1075 and 1200. This phase established the framework of the settlement system within which we now live, but, of course, exploring these roots is only part of the story. Once established, these villages and hamlets could suffer many changes in fortune during their passage through history. Some were wholly successful, and thrived and expanded, with monk and layman both benefitting from the region's better soils. Others were less successful, changing only slowly, while some were depopulated and destroyed, often as a result of late medieval change from arable to sheep farming. Land quality may have been one factor in their histories, but there is little doubt that a key factor was *lordship*. Who owned a village was crucial. Every settlement was part of an estate for which a succession of lords and stewards took decisions in the light of prevailing circumstances. Space forbids further exploration of this theme, but it becomes important when considering the development of the high grazings of the moors proper. Here decisions by lords were quite fundamental in directing development and the effects remain visible in the landscapes of today.

THE MOORLANDS

Discussion of the colonisation of the core area of the National Park must take account of two factors. First, very large areas were annexed to the surrounding villages. This high and cold land, often on poor rocky soil, was used as a reserve of grazing until rising numbers caused people to move into the moorland fringes. Secondly, within the moorlands there are some townships and parishes which have always been dominated by rough poor lands. In a few cases, notably in Fylingdales, Danby and parts of Lastingham, areas common to several parishes survived to be recorded upon mid-nineteenth century maps (Fig 14). Must we imagine an earlier situation, perhaps long before 1086, when all the inner moors were grazed by all the surrounding townships? If the uplands were at an early stage entirely exploited from the outer settlements (which seems to have been largely true in prehistoric times), then there may have been a stage intermediate to formal land division. Stock would have moved to the higher ground in April and down again in September, traditionally accompanied by the younger folk. The intervening months were used for feeding the animals, producing dairy products, and, inevitably, sowing wild oats! We do in fact have some place-names which imply seasonal movement. The Norse-Irish *airyh*, pronounced 'airey' and meaning 'shieling' – a hill pasture – appears in *Airy Hill* (Whitby), *Airy Holme* (Great Ayton) and *Coldman Hargos* (Guisborough). And the old Norse *'skale'*, meaning a temporary hut, comes down as *Burnolfscales* (Guisborough), *Laskill* (Helmsley), *Scaling* (Roxby), *Scalestedes* (Tocketts), and others. The evidence for seasonal pasturing is therefore quite strong.

By 1086 recorded farm settlements in the uplands were restricted to three areas. First, strings of settlements lay along the coastline on difficult broken terrains, the greatest concentration being near Whitby. Secondly, settled places are documented in the Esk Valley between Egton and Danby, and thirdly in upper Rydale, between Byland and Arden, on the north-thrusting limestone spur of the Hambleton Hills. However, the little settlement at lovely Dale Town, near Hawnby illustrates some of the general problems. There seems to have been a nucleation here, for there were 22 tenants in 1433, but in 1569 there was simply 'a house called Dale Town'. In 1086, Ulfr, Asketill and Frithgestr held 3 carucates of taxable land in Dale Town from the King, with two ploughs, worth 8s., nominally one manor. But Robert Malet also possessed a manor there, and Ulfr and Asketill (surely the same men of the royal entry) had one and a half carucates of taxable land belonging to him. This is a part of four entries of local Malet manors on which Domesday Book comments 'Robert Malet has these lands, but they are all waste'. What are we to make of these two entries? Why should one manor in Dale, occupied by the three royal tenants, have been spared, while another, occupied by two of them, have been devastated? In this case one cannot easily explain the devastation of part of one place by suggesting a post-1070 removal of tenants by one landlord, *because the same major tenants seem to be involved*. It is equally reasonable to argue that Ulfr, Asketill and Frithgestr, neighbours, perhaps even kinsmen, lived not in a single nucleation but in a small scatter or girdle of farmsteads. No easy explanation is feasible, however, but the presence of carucated land shows that the formal procedures of assessment for royal taxation had reached even this out-of-the-way Ryedale nook. And the evidence of long-term arable is provided by the massive bank of strip-lynchets (Plate 14) at Dale Town, one of the very

Plate 14 Strip lynchets at Daletown. These strips were formed by medieval ploughing on the sides of limestone hills, and are common in the Pennines. Other examples in the North York Moors are at Whisperdale (Hackness) and Hood Hill *(Photograph A. Staniforth, NYMNP)*

few still surviving in the North York Moors.

When we turn to the sandstones of the uplands, generally land lying above 240 metres (878ft), we find that in 1086 they are almost empty of recorded settlements. How much of the landscape was actually wooded in 1086 is relevant (Chapter 1) to the post-1086 colonisation: we believe that there was still ample woodland, perhaps concentrated in the valley floors and sides, with the tops being cleared. In 1086 Pickering certainly possessed 'woodland . . . . . 16 leagues in length and four of breadth', a league of 1½ miles suggesting the order of 24 miles by six. This was a block of country embracing the great strip parishes of Pickering, Thornton Dale, Levisham, Allerston, Ebberston and Brompton, stretching from the Derwent to the watershed and perhaps even to Goathland. The 24 miles is surely too long; perhaps it felt that distance to the herdsmen and woodmen. Of course, these wood pastures were as valuable for stock rearing as were the open moorlands, indeed they were more suitable for cattle. Whole settlements and their fields lay *within* this zone, which became the Royal Forest of Pickering, under the control of the Constable of the castle. The central Esk Valley, however, was a remote area. Here Hugh son of Baldric had three ploughs in the manor of *Crumbeclive* (Crunkley Gill, west of Lealholm), to which Danby and Lealholm were attached. But a schedule of lands later granted to Robert de Brus, from an earlier local draft of Domesday Book, also includes two settlements now called Hangton Hill Farm. Once again we face questions about assumptions: are we dealing with nucleated settlements, or do these terse entries really conceal farmstead scatters?

One way of evaluating Domesday Book is to look backward from later sources. In 1086 the only sizeable settlement of the inner moors is Danby in the Esk Valley, and this is assessed at 6 carucates. By 1272 it had, as one might expect, grown considerable and some 56 bovates of land were held by serfs and at least another 33 bovates by freemen. This would make approximately 90 bovates or 11½ carucates. Land assessed in this way is likely to have been colonised fairly early, certainly before 1200 and probably before 1150. As a general rule bovated holdings refer to arable land lying in open townfields, while all later holdings, often in consolidated blocks, were assessed in acres. Danby did indeed have an area of townfields at the northern end of Danby Dale, near the parish church. But there is no way that 90 bovates (of the order of 1000 acres) could be fitted into these small townfields. A solution may be seen in the farm until recently called Low Bramble Carr (Fig 20). It is at the north east of Danby Dale, with its lands running from the lower slopes of Danby High Moor (which here narrows to become Ainthorpe Green) down to a small stream called *Suwardholm*, beyond which the communal fields began. This farm in 1575 consisted of four closes, or enclosed fields, containing 12 acres, and in a deed of 1397 *this same farm is described as 'one bovate', and its boundaries are precisely delineated*. Beside Ainthorpe Green this boundary still exists, a huge wall of massive and primitive construction. This seems to be a 'ring fenced' bovate, never part of communal fields. Given the location on the better land of the dale floor, this could even be one of the farms subsumed under the six carucates of 1086. The land assessed in

Fig 20 Medieval peasant farms in the moorlands

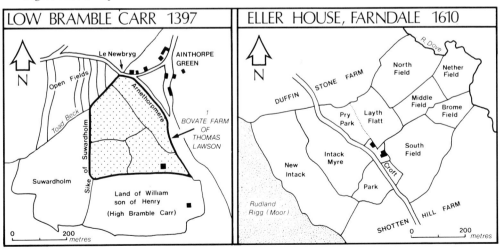

the Domesday text therefore consisted both of townfields and of smaller isolated farms. One point must be emphasised, that the present clusters at Danby, Glaisdale and Grosmont were only brought together by nineteenth century industrial development, and that at Goathland resulted from the coming of the railway. Eighteenth century maps reveal that the earlier settlements were loose scatters of farmsteads and hamlets, albeit associated with the place-names of the township and parish centres. Here is an unusual type of settlement, in between the truly nucleated village or hamlet and the dispersed farmstead. Fig 17 maps hamlets based upon small groups of farmsteads which appear on nineteenth century maps. Although some farmstead or hamlet clusters result from the decay of a former nucleation (the depopulated village of Newton Mulgrave is an example), these loose groupings appear in many other places – East and West Barnby, Roxby, High Hawsker, Hutton Mulgrave and Normanby. We may be seeing traces of a settlement type earlier than the villages, where a manor hall and other scattered farmsteads formed a focus for later growth. Add more farmsteads randomly, and an irregular cluster appears; add more and formalise the plan, and a regular village is created.

An area with features similar to Eskdale is Bilsdale, where, although there is no entry in Domesday Book, the presence of strip holdings and a chapel built by 1122 indicate early Norman or even pre-Norman colonisation. The terrain here is much more broken than in Danby Dale. Danby has a single area of open townfields and a possible village, with enclosed farms on the edge; in Bilsdale we have some scattered hamlets, several areas of townfield, and a small number of outlying farms. In the eastern arm of the valley – the Bilsdale Beck – there was a hamlet simply called 'Bilsdale'. Here was a chapel and a manor house (Fig 21), although the presence of 'Town Green' as a place-name suggests that this may once have been a small village. In addition there was a loose collection of farms around Seave Green, extending south to Chop Gate; further north lay the hamlet of Urra, an irregular cluster set at the boundary between improved land and moor. There seems to have been a further cluster, *Bradfield*, at what is now Broadfield Farm, with perhaps another, *Garthwait*, now Garfit Farm. In the western arm of the valley, Raisdale, were two clusters. Great Raisdale, with a chapel by the thirteenth century, may have lain near Raisdale Mill. Little Raisdale lay in a small valley between Cold and Cringle Moors, at or near the present Hall Garth Farm, where there is an impressive collection of earthworks and trackways. Isolated farmsteads are also recorded at *Aykeheved* (Akitt, near Seave Green, Fig 21), *Staynhouse* (Stonehouse Cote east of Chop Gate, Fig 21) and *Huhyrst*, (unlocated, but in Raisdale). These names are a mixture of Old English and Old Norse. The presence of strip holdings in medieval sources, with large numbers of serfs and freeholders and fragments of communal

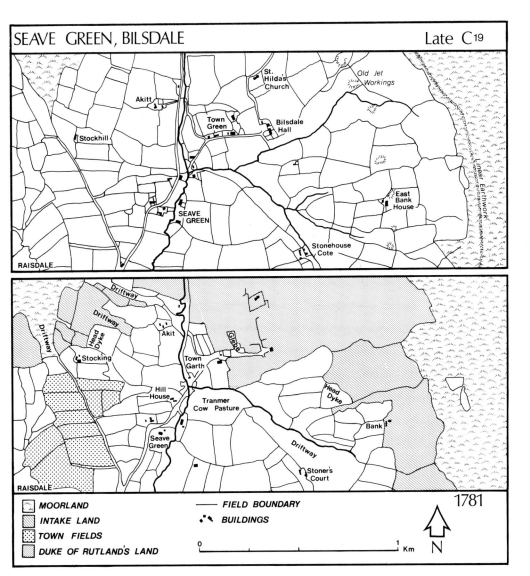

MOORLAND
INTAKE LAND
TOWN FIELDS
DUKE OF RUTLAND'S LAND

FIELD BOUNDARY
BUILDINGS

1781

0   1 Km

N

Fig 21 A landscape of hamlets and isolated farms with small areas of open fields amidst the ancient enclosures

townfields, all combine to suggest settlement well-established by 1150, even though it is not mentioned in 1086. It is odd to find this apparently isolated, scattered community drawn into the parish of Helmsley. Nevertheless, once Whorlton was abandoned as a strategic site, the custodian of Helmsley, with its castle guarding the Bilsdale route, must have sought to have trustworthy men in this key area. There they could keep watch over the Cleveland plain when Scottish armies were on the move.

99

EXPLOITING THE LANDSCAPE: LAND USE AFTER AD 1200

One of the key questions concerning Norman England is 'How many people were there?'. For Yorkshire we cannot even estimate the overall level, but we can suggest trends. It is clear from the Domesday settlements that the pre-Conquest communities of north-east Yorkshire were successful. Although the highest parts of the region were unsettled, population increase had already caused colonisation of some valleys by arable farmers. The Norman devastation checked this process, displacing thousands of peasants by destroying their livestock, agricultural implements, winter food supply and seed corn. William's troops were probably not able to carry fire and sword to all those remote places where waste is recorded; and some waste was the result of local lords moving people from remote areas to their lowland manors, where the returns on labour were more certain. However, the case of Dale Town (above) shows the problems of interpretation. The overall levels of population fell, reducing pressure on the land. Some migrants found their way to undevastated estates. In some cases these refugees, particularly the younger elements, were surely welcomed by the landowners, to take up empty but viable farms; others could have been directed to estates where farming was being re-established.

Such changes – and we can only speculate on the time scale and extent of human suffering and endeavour – laid the foundations for a new set of growing communities. Gradually nation-wide markets grew for meat, wool, hides, butter and cheese. The importance of the pasture grounds adjacent to the upland edge villages became clear. A lord with rights over woodland and moorland pastures might benefit from these in several ways. First, he could attempt to exclude men and domestic animals to create a private hunting area, termed a 'forest' if it was royal, but a 'chase' if it was held by a great lord. Within this enclosed area, deer parks could be created. Secondly, he could reclaim the land directly, using his own men, and establish great stock farms, or 'vaccaries', also an option involving little in the way of peasant settlements. Thirdly, he could allow a free-for-all, offering land on very easy terms to whoever would come to reclaim it. Or, fourthly, he could reclaim the land himself, and then colonise it with small tenant farms. Of course, given a sufficiently large estate a lord could follow two or more of these, while the last two really contain many options. If, for example, land was timbered, then it may have been profitable for a lord to *assart*, or clear, using his own men, sell the profitable timber (for every scrap was valuable) and then let the land to tenants. But where scrub or stone clearance was needed, it was easier to let tenants do the backbreaking labour, over a long period of time. Initially, at least, these people could not pay rents as high as those taking on land already cleared. Finally, land could be granted to a monastic house. This final option, because of the magnificent ruins left by the Dissolution of the Monasteries, is widely appreciated, although as Figure 23 shows, two-thirds of the uplands in fact remained in lay hands. All the options listed above were tried, at different times and places and in different combinations, but colonisation by tenant farmers was the main theme, at least in the more remote valleys.

By the end of the thirteenth century, local records show that many of the valleys had very large populations. Farndale provides a good example of the complex processes of colonisation. The earliest references, of the 1150s and 1160s in grants to Rievaulx Abbey, St Mary's Abbey, York, and Keldholme Priory, deal with the transfer of rights to take timber for building, or fence-making and fuel, provided this did not affect the lord's hunting. The Abbot of St Mary's asserted 100 acres of woodland, ie he felled the timber and dug up the roots and, presumably, cleared the land for cultivation, actions which involved him in a lawsuit. By the end of the thirteenth century Baldwin Wake, Lord of Kirkbymoorside, had 90 serfs in Farndale, and another 26 on the east side of Bransdale, paying a heavy rent, performing many labour services and holding 'not by the bovate but more or less', ie in acres (in 1610 the average holding was about 14 acres, none more than 30). These farms, like today's, seem to have formed wide bands, running down from the farmstead. This gave the farmer access to arable on the slopes below his house and meadow in the valley bottom. The farm buildings were sited on the valley side, at the junction of the improved land and the moorland.

As time passed, land was enclosed upslope, creating 'intakes', and leaving wide driftways between the farmstead and the moorland pastures for the passage of stock, but these intakes are often of the sixteenth or seventeenth century (Fig 21). The high rents and the low personal status of the tenants (for in regions beyond Yorkshire, colonists were normally freeholders) imply that Farndale was cleared by the lord. It was then let to land-hungry peasants who were unable to break new land themselves. Rising rent tolls suggest that this colonisation took place in the thirteenth century.

We are on much firmer ground in another remote area, the township of Goathland, in the northern portion of the vast manor and forest of Pickering. Domesday Book shows no activity here, but there was some cultivated land by the early twelfth century, for Henry I endowed a hermitage with one carucate (ploughed land). Later in this century this was given to Whitby Abbey, who ran it as a small vaccary, or cattle farm, on which 20 cows and one bull were kept. A massive programme of assarting – woodland clearance – was then undertaken by the King's officers. A document in 1334, reporting back to 1217, states that a bailiff of Pickering, Robert de Coniscliffe, asserted 190 acres in Goathland and that later bailiffs added a further 308 acres. The land was then rented

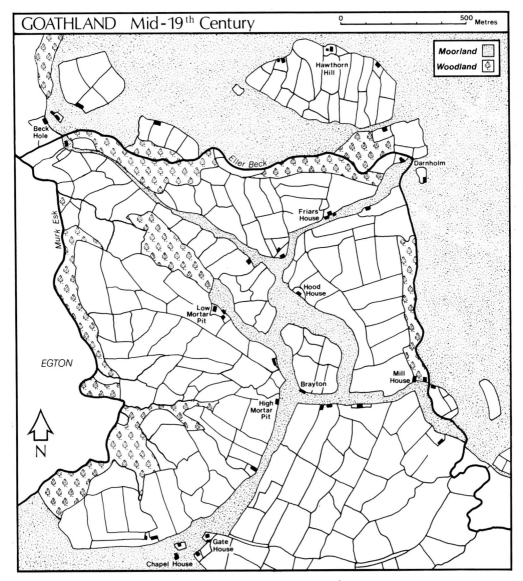

Moorland

Woodland

Hawthorn Hill

Beck Hole

Eller Beck

Darnholm

Murk Esk

Friars House

Hood House

Low Mortar Pit

EGTON

Mill House

Brayton

High Mortar Pit

N

Gate House

Chapel House

Fig 22 Colonising the wastes. New farmsteads of the 13th century. Note the strips of common left to provide trackways between the farms and links to the moorlands to the north and south

'. . . . . to diverse tenants for the need of the lord'. Most of this took place before 1298, for the rents of Goathland were then at their full level. A rental of 1599, giving the same level, names 32 farms, most of which originated in the thirteenth century and still appear, widely scattered, on the modern map (Fig 22). Similar policies were being adopted elsewhere. By 1336 the Lord of Danby enjoyed the rents of '42 cottages with various closes' in Glaisdale totalling no less than £25. For Pickering, the highly detailed review of 1334 shows that much of the assarting was undertaken by the great landlords to expand their highly profitable demesne (home) farms rather than for tenant occupation. The case of Goathland was an exception. Assarting and colonisation initiated by farmers rather than the great landlords did occur on the great estates in the centre of the moors, but generally on a small scale and in very limited areas. One instance is to be found in the remote valley of Hartoft Dale within the lordship of Cropton, where 32 men are recorded as the assarters of over 100 acres between 1312 and 1334. This could give each on average only three acres, to be sown with oats or mown for hay, and it is possible that these were merely additions to the township fields of the village, although by 1349 there were farmsteads in Hartoft itself. In a second instance, three energetic characters were compelled to pay the Earl of Lancaster 4 marks (£2.66) in 1334 for the trees they had uprooted at *Langedon*, Langdale. They then paid a formal rent for the reclaimed land.

In the villages around the edges of the moors much reclamation and colonisation were undertaken by the freeholders. Evidence for this is to be found particularly around the northern edges. Between Guisborough and Whitby there are a series of townships of strip configuration, extending inland from the coast to the watershed of the moors overlooking the Esk Valley. Here the land slopes back gently to the uplands, presenting no clearcut barrier beyond a decline in land quality. Even by the time of the Norman Conquest a second line of settlements had already been planted inland, with villages set on the moor edge like Moorsholm (literally 'the house on the moor'), Liverton, Ugthorpe and Hutton Mulgrave. Indeed in this zone names such as Normanby, Aislaby, Ugglesbarnby, Barnby, Mickleby, Ellerby, Borrowby, Roxby, speak of Scandinavian colonists avoiding the territories of older settlements such as Whitby, Hinderwell, Seaton, Easington and Brotton. Although this was a heavily devastated zone, in the course of the twelfth and thirteenth centuries a number of hamlets were created further out at places like Girrick and Scaling. In the manor of Skelton, right at the northern tip of the moors, where freemen were quite numerous, isolated farms were cut out of the wastes around Lingdale and Stanghow whose curved boundaries can often be seen on later large-scale maps. The farm called Kateridden ('the *ridding*, or clearing, of Kati') lay within a roughly oval-shaped enclosure on the moor south of Stanghow, and was held by a freeman, one Roger d'Aunou, in 1272, for a nominal rent of 1d. per annum. Near Lingdale, to the north, was another irregularly shaped assart known as Claphow, from the 'howe' or prehistoric burial mound still standing near the farmstead. Just south of Boosbeck there is a remarkable collection of curved field boundaries of freehold assarts. By the early fourteenth century these had given rise to a small hamlet called *Halikeld*, now Holywell Farm in Boosbeck. Nevertheless, we may even here be seeing the effects of lordly policy, for all of these holdings lie on the de Brus estates.

It is more difficult to see a general pattern in the expansion of settlement in areas of dispersed farms, but some examples can be quoted. One example (Fig 22) shows the central part of Goathland in the mid-nineteenth century, between Murk Esk Beck and Eller Beck. The settlement pattern is one of dispersed farms along the sides of wide strips of common which link the moors to the north and south of the enclosed, improved lands. Occasionally a few farmsteads coalesce to create small hamlets, as at Beck Hole in the north and around the Chapel to the south. Woodland is restricted to the steep sides of the streams and their tributaries. The presence of some 'master' enclosure boundaries, ie lines which are continuous over long distances, hint at former blocks, reclaimed as part of a single great effort. Many of the farm names have changed, but those recorded on Fig 22 appear in a late sixteenth century rental and are probably of medieval origin. Nucleation of Goathland village was caused by the coming of the railway in the nineteenth century. Secondly (Fig 20), one of the small farmsteads on the west side of Farndale, now Ellers House, formerly *Ellers*, is mentioned as early as 1301. The farm can be reconstructed by comparing a survey of 1610 with the Tithe Award of the 1840s. All the fields on the map appear in 1610, with the exception of 'New Intack', clearly a later arrival. The road along the side of the dale, formerly a mere track, links together many of the homesteads. It generally runs along the dividing line between the 'Intacks' and the other lands, which suggests that the farmsteads were placed on sites above the cold air flows down the valley. They were above the arable, so that manure could be carted downwards.

VACCARIES AND DEER PARKS

It is possible that landlords actually chose the more distant valleys in which to settle tenants. Closer to their residences they often used other methods of exploitation, with the intent of keeping their hunting preserves. The Mauleys of Mulgrave Castle held a vast and coherent estate stretching along the coast from Sandsend to Staithes, and inland across the Esk to the watershed of the moors. Most of their tenants were serfs living in sizeable villages as at Lythe and Egton or hamlet clusters as at East and West Barnby. The great upland tracts of this estate were exploited for the Mauleys themselves. In 1279 these comprised large blocks of land in out-of-the-way places such as Lease Rigg, above Grosmont, *Wivedale*, Wood Hill, in the south-west corner of Ugthorpe, *Cukewald*, Coquet Nook in Hutton Mulgrave, and the huge area south of the Esk known as Egton Grange. Given the problems of labour supply, these can hardly have been for arable use. By the fourteenth century great deer parks had been developed in all four corners of the estate – Julian

Park in the far south-east, above Goathland, Butter Park, south-west of Egton, Newbiggin Park, in the north-east between Egton and Aislaby, and *Cukewald* Park to the north-west of Egton. To this day farmsteads in Egton south of the Esk are few and far between, and bear names like Lodge Hill, Hall Grange and Grange Head, betraying their lordly origin. The boundaries of the deer parks themselves frequently survive in the landscape as banks or stone walls, and make interesting circular walks. Julian Park, in particular, has a spectacular park dyke running up the eastern slope of Egton High Moor.

A similar decision, to develop home farms, demesnes, rather than peasant settlement, seems to have been made by the de Brus family in their lands between Danby Dale and Glaisdale: this area embraced Great and Little Fryup Dale, the adjacent meadows around the Esk and a tract of pasture to the north called Oakley Side, in all an area of some ten square kilometres. In 1336 William Latimer held nearly 500 acres of meadow around the Esk, vital for growing hay to carry cattle, and in bad seasons even the deer, through the lean winter months. He also held huge cattle pastures called Fryup and *Le Heved*, ie Heads Pasture between Great and Little Fryup, and Oakley Side. In 1431-32 the lord kept some 200 of his own cattle in the pastures, but also drew a large income (over £50) from the leasing of grazing rights to others. One grazier had no less than 560 cattle 'nourished upon the pastures there' and paid over £18 for the privilege.

There appear to have been no houses on this great 'ranch', except the residential castle at Danby which the Latimers built for themselves in the late fourteenth century. The area remained a great consolidated block until it was sold off, enclosed and divided into tenant farms in the mid-seventeenth century. This pattern of extensive exploitation can be seen elsewhere, both on small and large estates. In Kildale the Percy family restricted peasant cultivation to a very small area around the village itself, keeping two thirds of the township, upland and lowland alike, for themselves, and using the long valley of Lounsdale as a vaccary. The Meynills operated a similar system from Whorlton where the long Scugdale valley was retained as demesne wood and pasture. In the remote area of Bickley, Thomas de Ebberston, lord of the manor, asserted 40 acres of land and built a house, which he retained in his own hands.

Thus, the medieval settlement in the area in 1300 showed great diversity. It was certainly not a land of opportunity for an upwardly mobile peasantry; land there was, but generally of very poor quality. As landlords usually made the decision and provided the effort for assarting, holdings were burdened with rents and services as high as those in the lowlands. To the lords went the bulk of the profits. That there were plenty of takers is due to the land hunger of this period. This, paradoxically, is a monument to the success of Norman resettlement in this wild and intractable zone. We should not overstate the case, for all the national measures of prosperity show that the medieval north was desperately poor compared with the prosperous south and east, a sombre precursor of present trends.

THE MONASTIC CONTRIBUTION

At the time of the Norman Conquest monasteries observed the rule of St Benedict, made in the great house at Monte Cassino in the sixth century. In the year 1098 a small monastery was founded at Citeaux in Burgundy and this became the mother house of an order which spread so rapidly that some 50 years or so later there were over three hundred houses scattered through Europe. The monks of this new order strictly observed the rule of St Benedict. At first, it attracted few recruits, but in 1112 it was joined by an organising genius, St Bernard, and from then on its success was remarkable. Why? The distinctive features of the Cistercians, a name derived from Citeaux, were insistence upon manual labour by the monks and simplicity in lifestyle in matters of dress, food, beds, building, the worship of God and the use of ornaments in services. Accordingly, Cistercian monasteries were founded on remote sites. The land was farmed by lay brothers, members who had not taken full vows, who lived in what were termed *grangia*, 'granges', in reality well-run farms. St Bernard's writing is unusual for the period (1091–1153): he combines a strong religious feeling with an appreciation of natural beauty and a frank, even exultant, appreciation of the role of man in changing the face of the natural world. But he was no mere romantic, for he shows equal enthusiasm for the way in which a stream course changed by labour so that 'the water is controlled to check inundations; it runs great mills and further on it fills the boiler for the brewer, and the fullers use it to operate the heavy pestles, mallets or wooden foot-shaped blocks, relieving them of heavy labour; the water then passes to the weavers workshops ... small streams wander in careless curves through the meadows, irrigating the fields before returning to the main stream'. No-one reading this can fail to be moved when visiting the scene of Cistercian labour at the great house of Rievaulx. Here, in truth, a waste place was made fruitful.

Whitby Abbey, with Anglo-Saxon roots, was destroyed by the Vikings and re-occupied in the period 1072–8 by Benedictine monks of the Order of Cluny. Like the Cistercians, this order emphasised community living, so that the sites of both are dominated by a great church, surrounded by communal dormitories; vast refectories and kitchens are characteristic, along with cloister walks, library, and chapter house for formal meetings. In sharp contrast, the Carthusian Order, established initially in a house at La Chartreuse, France, lived in individual solitude, so that their monasteries are dominated by single 'cells' arranged around a great

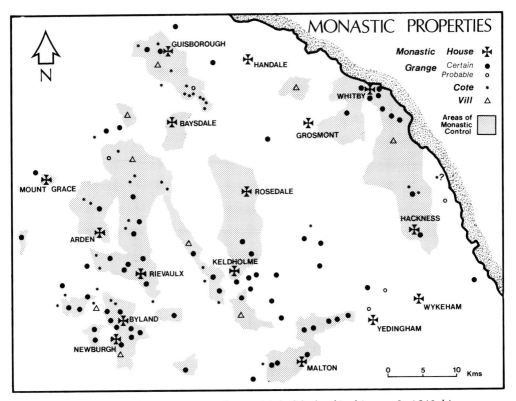

Fig 23 The monasteries came to own about a third of the land in this area. In 1540 this was sold in large and small holdings into private hands (*after B. J. D. Harrison*)

courtyard. Visits to Rievaulx and Mount Grace will quickly show the differences in practice. Nevertheless, all such houses had one thing in common: they contained large populations which had to be supported. No matter how ascetic the rule, grain and meat, skins and wool, timber and fuel, building stone and roofing materials, iron and lead had to be sought, and a supply sustained, as well as spices for preserving, fat for lamps and greasing tackle, pumice, vellum and gall for the preparation of manuscripts, lime for mortar and wine for guests and the sick, wood for trenchers, seats, handles and hods, heather for brooms, bone for toggles and spoons . . . the list goes on. Monks did not only pray, they were managers and accountants, engineers and craftsmen, dealers and artists. The paradox is that the more effective their production under the stimulus of poverty, the richer they could become. The concentration of intellectual energy and practical skills within a monastery, initially at least directed to the service of that house, could produce wealth greater than that of the ordinary secular castle.

Within a century of the Norman Conquest approximately one third of the area had been brought under monastic control (Fig 23). The process began in about 1077 with the refoundation of the Benedictine abbey of

Whitby, endowed by William de Percy with a great block of territory running southwards from the house as far as Hackness. The new abbey faced immediate problems arising from a combination of interference from the Percy family and raids from North Sea pirates. Within a few years many of the monks had left, first, for a new foundation at Lastingham (where the remarkable crypt and choir are a monument to their presence) and a little later for the more peaceful and civilised environment of York. More than a generation then elasped before the next wave of foundations. With the support of the reforming archbishop Thurstan of York (1114–1140) three great houses of Augustinian canons were established, at Guisborough (c1119) by Robert de Brus, at Kirkham in the East Riding (c1122) by Walter Espec, Lord of Helmsley, and at Newburgh (c1144) by Roger de Mowbray. The canons of this order were able to serve as parish clergy. The new houses were consequently endowed with parish churches rather than with landed estates, in the hope that they would raise the quality of church life generally and bring this remote area more firmly under the archbishop's control. However, by the mid-twelfth century, a time when the Augustinians were still at the height of their popularity, the new and more ascetic spiritual ideal was already commanding attention – the Cistercians. Even before monks from Clairvaux arrived at Rievaulx in 1131 word of the new order had caused such a stir in York that thirteen 'reformist' monks had broken away from the abbey of St Mary to form the community which subsequently settled at Fountains. Monks of the order of Savigny (later merged with the Cistercian order) beset by Scottish pirates and fleeing from their house at Calder in Cumbria were settled at Hood Grange above Thirsk in 1138. At first these communities lived in abject poverty; the monks of Hood (later Byland) endured the servility of living on one tenth of the victuals of the household of their founder, Robert de Mowbray. But by the 1140s there began a flood of land grants which within about twenty years gave vast tracts of North Yorkshire to the monks.

The initial land grants were made by the great lords. Some of the land was already settled and, particularly where the Cistercians were involved, arrangements had to be made to dispose of the sitting tenants. Other grants were of uncultivated moorland and wood. The Cistercian ideal, which was to affect the other orders to some extent, was to have no contact with ordinary tenant farmers and if possible to farm the land in large units or 'granges' staffed by lay-brethren. At Rievaulx the third abbot, Aelred (c1146–67) wrote that there were 140 monks and at least 500 lay-brothers in the mid-twelfth century 'so that the church swarmed with them like a hive of bees'. The huge naves of the abbey churches, exclusively for the use of these lay-brothers, and the great size of their quarters within the monastic buildings (seen spectacularly at Fountains) argue for the importance of this lower order of monks. And their labour was needed! The chronicler of Byland writing in about 1200 states that while the monks were still living at Old Byland (1143–48) they began to assart land in the wastes and woods of Coxwold. By 1152 they were in a position to build a stone church on the newly cleared lands, at Stocking (Oldstead), where they stayed for 30 years and '. . . vigorously began to uproot the woods and by long and broad ditches to draw off much water from the swamps so that eventually solid ground appeared . . . on which . . . they constructed their great and beautiful church', the present Byland Abbey, to which they moved in 1177.

In the outlying granges, even those close to the monastic house, the situation was very different. Rievaulx gave the peasants of Welburn the option of moving out or staying on, presumably as labourers. The monks from Hood did not wholly expel the villagers but in 1143 moved them to a new settlement at the place now called Old Byland. The earliest recorded Byland grange, at Wildon, was placed under the control of three knights, formerly members of Roger de Mowbray's retinue, who had become lay brothers. Described as '. . . of great name and prudence', they are more likely to have worked as farm managers than as labourers.

The Cistercian houses were not alone in their exploitation of waste areas by the grange system. Guisborough Priory's vast network of granges in the upper Esk Valley (Commondale township) was carved out of an area where no earlier settlement is known. The small priories of Rosedale, Arden, Handale, Keldholme and Baysdale (Fig 23) all seem to have assarted lands near their houses and to have farmed them directly from the monasteries. However, granges could be built up in other ways. Newburgh Priory profited from Robert de Mowbray's dispensing with his estate and manorial complex at Coxwold in 1144. The canons were granted a going concern on which to build their new monastery, embracing demesne lands, manor house, deer park and fish-ponds. Even their later grange sites at Brink and Ulthwaite seem to have been partially assarted by this time. Of course, granges could be accumulated piecemeal, so that the canons of Guisborough patiently assembled gifts and purchases of odd tofts and strips of land, and it took them over a century to acquire and engrange the large township of Barnaby, just to the west of Guisborough. Other granges on the lowlands – as at Marton and Ormesby – were slowly built up from the parish glebe (or parson's farm) which the canons controlled by virtue of their ownership of the parish church. Another line of approach, much favoured in areas of rich grazing like the Hambleton Hills, was for the monks to begin by acquiring rights of common pasture, followed by the construction of a sheep cote, and then to begin the process of reclaiming the land around it. Malton Cote, a sheep cote of Malton Priory, was surveyed before its recent destruction, and comprised a carefully planned structure (Fig 19). Eventually such a property could become a sizeable outlying farm, even if a little short of 'grange' proportions, as happened with the Rievaulx Abbey cote at Sproxton. Because every monastery was an undying corporation, maintaining careful records, the monks could afford to be patient, and by avoiding the inheritance problems to which lay estates were subject, they could take a long view of rounding off their estates. It took Byland Abbey several generations to acquire the whole of Osgodby from the Meynell family. And the monks had to wait until the fourteenth century to purchase the manor of Kilburn which was surrounded by lands they had acquired some two centuries earlier!

By the middle of the thirteenth century, scarcely a century after the foundation of most religious houses, the surge of expansion was practically at an end. The only way to increase estates was to buy land at the market rate – thus Malton Priory spent over £500 on land purchases between 1244 and 1257, mostly to develop its granges in the villages between Malton and Hovingham. By this time, however, many houses were heavily in debt, and indeed by the end of the thirteenth century probably none of them exceeded 30 monks and a dozen lay-brothers employed as grange-keepers and abbey servants. The epidemics of the mid-fourteenth century, by reducing population, made direct farming unprofitable. So that, while the home farms and granges were still kept in hand to feed the monks and their servants, outlying granges were leased out, sometimes *en bloc*, but often split into many small units. In Bilsdale, where Rievaulx Abbey had held four granges and four cotes in 1301, no less than 50 small farms had emerged by the early sixteenth century. At Byland the former grange-labourers' hamlets at Wass and Oldstead had been divided among some 25 tenants, and were well on the way to becoming agricultural villages.

MEDIEVAL CHURCHES

In the Middle Ages there were about 65 parish churches serving a network of parishes which was probably almost complete by early Norman times. On average there was only about one parish church to every three villages. But there were at least 29 chapels of ease (unendowed chapels served by the clergy of parish churches) and some 50 private chapels (perhaps many more) most of which probably provided some services for local congregations. Only 11 new parishes are known to have been created in the medieval period: Husthwaite, Kilburn, Thirkleby and probably Scawton seem to have been severed from the mother church of Coxwold in the twelfth century, and Sneaton and Fylingdales probably became independent of Whitby at the same period. Allerston, Ebberston and Wilton were carved out of Pickering parish by its patron, the Dean of York, in 1252, as an enlightened act of policy. Thereafter some of the chapels of ease acquired certain parochial functions but none succeeded in splitting away

Plate 15 Kirkdale Late Saxon Church in its quiet woodland setting. The tower was added in 1827 *(North Yorkshire County Library)*

Plate 16 Ingleby Greenhow Church. Early Norman nave with north aisle added in the late 12th century *(North Yorkshire County Library)*

Plate 17 Coxwold perpendicular church. Laurence Sterne's grave is here *(NYMNP)*

from their mother parishes before the Reformation.

Many former medieval churches were rebuilt in the late eighteenth and nineteenth centuries – particularly in Cleveland and the Esk Valley – but there are still some 53 parish churches and 17 chapels containing substantial medieval work. Of these a very high proportion (38 churches and 11 chapels) contain Norman work. The Norman parish churches were probably mostly rebuilds of earlier Anglo-Saxon churches – such as the 'wooden church' which Domesday Book mentions at Old Byland – but the scale of rebuilding is a testimony to the speed with which the Norman lords re-developed the area. For the most part the Norman churches are very basic structures. The large cruciform parish church, favoured by the Normans for their great estate centres, is represented only by Pickering and perhaps Whitby (other examples – Lastingham and Old Malton – were built to house monastic communities). The most common plan was a simple structure of nave, lower chancel and west tower. Aisles were not normally added until the late twelfth or early thirteenth centuries. A large and remarkably complete example of this type can be seen at Salton, a small but wealthy parish given by the Archbishop of York to the Prior of Hexham in the mid-twelfth century. Many churches were much smaller than this – the church of Great Ayton (a relatively large and mainly low-land parish) is a remarkably humble structure. The churches of small parishes could be miniscule, not even boasting a tower. The church of Scawton is a magnificently preserved example. Many churches acquired one aisle (usually on the north side) in the late twelfth century (Plate 16) and perhaps another in the thirteenth. Two aisles built at the same time are very rare, although Stonegrave seems to have them, as well as the chapel of St Michael which was built for the burgesses of the newly founded town of Malton. As one might expect, most of the chapels of ease were very small and basic; they have often been completely rebuilt in recent times, but St Peter's at Hilton-in-Cleveland is a relatively unspoilt example. Although most of our Norman churches are small, they occasionally have quite expensive decoration. The sumptuous carvings of the doorways at Barton-le-Street and of the chancel arch at Liverton (a mere chapel) are quite outstanding.

Later medieval churches are not well represented in the area. Thirteenth century work is mainly a continuation of late-Norman aisle construction and the rebuilding of chancels to cater for more elaborate rituals. The only near-complete church of this period is St Mary's at Scarborough, which has a fine west front and arcades of about 1200. There is very little fourteenth century ('Decorated') work to be found in the area; the almost complete Decorated church at Thornton Dale is quite exceptional. In the fifteenth century there was rather more activity but it was largely confined to rebuilding west towers – about 17 churches have a 'Perpendicular' west tower and others were heightened at this period. The best complete churches of this period are at Coxwold, with its octagonal tower and the great hall-church built for the townsmen of Guisborough around 1500.

This account of the evolution of the medieval landscapes reveals one fundamental fact: to a surprising degree, even many of the fine details of today's landscapes were already present by 1300. Building upon the prehistoric, Roman and Anglo–Scandinavian foundations, knights, monks and above all a host of peasant farmers and humble labourers created lasting patterns. The later changes to this landscape are the subjects of our following chapters.

6

AFTER THE MIDDLE AGES: AGRICULTURE AND SETTLEMENT

FOR the villager in Hinderwell or Helmsley, the end of the medieval period (c1536, as defined by tidy-minded historians) made no perceptible difference. He still lived in his flimsy one-storey cottage. He still paid rent, and in some cases remnants of feudal labour services, to his lord; though with the dissolution of the monasteries he might have exchanged a reasonably easy-going monastic lord for a more demanding layman. As yet he still went out to the common fields to plough his own or his lord's strips, while his children led the family cow to the common pasture. The staple of his diet was oatmeal and his family rarely tasted meat. He still lived on the edge of destitution; a couple of bad harvests could plunge him, his kin and his neighbours over that edge.

For the owners of land, down to and including the comparatively new and ebullient class of 'yeomen' – small farmers who had broken out of the rut of villeinage and acquired freehold or leasehold land – the end of the monastic era provided a unique opportunity to buy in more land. Purchases ranged from broad estates surrendered by a great abbey like Whitby or Rievaulx, down to an odd acre here and there in some fenced-off corner of the village fields or pastures. It was the modest but 'upwardly-mobile' yeoman section of the population which was to do most, over the next hundred years or so, to snap the remaining bonds of feudalism and open up society. A steadily expanding population in the sixteenth and seventeenth centuries, the price-inflation which went with the expansion, improvements in domestic architecture (Chapter 7), in new and revived industries (Chapter 8), and in communications (Chapter 9), all had their impact on the landscape.

ENCLOSURE OF THE COMMON FIELDS AND PASTURES

By far the most radical alteration on the face of the country as a whole came about in the ensuing centuries as a result of the enclosing of the

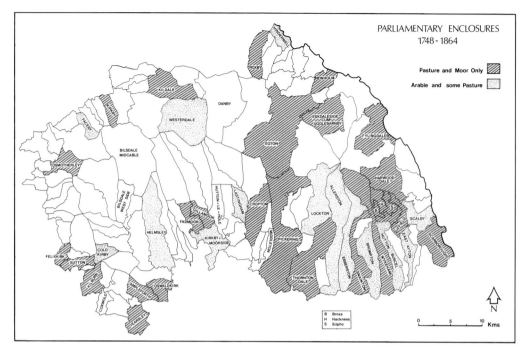

Fig 24 Enclosure of common fields and pasture was done by common agreement in the unshaded areas, sometimes over many centuries. In the shaded areas the landowners financed Parliamentary Acts

commons – arable, meadow and pasture. In this process the North York Moors differed significantly from the general pattern. Much of lowland England experienced enclosure mainly in the eighteenth and nineteenth centuries by means of parliamentary acts for individual parishes – what is generally termed the 'Enclosure Movement'. Even in the Midlands, however, there had been considerable earlier enclosure of commons by less formal and expensive means: notably by decree of Chancery, where the lord of the manor and the principal freeholders were in agreement.

Fig 24 reveals that within the Moors the role of parliamentary enclosure was small, save in the south-east quarter and to a lesser extent in the cliff-top townships of the coast. The one or two moorland parishes elsewhere which were the objects of a parliamentary act were exceptional: Kildale (to which we shall return later) was owned in the late eighteenth century by an enthusiastic 'improver', Sir Charles Turner; while the even remoter Westerdale – also at one time owned by Turner – had an act applied to it which covered a mere 171 acres (69 ha) out of nearly 10,000.

The relatively frequent parliamentary enclosures in the parishes between Pickering and Scarborough correlate closely with the old Forest of Pickering, where remnants of medieval forest laws and Crown ownership had for a variety of reasons inhibited the establishment of full-blown manorial townships; they tended now to be owned by families wealthy and powerful enough to over-ride tenant opposition by resort to a parliamentary act. The same was true of major manors like Helmsley – though here too the act was applied to only a tiny fraction (905 acres, 366 ha) of that massive parish.

As to the coastal strip between Hinderwell and Stainton, the significant feature of the terrain here is that, save where the boulder-clay is too wet and cold, the land is mainly arable, and the communities face landwards: fishing villages like Staithes, Runswick Bay and Robin Hood's Bay are odd men out on a coast remarkable for its lack of safe havens, and often began as mere appendages to cliff-top farming communities like Hinderwell and Fylingthorpe. The whole coastline, except at points where a buttress of sandstone stands up, as at Whitby and Scarborough, is composed of erodable clays and shales, and discourages maritime endeavour. Poorly served by roads as by coastal sea-traffic, it was in the main not until the nineteenth century that improved communications and the impact of industrial demands (see Chapters 8 & 9) brought the district fully out of a subsistence economy and made enclosure worthwhile.

What, then, of all the other parishes, on and around the moors, which were never the object of a parliamentary enclosure? Some, like Danby and Bilsdale, had developed an agricultural pattern which included little or no common arable, though with a good deal of open common pasture on the surrounding moors. Others had experienced piecemeal enclosure from the late medieval period onwards. The manor of Whitby, for example, was entirely parcelled up before the Abbey was dissolved in 1539, and Coxwold had lost most of its common fields by 1605.

What happened in most of the moorland dales was that in effect they skipped a stage in the 'classic' evolution of English landscapes. The normal pre-enclosure pattern in lowland England consisted of villages ringed by two or three common fields, with common waste, woodland and pasture beyond these. The inhabitants lived in the village and went out daily to work their scattered strips and graze their animals. Enclosure, by whatever process, broke this concentric pattern by dividing the great open fields into blocks where each man's holding was coalesced. As a result, the more prosperous villagers moved out of the settlement and built farmhouses on their new land, so creating the familiar arrangements of ring-fenced farms, each compact and self-contained around its new farmstead. Those who remained in the village, therefore, were mainly the landless labourers, smallholders, craftsmen and shopkeepers, along with the squire, if resident, and the parson.

In our moorland dales, by contrast, villages were always rare and small. Moreover the lie of the land generally demanded that the inner and outer rings of lowland village patterns be replaced by a linear arrangement across the contours, with meadow and winter pasture on the low ground, arable on the lower slopes, and rough pasture above. In the case of Bilsdale, much of which in the thirteenth century had been a chain of sheep-farms managed by lay-brethren of Rievaulx Abbey, there was a scatter of tiny hamlets in the north and none at all in the southern part of the dale. When the monks abandoned direct management of their lands, the granges were broken up into family-sized holdings and let to lay tenants who, from the fifteenth century onward, established separate farms, and so anticipated by several hundred years the post-enclosure pattern of the lowlands. Nor was a history of monastic ownership needed for such a system to develop; the same process had occurred in Danby parish by 1300, and there are even instances in remote areas like Raisdale (the north-west branch of Bilsdale) with its string of Norse farm-names, where one can still glimpse the layout of the original early medieval steadings.

Around the fringes of the moors, true villages and small market towns had become firmly rooted during the Middle Ages. But even though in a few cases their commons did survive long enough to require enclosure by act of parliament, the contents of many awards, like that of Helmsley, make it plain that both arable and pasture had already been subject to attrition and major reduction long before Parliament was called in to administer the final quietus. The most frequent terms for areas of land already separated off from the commons in these awards are 'croft' and 'close'. An estate plan of Coxwold drawn in 1605 records ten or more closes round the edges of the 'Whaytendailes' – former open fields now themselves partitioned. In Hackness half a century earlier 37 tenants had between them numerous 'little closes' of up to 12 acres (5 ha) in the town fields, and the common pasture was also divided up. Such creeping enclosures were the product sometimes of individual enterprise, sometimes of the need, as the village economy diversified, for paddocks or crofts for specific purposes, as evidenced in Coxwold by names like 'Horse Close', 'Fattinge Close', 'New Cowe Close'. Hutton-le-Hole in the seventeenth century had a six-acre patch in the common arable, then about to be enclosed by Chancery decree, called 'Linecroft', set apart for the growing of flax for the village linen-weavers. One of the fascinations of the whole area, indeed, is the variety of historical landscapes still visible. Between the very early parcelling-out of Bilsdale (Fig 25) and the seventeenth century enclosure of Hutton-le-Hole (Fig 26), for example, one can go to the township of Middleton, near Pickering, and see for one-

Fig 25 Small or medium sized farms carved out of the former monastic Laskill Grange. Note the many names referring to sheep farming

Fig 26 Hutton-le-Hole's open fields were enclosed by local agreement in 1671. Lund House and Douthwaite Hall had existed as separate farms long before this

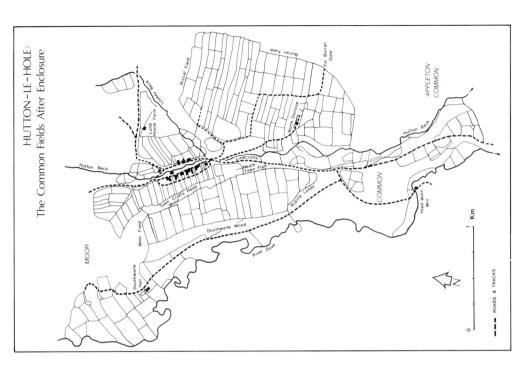

HUTTON-LE-HOLE:
The Common Fields After Enclosure

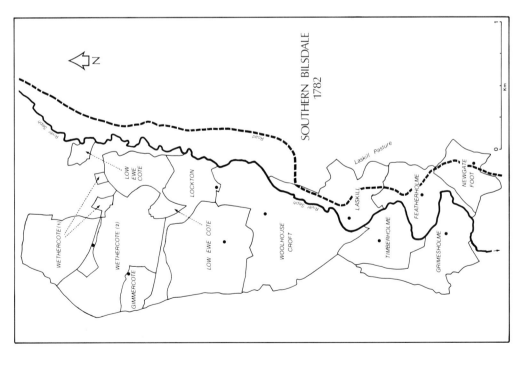

SOUTHERN BILSDALE
1782

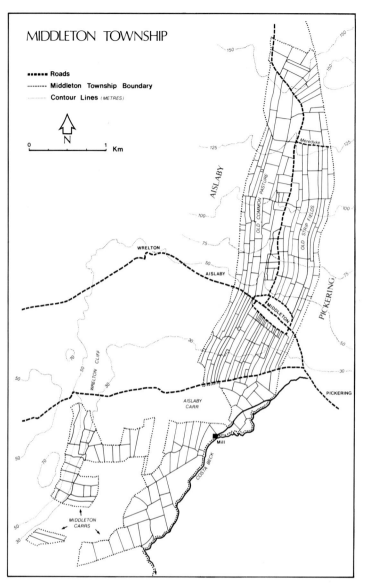

Fig 27 Middleton retains the pattern of curved medieval strips, fossilised by hedges planted after the Enclosure Act of 1765. The straight hedges north of the Meredyke divided up the previously open moor

self, on the ground, the curving pattern of the pre-enclosure furlongs embalmed in today's hedge-lines (Fig 27).

Most of our local enclosure awards and kindred documents, then, record a gradual process of enclosure of a long time-scale. Furthermore, on the outer perimeters of settlements there are numerous cases of larger 'assarts' or intakes from the waste which from medieval times have developed into separate holdings. Lund House Farm, north-east of

Hutton-le-Hole (Fig 26), seems always to have stood detached from the commons, while on the other side of the same village Douthwaite Dale, mentioned in medieval documents as a separate yet associated part of the township, appears to have evolved equally early as an independent sub-manor. By now the seat of a prosperous family called Shepherd, it had been at one time the base of officials supervising the hunting forest of Spaunton; Hutton's original name was not 'in the Hole' but 'Underheg' – under the park boundary.

Reclaiming Waste and Felling Woodland

Despite periodic recessions and climatic variations, the seventeenth century saw a major acceleration in the reclaiming of marginal wastes. Such holdings as High Hamer at the head of Hartoft Dale, Carr Cote above Bilsdale, and farms in the chilly recesses at the north-facing heads of Danby and Fryup Dales, are examples of this type of colonisation. We must recall, however, that many such sites had had a previous lease of useful life in the high-farming era of the thirteenth century, and should therefore be regarded as re-occupations rather than first-time settlements. One apparently new reclamation of some significance, however, was that of Langdale near Hackness, waste and wood-pasture in 1603, but leased a decade later with licence 'to convert the same to tillage . . . also to erect howses to dwell in . . . so as ther weere ten acres of ground laidd to every howse'.

This conversion of Langdale to arable is a reminder that, both inside and outside the royal forest of Pickering, woodland, as well as upland waste, was under threat from farmers seeking new land. Wooded areas have always been used by farmers, for pannage for pigs in the acorn season, for example, and also for sheltered winter grazing of stock in rides and clearings. The enduring problem has been to balance the needs of timber production with those of livestock. Numerous entries in the Pickering Forest records from medieval days onward show that this balance was steadily being tilted against woodland management, not merely by letting stock in to graze regardless of stands of saplings and coppice-wood, but by thefts of timber and by deliberate neglect and clearance to provide more grazing and occasional arable. A parliamentary survey of Pickering carried out in 1651 noted 'decayed and shaken' trees in Newtondale, and old 'dotterels' (pollarded trees allowed to re-grow without being lopped at the proper time) in Blansby Park, while timber trees worth £100 had been felled and cut up by the men of Pickering town. Some of the spoilers, too, should have known better. Sir Richard Cholmley of Roxby (Thornton Dale), one of the major landowners in the eastern moors and, like his forebears, a holder of royal office as master forester, was accused in 1580 of illicit assarting in the forest. Another survey, of the

Helmsley estates in 1642, includes a 'Wood Book' enumerating every major tree on the properties; the record here tells the same story of depredation and failure of management.

One recurring incentive for felling woodland regardless of long-term interests was that in time of financial crisis standing timber was often the only readily available cash-crop. If an heir like Sir Hugh Cholmley of Whitby in 1626 found debts encumbering his new estate, or if a mercenary custodian of a wardship wished to milk the property without blatant misappropriation, the sale of woods offered a prompt and less drastic alternative to the mortgage or sale of land.

A further reason for woodland mismanagement in this period was the decline of charcoal-burning iron-furnaces in the area, especially in Bilsdale and Rosedale. These had encouraged a positive regime of coppicing to ensure a continuing supply of charcoal, but with their abandonment there was little incentive to continue the practice beyond a minimal supply of small timber for agrarian requirements like hurdle-making. John Norden, the cartographer, surveying Pickering Forest in 1619, evidently regarded timber conservation as a lost cause. He remarked that 'there is little (large) timber left in the Forest. It hath been taken and felled long since', and went on actually to recommend the clearance and improvement of scattered pockets of woodland, pointing out that the rent of copses in Dalby Hagg, for example, brought in only a quarter of what the land was potentially worth. Such short-sighted views were to prevail, indeed, until the day of the late eighteenth-century reformers, to such an extent that in parts of the moors only steep, unimprovable gill-sides, as on Lythe Beck and West Beck in Goathland parish, were left unfelled.

Meantime, over the area as a whole, the vigour of yeoman reclamation did not always last. Inevitably cycles of economic depression affected also the 'new' farms. Even prosperous freeholders might get into debt and have to sell up, and the seventeenth and eighteenth centuries saw frequent cases of speculators buying up farms and quite often amalgamating holdings. Abbot's House in Goathland (then a staging-post on the Whitby–Pickering highroad as well as a farm) had a typical history of successive re-purchases. At various times between 1617 and the end of the eighteenth century it was bought by two Whitby businessmen, a London haberdasher, a local weaver, and a farmer from near Filey.

Enclosure itself could lead to speculation and amalgamation, and at the very least to bad feeling in the community, particularly if the poorer tenants found it beyond their means to carry out the necessary fencing and improvements to their new allocations, or if they had been persuaded into the scheme by richer neighbours against their better judgement. By no means all enclosures proceeded smoothly into operation, as witness the case of one 'awkward cuss', William Watson of Great Broughton. He had signed his name to the new arrangement and received his due allotment in 1629, but some time later a neighbour was startled to find, on arriving at his own new parcel, that Watson had begun ploughing right across it, along the line of his old common strips. The dispute dragged on for some years in the courts, even though Watson was quite clearly in the wrong; as his fellow-villagers testified, 'after he had taken the profits for a certain time of the grounds allotted to him, he did break the partition and division and entered his own former lands as they lay in common, and did sow and reap them which formerly he had exchanged, after he had received divers sums of money for fallowing of lands and for quickset fences'.

AGRICULTURAL IMPROVEMENT BY LANDOWNERS

With the eighteenth century the colonising efforts of yeoman farmers began to be overshadowed by larger-scale pioneering projects undertaken by 'improving' lords of the manor. 'Improvement' – the introduction of new crops, better strains of livestock, more scientific manuring – was very much in the air. The enclosure of common arable fields provided one source of such advances. But in an area like the Moors, with so great a preponderance of marginal land, local landowners also sought ways of exploiting such land more intensively and profitably. What could best be done with the rough pasture of dale-sides and the open moor above, much of it over 305m (1000ft) above sea-level?

Some improvers concentrated on breeding superior stock, especially cattle as the growth of industry in West Yorkshire and, later, Teesside brought a greater demand for beef to feed expanding populations. Sir Thomas Dundas of Upleatham in Cleveland was particularly noticed by contemporary commentators like John Tuke for his stock-breeding. Others, like Sir Charles Turner of Kildale, turned their attention to the unpromising soils of their moorland terrains. Turner's efforts – the marks of which can still be seen on the ground (Fig 28) – were at times over-ambitious and did not always survive their originator; but they were followed with close attention by contemporaries, and still merit study as an exemplar of what energetic land-management could achieve.

Kempswithen, Fig 28, the scene of Turner's most spectacular reclamation, is a ridge of moor dividing Commondale from Baysdale. It reaches about 305m (1000ft) above sea-level, whereas 240m (800ft) has generally been regarded as the limit for cultivation in this area. William Marshall, the eighteenth-century agricultural writer (himself a native of Pickering and well acquainted with the district), noted that Kempswithen is distinguished from neighbouring moors by a good deal of loamy soil 'much superior in natural qualities to the "high moors"'. It was presumably this factor which persuaded Turner that the ridge could be brought into productive use, not just for improved pasture or hay, but for cereal crops. To

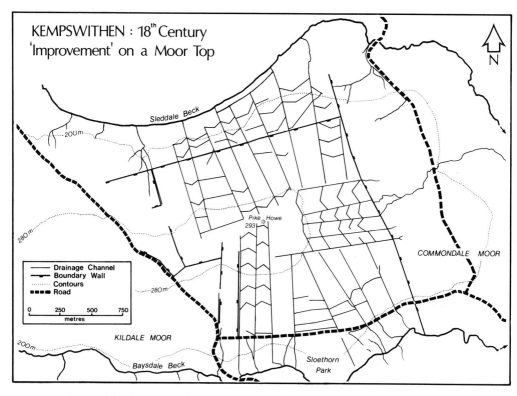

Fig 28 The drainage lines made by Sir Charles Turner in 1773 are still clearly visible. The improvement was unsuccessful and the land reverted to heather moor

this end in 1773 he had the crest and both flanks 'pared' – vegetation cut down to ground level – and the parings burnt and spread. Radial drains (see Fig 28) were opened down the hillside to take off surface water, then large quantities of lime were carted in at great expense and ploughed into an area totalling many hundreds of acres. The whole was enclosed within stone walls, lengths of which survive. Part was then laid down to grass and part to corn.

Marshall, who visited Kempswithen in Turner's lifetime, about four years after work began there, was a trifle contemptuous of the enterprise, criticising the initially successful attempt to grow cereals, but noting the good quality of the grassed portion. Another expert observer, John Tuke, coming a few years after Turner's death in 1783, was rather kinder, but confirmed that the yields of corn never matched the costs of labour and materials brought in to create the cornfield. Even though the Kempswithen enclosure was by then abandoned, Tuke notes the vegetational difference inside and outside the boundary wall, and concludes that if 'green crops and grass, for the support of small cattle and sheep, had been the object, the land would have been much improved, at an expence of perhaps not more than one-sixth part of what was laid out'.

122

Turner had better fortune on lower ground on Kildale, however; both Tuke and Marshall comment favourably on his improvements there, and on comparable measures by other landowners, as at Saintoft Grange (Middleton) and Lockton Moor where, on limier soils and at somewhat lower altitudes, both grassland and arable were successfully carved out of the waste. All these experiments, indeed, echoed on a larger scale the energy and enterprise of the earlier yeoman-led expansions, and they have left a lasting mark on the landscape of the moorland area. Along the rim of every stretch of moor the stone walls have crept steadily higher, and many of the upper fields still bear the name of 'Intakes' or 'Intacks'.

The importance of alkaline dressing in soil-improvement is well illustrated by the foregoing examples. A growing traffic in lime, both carted in from the southern edge of the Moors (see Chapter 9) and brought by sea from County Durham, was a feature of the whole modern period up to the nineteenth century. But there was a disadvantage for the dweller on the limestone subsoils of the Tabular Hills: he might not have to go to such expense in dressing his fields, but the pervious nature of the oolitic limestone has always meant problems of water supply. A feature of many settlements in this southern area between Black Hambleton and Burniston, though often infilled in recent years since mains water supplies became available, is a clay-pond. Nevertheless some villages, like

Fig 29 The watercourses conveyed water from the moors to the Tabular Hills, surmounting the scarps by routes brilliantly engineered by Joseph Foord from 1773 (*N. R. Staley, NYMNP*)

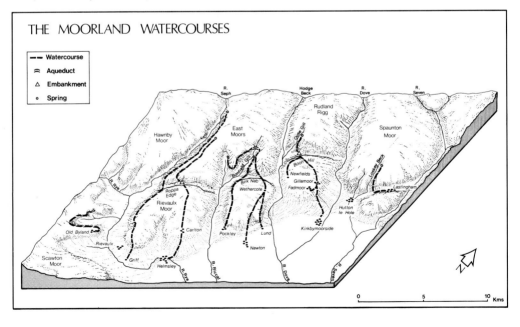

Newton-upon-Rawcliffe near Pickering, have retained quite large ponds, mostly dating from the eighteenth century when the technique of construction (rather on the lines of Sussex dewponds but without all their self-replenishing capability) became generally known.

Ponds, however, can fail in a dry summer, and the lack of a plentiful and reliable supply tended to inhibit cattle farming in particular (sheep can get by with a less regular supply) on the otherwise very suitable limestone slopes. Wells had long been dug where practicable, but the eighteenth century also brought to the district a more unusual technique which has still left traces around various hilltop villages in the south-west sector of the Moors. It was pioneered by a self-taught surveyor, Joseph Foord of Kirkbymoorside. He brought water 'on its own legs' by means of narrow, clay-lined channels or 'made rills', in a way graphically described by John Grayson, a contributor to the *History of Helmsley, Rievaulx and District*:

> Foord built his first watercourse in 1747, to supply Gillamoor and Fadmoor. Both villages stand at about 154m (500ft), and Foord had to bring the water from good springs rising some 92m (300ft) higher on the moors to the north . . . The water had to flow several miles on its course, and moreover had to be made to surmount the steep, scarped edge of the Tabular Hills . . . From the 'Surprise View' at Gillamoor the steep drop to the northward makes his difficulties quite apparent. It would at first seem impossible that water could ever have been brought to this village, standing as it does on the edge of what is virtually a 200-foot cliff. Foord, however, noticed that the plateau dipped gently eastward; he had therefore to find a point where the foot of the escarpment was higher than the village itself. He then laid his channel along the side of the hill from foot to edge with a gentle fall all the way. (When seen from below this stretch appears to be running uphill owing to the steeper gradient of the skyline.) To make certain that he got a satisfactory fall away from the hill foot, he constructed a strong bank two feet high from moor to scarp foot and led the water along the top of it.

Foord's calculations and execution were so successful that shortly after the channel reached Gillamoor and Fadmoor, Kirkbymoorside – the only market town on the southern flank of the Moors which does not adjoin a sizeable stream – applied to join in the scheme. So, via a settling-tank and a

(opposite) Bransdale, one of the most remote and lovely dales (*Ian Carstairs, NYMNP*). (over page) The Tabular Hills above Langdale End (*A. Staniforth, NYMNP*).

trough with three apertures cut in the lip, 2.5, 5.0 and 17.5cm (1, 2 and 7in) wide respectively, water was distributed to all three places, with Kirkby receiving seven-tenths of the flow, Fadmoor one-tenth, and Gillamoor.

Other courses followed (see Fig 29) on the Duncombe estates, and several survived into this century. At Lord Feversham's shooting-box, Cockayne Lodge near the head of Bransdale, it was even possible, by piping the last stretch of a late private course, to supply enough head of water to raise it to the upper floor of the lodge.

The one drawback of these open courses was their vulnerability to damage, from stock, rabbits, cart wheels, or just frost. Each course therefore had its surveyor or 'waterman', responsible for maintenance. Towards the end of the nineteenth century the waterman for the Nawton course was paid £25 a year for his pains. Thanks to his and his colleagues' efforts, the lines of several of these courses can still be traced on the ground, and some of the engineering works, like the 'floating' embankment below Roppa Edge, and the abutments of an aqueduct crossing Bonfield Gill on Pockley Moor, are still preserved – the latter thanks to conservation work, first by the Helmsley Archaeological Society and subsequently by the National Park Authority.

The increases in stock numbers made possible by enclosures, improvements of water supply and other advances, were largely responsible for a major change in land use that came about in the later eighteenth century. As noted earlier, the old pattern of husbandry in the parishes lining the north edge of the Vale of Pickering had followed the medieval practice of hay-meadow and winter grazing on the carrs of the vale bottom, arable fields and sheep folding on the south-facing limestone slopes, and rough summer grazing, especially for sheep, on the moor above. Improved drainage on the carrs, and the ability to graze more beasts on the higher and drier land, brought about some reversal of roles. In several parishes, as Marshall commented, carr-land was ploughed, and proved to yield heavier crops than the thin limestone soils above, while the latter were enclosed and put down to grass to feed the growing herds of beef and dairy cattle now being grazed on the Tabular Hills. There are signs, in the 'reversed-S' fence lines south of Middleton village (see Fig 27), that the new arrangement was practised there.

One of the most conspicuous features of the landscape in most parts of the Moors is, of course, the network of stone walls running up and along the dale sides. In contrast to similar drystone walls in many of the Pennine

---

(opposite above) Coppiced woodland in Bilsdale. *(opposite)* The Tabular Escarpment from Blakey Rigg *(A. Staniforth, NYMNP)*

Plate 18 Field pattern in Bransdale. The curved field walls are older than the straight ones, which usually date later than 1750. Notice the intake fields bordering the moor on the far bank. Some of them are becoming infested with bracken *(NYMNP)*

Dales – straight, geometric lines for the most part – which are largely the product of eighteenth-century enclosure, our moorland walls can be dated to a variety of periods from this century back to the medieval and perhaps in a few cases even earlier. In general, the more irregular their lines, the older they are likely to be. Recent fieldwork in Bransdale and Westerdale suggests that the irregular walls containing some orthostats – vertical, earth-fast stones – in their structure represent an earlier style of building than the more familiar horizontally layered type which developed with the advent of professional wallers during the 'Enclosure Period'.

As already remarked, the uppermost of these walls, the head-dykes bounding open moorland, mark successive 'advances to the margin' (notably in the thirteenth, early seventeenth and nineteenth centuries) as dale farmers pushed their pastoral and even arable activities up to and beyond the 800-foot contour in eras of prosperity, only to be driven back by climatic deterioration or economic recession. The highest levels of these 'intacks' may well have gone into and out of use half a dozen times in the past thousand years. The work of the adventurous dales communities is epitomised in one walled enclosure, high on Bilsdale East Side and just at the thousand-foot mark, which on an eighteenth-century estate map bore the name of 'Plowed Land'. Sir Charles Turner was not the only

130

pioneer with 'Excelsior!' as his device. Equally, of course, there are traces of prehistoric field systems discussed in Chapter 2, like the cairnfield at Iron Howe, surviving from very early attempts at arable cultivation at comparable heights.

Stone walls also mark that other type of enclosure, the gentry's private parks. The A170 road running east from Thirsk climbs Sutton Bank and continues towards Helmsley for several miles with a sometimes dilapidated stone wall on its north side. This is the old limit of the Duncombe Park deer park, which despite periodic culls still harbours some deer in its remoter corners. In the late Middle Ages there were upwards of thirty deer parks round the skirts of the Moors. By the time Saxton and Speed drew their maps at the end of the sixteenth century the number was down to single figures, and today their memory is often only preserved in place-names like Blansby Park near Pickering. The present-day Duncombe Park, laid out in the eighteenth century with its carriage drives and neo-classical temples overlooking Rievaulx Abbey, is one of few to survive as private domain, though the equally elegant Newburgh Park lies only a few miles to the south.

Two further sorts of wildlife preserves have left occasional traces. Names like 'Warren Farm' on the map are the mark of, usually, eighteenth-century artificial rabbit warrens. Most lie on the south-facing slopes of the Tabular Hills in places like Dalby Forest and Allerston, with some higher up around the Scamridge and Cockmoor Dykes area. Young, the historian of Whitby, noted over 6,000 acres in all given over to warrening in 1817. Though the vogue declined rapidly in the nineteenth century the alert walker can still spot the humps of artificial burrows or 'pillow-mounds', relics of an earlier style of warren. The extensive warrens of the eighteenth to twentieth centuries, up to 1000·acres, can be detected by their stone or turf walls and 'rabbit-types'. These are stone-lined pit traps, originally fitted with trapdoors that tilted under the animal's weight; about a hundred survive in the Dalby-Allerston forests, and there are some in remote High Langdale End.

Upright stones, tall enough to stand clear of ground cover and carved with landowners' initials on opposite sides, frequently mark the boundaries of those other lordly preserves, the grouse moors. The deliberate conservation, with periodic burning to clear the old, coarse stems, of thousands of acres of heather moorland to give shelter and sustenance to grouse, has been a feature of the area for some three centuries, and it now contributes not a little to the enjoyment of visitors, whether or not armed with shotguns. The seas of purple that greet the eye around Ralph Cross or Goathland in early autumn contrast markedly with the more sombre moods of the moors a month or two later, when clouds lower above darkened slopes. This latter, more typical aspect helps to explain the label 'Black' or 'Blakey' which recurs in place-names. Helmsley was widely

131

known until the last century as 'Helmsley Blackmoor', among other reasons to distinguish it from two other Helmsleys in the Vale of York.

The stone pillars that mark grouse-moor boundaries are only the latest in a succession of marker systems used by landowners to delineate their territories. Everywhere on the unfenced moors, and usually recorded on the larger scale ordnance maps, parish, township and manorial boundaries are marked by widely separated standing stones, some very old but most the handiwork of the eighteenth century. In 1716, for example, Edward Chaloner rode the bounds of his Gisborough estate with a company of 200 people on horse or foot. The record of this 'perambulation' – a standard practice in parishes at Rogationtide – described on Gisborough Moor a series of marker stones in addition to natural features or much earlier man-made landmarks like Tod Howe or the barrow called Hob on the Hill.

These newer boundary stones are often inscribed. The Hall Cliff Stone on Busby Moor, for example, has carved on it 'Duncomb Estate Bounder – Ye H. . . C. . . Stone', and another surmounting Breckon Howe, close to the A169 above Goathland, is marked 'Goathland Boundary determined at York Assises 1818'. In earlier days, when boundary descriptions often made use of comparatively perishable landmarks like trees, disputes over bounds were more frequent. Even sizeable standing stones might not be immune to tampering. In one lawsuit the plaintiff accused the defendant of having had a whole line of stones shifted bodily to take in a two hundred yard strip of ground. So as time went on landowners invested in more solid and identifiable markers. In several places along the Snilesworth-Osmotherley Moor boundary there are still pairs of stones side by side: a rough, unmarked stone of presumably medieval date, and a newer, more massive one, sometimes with its name – 'Nelson Stone', 'Robinson's Cross' – carved on it together with landowners' initials, as on grouse moor markers. There are stones with strange, often wildly corrupt names like 'Water Dittins', 'Slavering Ciss', 'Good Goose Thorn' (perhaps substituted for a vanished bush marker), as well as the better known 'Jenny Bradley', 'Margery Bradley' and 'Hob on the Hill'.

Along with such moorland crosses as Cockan Cross between Farndale and Bransdale, which has directions ('Stoxle Rode', 'Bransdale', etc.) carved on the remains of the medieval cross-shaft, and other stone waymarkers similarly inscribed, boundary stones are quite a conspicuous feature of the moors, at least when the heather and bracken are not high enough to mask them. They offer an opportunity for the keen walker to 'beat the bounds' in the steps of Chaloner and his ilk.

So during the period under review enclosure boundary-marking and agricultural improvement were all in their own ways helping to improve the lot of at least the larger farmers and landowners. New crops like potatoes made some difference even to the cottager's diet, and in one localised area Foord's watercourses had come to the aid of both farmers' and housewives' problems over water supply. What effects were such changes having on the pattern of human settlement in and around the Moors?

SETTLEMENT IN AND AROUND THE MOORS

The basic pattern of small market towns round the fringes of the moors, and even smaller and more scattered communities in the hinterland operating a mainly pastoral husbandry, remained largely unchanged in the post-medieval period. A conspicuous feature of the towns is that, especially on the south side of the Moors, they remained static in size and population right through the nineteenth century, in contrast to vigorous urban growth in the country generally. Some indeed, like Helmsley and Kirkbymoorside, even witnessed a modest decrease in population between 1801 and 1901, often as a result of declining local industry such as linen-weaving. In essence they remained what they had always been since their founding – providers of essential services for their hinterland, from grocers and tanners to lawyers and doctors, with, of course, a weekly market for produce and usually one or more annual fairs. It is little wonder that even today, despite the suburban skirts they have acquired in this century, visitors tend instinctively to talk of Helmsley, for example, as a 'village': a population of one and a half thousand may hardly seem to merit the label of 'town'. Yet in practice Helmsley is as much a market town as Thirsk or Pickering. Pickering in fact, thanks to its mid-way position between Thirsk and Scarborough, to a minor role as a railway junction (see Chapter 9), and to a slightly more substantial industrial base, did nearly double its population from 2,000 to 3,500 during the nineteenth century.

A roughly parallel situation is to be found in towns like Stokesley and Guisborough on the north side of the Moors, though distorted in part by industrial development (Chapter 8). Yet if in terms purely of numbers most of the moor-fringe towns failed to develop, some variations in their functions are apparent. The economic relationship between them and the rural communities they served inevitably underwent adjustments as the latter moved from an essentially subsistence economy to one of higher production.

The dominance of sheep in the dales, grown primarily for their wool, gave way to a mixed cattle/sheep husbandry. Hardy cattle bred in the moorland dales were sold to lowland farmers to fatten for beef. Later, in the nineteenth century, dairy cattle also figured more prominently, as improved communications between local markets and developing centres of population like the West Riding made it possible to send out cheese (especially from the Esk Valley), butter, and eventually even milk.

While the outer ring of towns prospered with this new traffic, the benefits within the Moors tended to accrue less to the villages and hamlets than to the families on the newer farms who, as we have seen, established themselves outside the traditional foci of habitation on their separate holdings. An extreme case in point is the huge moorland parish of Danby (including Castleton, the two Fryup dales and, for a time, Glaisdale lower down the Esk). Here, by the mid-seventeenth century, the bulk of the population was spread over more than 150 several holdings, and neither Castleton nor any other settlement in the parish contained more than a handful of dwellings. When the lord of the manor, Sir John Danvers, got into financial difficulties and put the manor up for sale in the Commonwealth period, all but a score of the farms were purchased by the sitting tenants, which indicates a fair degree of prosperity among the yeomen of the district.

By contrast the villagers and hamlets experienced increased economic fragility, and a tendency for population to exceed the employment available. This led to a considerable amount of migration, to the coast, to industrial centres, or even (particularly with religious dissenters in the eighteenth century) to America. Cleveland (Ohio) is a legitimate descendant of the north Yorkshire district, for example.

For the deliberate obliteration of a village one must seek the lowlands, as at Castle Howard, where the former village of Henderskelfe lies under the formal gardens and park. There are no instances of whole settlements being deserted within the moorland area. But some, like Pockley, undoubtedly shrank; landlords might well pull down surplus cottages to deter squatters who could become a charge on the poor rate. The mid-nineteenth century historian of Cleveland, John Ord, described one hamlet, Moorsholm, on the northern edge of the National Park area, as a 'dismal prototype of Goldsmith's *Deserted Village*'. He did not, however, mean that it was uninhabited, but simply primitive and wholly unimproved in his day. The speech of the inhabitants, Ord claimed, was unintelligible, they ploughed no land round about, and he questioned whether the appearance of the hamlet had changed since Norman or even Roman times. Fieldwork in the locality has disclosed the sites of several longhouses, which would have contributed to the hovel-like aspect of the cottages. Ord's asperity on the subject may be due to the fact that the Moorsholmers had at the time succeeded in blocking the execution of the Skelton enclosure act, promoted by Ord's friend, John Wharton of Skelton Castle. The lack of arable adjacent to the village was due to an historical accident rather than shiftlessness on the part of the inhabitants, since the cultivable land on the west of the settlement had been taken in as part of a Guisborough Priory grange in the course of the medieval period. We may wonder, nevertheless, how the hamlet survived without any ploughland: shepherding at best, one suspects, but at worst no doubt a hand or two in smuggling, poaching and other less legitimate pursuits.

Villages might also 'drift', in part or in whole, temporarily or permanently. Isolated churches, as at Leake, below the western Hambleton escarpment, are often evidence of this process, though in this case the disappearance of houses near the church took place before the modern period. A more recent and complex instance is to be found at Egton in the Esk Valley, where there has been a long-drawn tug-of-war between Egton proper, up on the moor edge, and Egton Bridge, down by the Esk and adjoining Egton Manor. Here too the old parish church (demolished in the nineteenth century) stood well to the west of either settlement. A complicating factor in this case was the strong element of Roman Catholic recusancy in the district, and the mid-eighteenth century purchase of the manor by a rigorously Protestant family of London goldsmiths. In the following century the development of Egton Bridge received a new fillip with the arrival of the railway.

'Temporary drift' can usually be identified, if only in faint and indirect glimpses, through parish registers and other records. In the previously discussed case of Danby, a good half of the total population was firmly anchored on the dispersed farms of the parish. But a sizeable element – cottagers, 'daytalmen', younger sons of farmers – seems to have been notably more volatile, moving, perhaps for only one generation, to wherever a new source of livelihood offered. The subsidiary townships of Danby parish, such as Ainthorpe and Fryup, seem to have experienced distinct fluctuations, as when Glaisdale in 1673 had just about as many inhabitants as all the rest of the parish put together. Little trace of such movements survives, of course, in the form of permanent building.

In contrast to shrinkage and drift, settlement growth generally coincided with improvements in communications and, especially in the nineteenth century, with the intrusion of industry into the moorland area. Whitby, thanks to ship building, fishing, coastal trade and the comparatively short-lived whaling industry, doubled its population in the hundred years from 1750, and was able to sustain much of the increase – despite the demise of the whaling fleet about 1837 – thanks to its emergence as a watering-place after the coming of the railway. By the 1850s George Hudson, the 'railway king', was building a hotel and the crescent on the West Cliff (Plate 45). Alum, jet and iron (Chapter 8) were the main extractive industries, with iron-mining attaining remarkable proportions in the mid-nineteenth century. On either side of the Esk population grew explosively in mining centres like Liverton and Skelton to the north of the river, and Rosedale to the south, where the population increased five-fold in the course of the century. The iron-mining boom had its repercussions in many a township less commonly associated with the industry. Swainby in the west, Grosmont, and many another isolated community witnessed an influx of miners from as far away as Wales and Cornwall as the ironmasters of Teesside and Tyneside sought new supplies for their furnaces. Even remote Beck Hole in Goathland parish saw Scar Wood ripped open in 1860, and two farms bought by an iron company to build a smelting works and cottages for the miners; but here, after a mere three years, the seams of ore proved unprofitable, and the Beck Hole boom collapsed in less than a decade. Elsewhere, when the ore was satisfactory, the industry endured for generations.

Viewed with hindsight, of course, nineteenth century mining has left a not wholly beneficial mark on the landscape, notably in the shape of spoil heaps and terraces of cottages of undistinguished aspect. Much building in Rosedale, for example, is roofed with Welsh slate brought in on the ore trains returning from Teesside, and cheaper than the more 'typical' pantiles which were gradually replacing thatch in other dales. Time, however, has wrought its customary healing, and thanks in part to the current interest in industrial archaeology the surviving evidence of mining activity, such as the Rosedale East Side calcining kilns, is now accepted as 'picturesque'. There was even sentimental regret over the demolition in 1972 of the towering chimney of the stationary winding engine on the other side of Rosedale. Its companion at the other end of the moor railway above Ingleby Greenhow, where the ore trains were winched down to Battersby Junction on their way to Middlesbrough, had already been felled during World War II as too helpful a landmark for German bombers heading for Teesside. In time the scars of more recent mining activity north of the Esk will likewise blend acceptably into the landscape, its polluting potential conveniently forgotten.

Even before the iron boom other extractive industries like stone quarrying had had their effect on population within the Moors. Canon Atkinson, the historian and long-time vicar of Danby, recorded in his classic *Forty Years in a Moorland Parish* (1892) that 'both Castleton and Dale End' (the present Danby village, north of river and railway) 'have grown up to what they are within the present century . . . The number of habitations at Castleton a hundred years ago was not more than six; while at Dale End there were but two.' In the case of Castleton at least, this statement is a little surprising; if Atkinson's figures are based on his parish registers he may have underestimated nonconformist elements. By the second half of the nineteenth century Castleton had, in addition to an iron-framed Anglican church, Wesleyan and Primitive Methodist chapels, and a Quaker Meeting House. Certainly, however, the development of Castleton into a small but thriving market town was not initially the consequence of either iron-mining or even the arrival of the railway. Already, in the first half of the century, stone quarrying, a little coal-mining, and also a short-lived silk mill (later adapted to flax spinning), had supplemented the activities connected with its annual cattle, wool and cheese fairs. Thus between Castleton's first apparent emergence from a hamlet phase some time in the eighteenth century and its apotheosis as an agricultural and industrial focus for the upper Esk Valley in the nineteenth, it grew, for no one paramount reason, to take over Kildale's old function as a market and to dominate the rest of the sprawling Danby parish.

THE PEOPLE: LANDOWNERS, WORKERS AND TOURISTS

The appearance of an installation as exotic as a silk mill raises a significant, and so far not fully investigated, aspect of economic development in north-east Yorkshire: the role of the landed gentry in the encouragement of local industry. A feature of the area in the post-medieval era has been a large proportion of comparatively modest landowners who were customarily resident on their estates. There is no evidence that such men involved themselves in the promotion of, for example, cottage weaving industries. The role of entrepreneur in such circumstances was usually taken by the 'brogger', the middleman who distributed raw materials to individual weavers and who in his own interests would assist them to acquire looms and other equipment on credit. But where greater capital investment was needed, as in the case of a silk mill or a coal mine more advanced than the bell-pit type, it is likely that the landowner (whose revenues would benefit in rents or royalties) was frequently a partner in such enterprises.

Certainly there is some evidence to suggest a closer and more enlightened interest by north Yorkshire squires in the social and economic well-being of their communities than was the case in other parts of England: we may surmise at least a brisker leaven, in Henry Fielding's terms, of Squire Allworthys among the Squire Westerns. Village schools, for example, were often set up and endowed long before the 1870 Act in places like Hinderwell, Fylingdales, Ugthorpe and Ingleby Arncliffe. For an atypical but revealing illustration of this tendency in the squirearchy we may turn once more to the Turner family of Upleatham and Kildale. A seventeenth-century forebear of Sir Charles Turner, the Kempswithen improver, had been Lord Mayor of London, and also built and endowed Turner's Hospital in Kirkleatham. Subsequent members of the family endowed a free school (1709) and enlarged the hospital (1742). Sir Charles himself was MP for York City from 1768 until his death in 1783. The independent quality of his mind is epitomised in a speech he made in Parliament a year before his death. The House was debating the Game Laws, and Sir Charles, almost uniquely among his fellow members, opposed increasing the already harsh penalties against poaching. 'The House is too fond,' he said, 'of making laws for gentlemen and not for poor men. Had I been a common man I would certainly have been a poacher.'

His sympathy for poachers was perhaps due to his own lack of enthusiasm for preserving game. His preferred sports were horse racing and hunting. Local hunts have a long history on the Moors, notably in Bilsdale, where the famous (or notorious) gravestone carved for the nineteenth century whipper-in, Bobby Dowson, can still be seen outside the Sun Inn, having been refused erection in the churchyard. Racing too had a respectable ancestry. In its heyday (early eighteenth century) the Hambleton Racecourse, north of Sutton Bank where race horses still train, was a favourite of the racing fraternity, with a Royal Plate run for a trophy presented by Queen Anne; and there was a later course, no doubt frequented by Sir Charles and his string, at Egton on the high ground north of the village.

All in all the gentry of our area have had a considerable, and on balance beneficial, influence on the appearance of the area. It was they who began to encourage and practise the revival of tree planting, if principally in the form of shelter belts, which became fashionable under the urging of writers like Marshall. They have been less prone than in other parts of the country to pour money into ostentatious pleasure grounds and self-advertising monuments like follies. Apart from the eighteenth century neo-classical temples of Duncombe Park, the few such structures tend to have an improving object, like the monument to Captain Cook on Easby Hill above Great Ayton, erected nearly fifty years after the great navigator's death by Robert Campion, Esquire, or the 'observatory' above Oldstead which bids the visitor

> see rich industry smiling on the plains,
> and peace and plenty tell Victoria reigns.

Another facet of community life in which the gentry played a key part was the great nineteenth century rebuilding of churches. The mid-Victorian era saw a notable counter-attack by the Church of England against the influence of other denominations, and its mark can be seen in the large number of local churches which were either wholly rebuilt or heavily restored. Few remnants of medieval work survive in any of the churches of Eskdale, for example. The results, even when architects of the stature of Barry (Helmsley All Saints and Bilsdale St Hilda) and Gilbert Scott (Kirkbymoorside All Saints and Pockley St John Baptist) were involved, are not always to our taste today, but they are there for all to see. There was also a considerable amount of new church building, as at Great Ayton, Swainby, Egton and Skelton, on the Cleveland side, while a dozen more, particularly in villages around Helmsley, went up on the south side of the Moors.

Even some of the enclosures encompassed by landowners were not wholly to the disadvantage of their tenantry, for while the exclusion of cottagers from former commons was undoubtedly damaging to their livelihood, the conversion of pasture to productive arable, as Turner aimed to do on Kempswithen, would create rather than diminish employment. Such often benevolent intentions, however, did little to mitigate labouring-class hostility to enclosures. Quarter Sessions and manor court records make regular reference to the activities of 'hedge-breakers' – individuals or occasionally gangs engaged in throwing down the hated enclosure boundary fences.

This form of protest seems to have been most rife, perhaps due to Leveller influence under the Commonwealth, in the seventeenth century, but a local chronicler of Victorian times claimed that Kirkbymoorside was 'still remarkable' for its hedgebreakers in his day. The later manifestations of the practice seem in fact to have been less a deliberate political act than an illicit means of gathering sticks for cottage fires. It has to be remembered that the loss of their commons deprived villagers not only of pasture but of rights of turf and wood gathering. Some landowners indeed were careful to reserve areas for cottagers to exercise these rights, but the majority were less scrupulous. More and more it was only the prosperous tenants and freeholders who were in a position to rent grazing land. The poor, as so often, tended to get poorer. By 1800 there were few true commons left in the area. Appleton-le-Moors Common is one such survival, with grazing rights still shared among householders. Over the moors as a whole common land dwindled away to tiny fragments.

Even the labourer's cabbage patch was often threatened too, despite optimistic provisions in some post-enclosure leases, such as the one quoted earlier in this chapter for Hackness, where the lessor stipulated that each new cottage erected should have ten acres of land attached.

With the nineteenth century the growth of West Riding and Teesside populations gave a new stimulus to arable production around the moors, just as it did to meat. Oats, a hardy cereal, could be grown at the limits of cultivation on previous rough pasture, and oatmeal found a ready market in the new industrial districts. The acreage devoted to cereal crops in the Esk Valley and elsewhere increased both absolutely and in proportion to grassland. Tithe schedules of the mid-century show an average for the region of 32% arable as against 67% grazing. But the exploitation of high marginal land for crops brought its own hazards. John Tuke, writing at the beginning of the century, was already commenting that 'it frequently happens that the crops are cut long before they are ripe, and are still in the field when the ground is covered with snow'.

In a period of generally expanding population, numbers locally held reasonably steady, with slight falls noticeable in the western sector of the Moors. In the east, coastal settlements like Staithes, which had first emerged as fishing communities about the sixteenth century, grew markedly, as rail transport to London and northern cities gave a boost to the fishing industry. The railways also brought about a burgeoning of

139

what would later become known as tourism. By the end of the century gazetteers like *Kelly's Directory* were discreetly recommending 'first-class' hotels in the major resorts. Scarborough, of course, had been a spa town since the discovery of mineral springs south of the old town in the seventeenth century. Even in the heart of the moors the Mallyan Spout Hotel was open in Goathland, though it did not then rate as first-class, and the hotel owner doubled as a farmer in the list of village tradesmen; Goathland also contained two landladies offering 'apartments' for more modest or family-burdened visitors.

At the beginning of this chapter we considered the lot of the ordinary labourers in the sixteenth century, in their turf-walled or rubble-stone bothies, with starvation an ever-present possibility. The Helmsley labourer's descendant in the latter nineteenth century probably lived in a sturdy cottage built in local stone by his landlord and employer. He doffed his billycock hat just as promptly, no doubt, as Lord and Lady Feversham turned out of their park gates in their carriage. Under the paternalistic eye of Vicar Gray and his squad of curates from the commodious vicarage which now houses the National Park headquarters, our cottager was comparatively free from extremes of want. If he had led a loyal and blameless life he might even hope to remain in his cottage at a token rent when he grew too old to work. In 1901 the Helmsley workhouse, rebuilt to house 65 inmates, contained only 29.

The Helmsley man's counterpart in Hinderwell (where enclosure of the commons had come exceptionally late) might well have gone to sea with the Staithes cobles, or have migrated to Boulby or Liverton to mine alum or iron. If he stayed on the land he too would be rather better off than his sixteenth-century forebears, even though council-built housing and old age pensions were as yet little more than dreams at the back of a few Liberal politicians' minds.

Between the early sixteenth century and the end of the nineteenth, then, the appearance of the land in which our labourers and their social superiors lived, worked and sported had undergone quite considerable changes. Houses, for all classes, grew in size, solidity and convenience. Much more land was parcelled out, almost all of it among the better off. All but the highest moors – from which the last wolf may only have vanished some time in Henry VIII's reign – were taken in for ploughing or pasture. Woodland too was depleted in the quest for more intensive use of every farmable acre. Quarries and mines were dug, limekilns and smelting works constructed, and eventually abandoned, for lichen and stonecrop to recolonise in the van of nature's own reclamation. A number of mostly small reservoirs were installed from the mid-nineteenth century, to supply water to the growing towns below the moors. The following chapters go into detail on the most significant aspects of all these developments.

7
DOMESTIC BUILDINGS

O<small>F</small> all landscape features, buildings bring us closest to real people, to the way they lived, thought and presented themselves to the world. Rievaulx Abbey with its quiet setting in the dale, and its noble architecture, represents one way of living; Duncombe Park and the exuberant Baroque of nearby Castle Howard set on hills to dominate the countryside, proclaim in Pevsner's words the 'unquestioning sense of being on top of the world' of the eighteenth century aristocrats. For most people, however, such notions were out of place. Farmhouses and cottages were at the centre of working life, and elegance was a lesser consideration. At the bottom of the scale, it was a question of keeping some sort of roof over the family's heads. This chapter will describe the whole range of the surviving houses.

The earliest standing buildings are of medieval date – castles, churches and monasteries. Among the important castles are those at Helmsley (Plate 9) and Pickering in the south and Danby in the north, and the principal monastery is Rievaulx Abbey, one of the most complete survivals of such a site in England. Lesser buildings of the Middle Ages include the vicarage of Canons Garth, Helmsley, parts of which date from the late thirteenth or early fourteenth century, what may be the chapel of a manor house at Sinnington, and a late medieval tower house, Ayton Castle. Medieval manor houses have otherwise been rebuilt or demolished; sometimes in the latter case, as at Cropton and Roxby (Thornton Dale), they survive as earthworks. A wider range of buildings remains from the post-medieval period. Houses of the nobility and gentry date from the sixteenth century and later, yeoman farmhouses survive from the seventeenth, the professional middle-class houses from the late eighteenth, and many workers' cottages were built in the nincteenth century.

HOUSES OF THE NOBILITY AND GENTRY

The dissolution of the monasteries changed the pattern of landholding but did not upset it. The Manners, earls of Rutland, acquired many of the lands of Rievaulx Abbey in Bilsdale, but as they already possessed Belvoir and Helmsley Castles, they did not convert buildings at Rievaulx to

141

domestic use. This was not so at all other monastic sites. Rosedale Priory was robbed and survives only as a fragment, and Baysdale Abbey was rebuilt. The new landowners at Arden Priory, Wykeham Priory and Whitby Abbey made houses from their buildings, which remain as the cores of the present Arden Hall, Wykeham Abbey and Abbey House, Whitby.

Later in the sixteenth and in the seventeenth centuries there was more building by the nobility and gentry, and this is interesting both for its form and for its distribution. In the south-west and over much of the north of the region, areas dominated by great estates, there was only limited building work. At Helmsley Castle (Plate 9), from 1572 to 1582, Edward Manners, 3rd earl of Rutland, spent large sums rebuilding and up-dating the west tower and west range. Surviving from this period are the fireplaces in the tower, as well as panelling, plasterwork, windows and fireplaces in the great chamber and withdrawing chamber. Danby Castle was refitted in the Elizabethan period by the Earl of Danby. The Rutlands also provided houses for agents, family stewards and the like, as with such buildings as Rectory House, Helmsley, and High Hall and Buckingham House, Kirkbymoorside. The main building by the upper gentry at this time was, however, away from these great estates. These houses were mainly in the south-east where a series of smaller estates had been established (Chapter 6). Surviving and demolished gentry houses of this period include Welburn and Riseborough Halls near Kirbymoorside, a series of houses to the east of Pickering, including Thornton Hall at Thornton Dale, Ebberston Hall and Church House in Ebberston, High Hall and Low Hall at Brompton, Wykeham Abbey, Hackness Hall and Newbiggin Hall, Egton.

The nature of the building work, which was mainly new construction rather than adaptation, varied from established plan forms to more innovative layouts. The late medieval form of manor house formed the model for what was, until it was rebuilt in 1891, the earliest part of Welburn Hall. It was probably of mid-sixteenth century date, and was timber-framed. It had a hall, open to the roof and with a screens-passage at one end, set between two-storeyed cross wings, that next to the screens-passage principally for service use, and the other with private family rooms. This basic form of building, but with a hall with an upper storey, was used in the sixteenth century at High Hall, Brompton and at Wykeham Abbey. Though the parts likely to be original are now largely hidden by remodelling, their form is known from eighteenth century drawings by Samuel Buck. Each had storeyed porches in front of off-centre screens-passages, and mullioned and transomed windows. Near-contemporary houses of the lesser gentry follow the same plans. The late sixteenth century Rectory House at Helmsley, which now forms part of the Black Swan, has the storeyed hall and end screens-passage of these houses but, as befits its status, it was built on a lesser scale and was

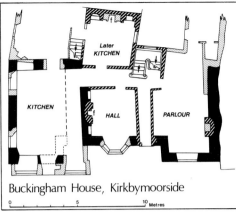

Buckingham House, Kirkbymoorside

Plate 19 & Fig 30 A seventeenth century house built for a steward of the Helmsley Castle estate *(RCHME)*

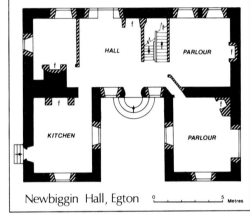

Newbiggin Hall, Egton

Plate 20 & Fig 31 A later seventeenth century gentry house *(RCHME)*

KEY TO BUILDING PHASES	FIRST PHASE	SECOND PHASE	THIRD PHASE	FOURTH PHASE

originally wholly timber-framed. Two other Rutland properties, High Hall and Buckingham House in Kirkbymoorside, both built in the first half of the seventeenth century, are similar in plan and size, the former originally timber-framed, the latter (Plate 19 & Fig 30) of stone.

The off-centre positions of the screens-passages and consequently of the entrances to these houses conflicted with the fashionable seventeenth century desire for symmetry. Two surviving houses with symmetrical elevations, Newbiggin Hall, Egton (Plate 20 & Fig 31) and Thornton Dale were built in the late seventeenth century; their halls, though still used for

143

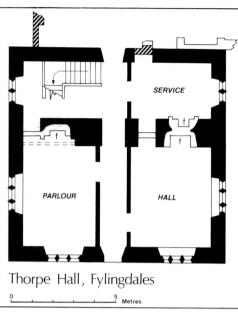

Thorpe Hall, Fylingdales

0   5 Metres

Plate 21 & Fig 32 Built in 1680, the first double-pile gentry house in the region (*RCHME*)

some domestic purposes, also served as a more formal entrance hall. The origin of the plan of all these houses lay in the medieval period, although there were some improvements and changes in room use; they have no centralisation of circulation which is found in some other houses of the seventeenth century. This was introduced in double-pile houses, that is houses built two rooms deep and two rooms wide, in which a central entrance hall and staircase enabled all the main rooms to be reached independently. The first house in the region built to this plan, in 1680, was Thorpe Hall, Fylingdales (Plate 21 & Fig 32). Quite different in plan from all preceding houses, it was traditional in detailing, with mullioned windows rather than the more fashionable cross-windows of the near-contemporary Thornton Hall. There is no sign of the classical internal detailing which a few years later was a feature of the fine south block added to Arden Hall.

The geographical spread of upper-class building of the sixteenth and seventeenth centuries was similar in the eighteenth and nineteenth. From the late eighteenth century houses were built for professional men which in form and size are often similar to those of the lesser gentry. Most of these were double-pile houses which were compact, symmetrical and convenient. This plan was also adopted for the main block of the greatest new house of the eighteenth century, Duncombe Park, near Helmsley.

The Helmsley estate, owned at this time by the dukes of Buckingham, was bought, on the death of the second duke in 1688, by the London

144

banker, Sir Charles Duncombe. He died in 1711 and his brother-in-law Thomas inherited the estate, changed his name to Duncombe, and began to build Duncombe Park. The house was erected about 1713 to the designs of William Wakefield, a gentleman architect from Huby. The wings now date from the nineteenth century, as too does the main block, which was rebuilt close to the original design in 1895–6 after being gutted by fire in 1879. Duncombe Park, lying west of Helmsley Castle, which it replaced as the residence of the Helmsley estate, was more than just a mansion since its grounds were planned on an equally ambitious scale (Plate 22). A gently curving terrace south of the house, with a temple at either end, overlooks the steep valley side of the River Rye which breaks in the centre over a cascade. This and an eastern terrace and a broad walk passing the garden front are bordered by plantations which came to have winding walks and formal clearings. Thomas Duncombe's work was probably completed after his death in 1725 by his son, Thomas Duncombe II. Thomas Duncombe III, who inherited in 1746, made another terrace, complete by 1758, overlooking the ruins of Rievaulx Abbey. The Rievaulx Terrace, also with a temple at each end, is not as formal as the earlier one, winding along the contour and unfolding a series of picturesque views.

The grounds of Duncombe Park can be claimed as among the most extensive and boldest landscaping enterprises in England, but they are not the only ones in the region. Ebberston Lodge, now called Ebberston Hall, was built in 1718 for William Thompson, MP, to the design of the architect Colen Campbell. Thompson's main dwelling was near Beverley, and Ebberston Lodge was a summer residence set in a well-planted park at the end of a cascade and canal. This small house is of one storey over a

Plate 22 Duncombe Park, Helmsley. First built about 1713, it was destroyed by fire in 1879 except the façade. Rebuilt 1895 *(RCHME)*

basement. The main floor has an entrance hall and loggia between a parlour and bedroom, each with a closet. It was originally flanked by blocks for stables and offices. Ebberston Lodge was a rural retreat, but to Squire George Osbaldeston, who lived at nearby Allerston Hall and acquired it in 1814, it became a base for sporting activities. Danby Lodge in the Esk Valley, now the National Park Centre, served a combination of both functions for the Dawnays of Wykeham Abbey. An inventory of 1761 includes stables, dog kennels and a pheasantry as well as domestic and service accommodation. In 1808 it was observed that Lord Downe occasionally lived there during the shooting season, the house being 'calculated merely for a small party to enjoy the sports of the field or to explore the wild mountain scenery in the neighbourhood'. The use of the moors for sport is reflected in other mainly nineteenth century shooting lodges, most of them along the southern moorland edge, including Nawton Tower, Bransdale Lodge, Bumper Castle, Spaunton Lodge, Sutherland Lodge and Keldy Castle.

Household requirements and fashions changed with time, and during the eighteenth and nineteenth centuries most of the large, gentry houses of the sixteenth and seventeenth were remodelled, extended or replaced. Alterations and infilling between the cross-wings in the late eighteenth century transformed Wykeham Abbey's irregular front into a classical style which was reflected in the interior. The Elizabethan Hackness Hall was replaced on a new site in 1797 by a two-storey, seven-bay long classical house designed by the York architect, Peter Atkinson, and at Welburn Hall, W. H. Brierley, a later successor to Atkinson's practice, replaced the timber-framed hall with a Jacobean-style structure in 1891.

Houses of the lesser gentry are found mainly, as in previous centuries, in the east and south-east of the region. Some were sited in villages and were equivalent to historic manor houses, which some indeed were, and others in the open landscape, more like country seats. Esk Hall, Sleights, of early eighteenth century date, is among the first. Fully double-pile, with front and back rooms of equal size, it was built with a recessed centre at the front. Mid- and late-eighteenth century houses, such as Aislaby Hall, Middleton Hall and Wydale Hall, all double-pile, are essentially pure rectangles. Their central front doors open on to entrance and staircase halls from which reception rooms, service rooms and bedrooms could be reached. Woodlands at Aislaby, near Whitby, which has a slightly less regular plan due to its situation, was rebuilt in the late eighteenth century by Henry Walker Yeoman. Yeoman, whose family formerly lived at nearby Newbiggin Hall, used his inherited wealth and profits from local alum workings to build his home on a better site. The house with its crenellated parapets (Plate 23) exploits its picturesque setting. Hawsker Hall at Hawsker-cum-Stainsacre is again more irregular in plan due to its unusual evolution, like Kingthorpe House, from an original longhouse.

Plate 23 'Woodlands', Aislaby. A late eighteenth century gentleman's house financed by profits from the alum industry *(RCHME)*

Houses of the nineteenth century, like Kildale Hall, said to be by Salvin, were more rambling.

HOUSES OF THE PROFESSIONAL CLASSES

The first houses of professional people to emerge, and overall perhaps the best documented and easiest to identify, were those of the clergy. They varied greatly in their wealth, and their dwellings reflect a wider range of society than might be expected. Those in towns, such as the Old Rectory, Pickering, built to a T-shaped plan in 1698, are the most substantial. In contrast, surveys of the early eighteenth century suggest that many country vicarages differed little from contemporary farmhouses, as the seventeenth century former vicarage of Ellerburn, Old Ellers, built to a version of the longhouse plan, confirms. Rebuilding in the eighteenth century brought improved living conditions. The rectory at Hawnby had, in 1733, a central entry between two rooms; service rooms were added behind and a second parlour to one side in the middle of the century. The house built in Sleights in 1765 for the curate of Eskdaleside (Plate 24 & Fig 33) is not unlike that at Hawnby, although it has greater architectural qualities as well as two original rear wings, one a back kitchen, the other a stable. The double-pile plan, or a version of it, was adopted by several nineteenth century vicarages, including those in Pickering,

147

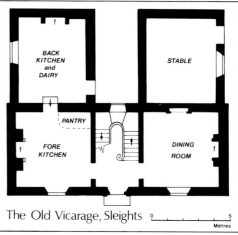

The Old Vicarage, Sleights

Plate 24 & Fig 33 Built in 1765 by Robert Bower who in 1762 had rebuilt the chapel in the village *(RCHME)*

Sinnington and Great Edstone. The rectory at Thornton Dale, now Comber House, designed in 1841 by the York architect, J. P. Pritchett, was built to an elongated plan. Its rooms included a study, a use appropriate to a parsonage, but not found in surveys until the mid-nineteenth century.

The houses of men working in the professions or business, who often styled themselves 'gentlemen', can first be identified in the second half of the eighteenth century. They are, as one would expect, mainly found in the towns, but they are also found in some villages and even rural positions. The houses are all built to central-entry plans, most of them double-depth. All have fine exteriors, and interiors with fashionable and high quality fittings. Prospect House of 1764, now The Bay Tree in Fylingdales, is one of the earliest, although the source of its builder's wealth is uncertain: Isaac Storm is described merely as 'gentleman' in his will. There is more certainty about other houses. In Helmsley in the late eighteenth century, James Fawcett, brandy merchant, and Humphrey Sandwith, apothecary and surgeon, respectively built Ryedale House, Bridge Street and 19 Bridge Street. Both are tall, three-storey houses which stand out from their humbler neighbours. John Petch, a solicitor, built the similar Petch House, Kirkbymoorside at about the same time as these Helmsley houses. The occupations of the builders of two other up-market houses in the town, Low Hall of 1797 and Vivers Lodge of the early nineteenth century, are not known. In the villages, High Hall at West Ayton, built in 1783–6 by a master mariner, was sold in 1787 to a schoolmaster; Cliff Grange at Snainton of about 1800 was the residence of doctors for much of the century; and the early nineteenth century Carr View in Sleights may have been built by a Whitby business man. Fyling Hall, Fylingdales (Plate 25 & Fig 34) built shortly after 1819 by John

148

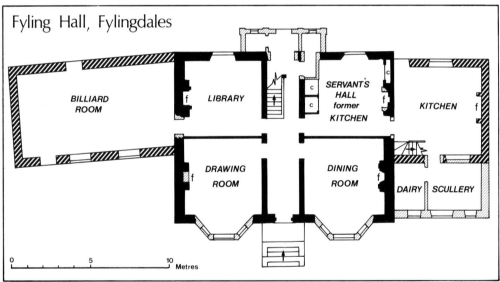

Fyling Hall, Fylingdales

BILLIARD ROOM

LIBRARY

SERVANT'S HALL former KITCHEN

KITCHEN

DRAWING ROOM

DINING ROOM

DAIRY SCULLERY

0 5 10 Metres

Plate 25 & Fig 34 Built in the early nineteenth century for a Whitby shipbuilder (RCHME)

Barry, a Whitby shipbuilder and ship owner, has the grandest setting of any of these houses, being sited in its own grounds, overlooking the sea. Most of these houses had plans and room uses similar to those of the lesser gentry, except perhaps that some ground-floor rooms were used for their owners' professions. In time the kitchens of several were moved out into wings, sometimes with the servants' accommodation, and at both Carr View and Fyling Hall, billiard rooms were also added.

149

FARMHOUSES

From the seventeenth century the houses of yeoman farmers were built so well that they still survive today. These were stone-built, thatched, generally single-storeyed, and had internal 'cruck' trusses, that is pairs of curved timbers rising to meet at the roof top. A great majority of the seventeenth century farmhouses, built in towns and villages and in the countryside, were 'longhouses'. These sheltered the family at one end and its cattle at the other, both sharing a common central entrance. A splendid example from Danby has been rebuilt in the grounds of Ryedale Folk Museum at Hutton-le-Hole. The longhouse has an old ancestry in medieval Britain, as shown by archaeological excavations. It must have been common in this region, and the surviving examples should be seen as the heirs of a long tradition. The seventeenth century longhouses had house-parts, in which the family lived, of varying size, two or three rooms long, and similar byre-ends. These differences in size reflect the fact that the longhouse was the dominant house-type in the region at the time, and that it served a broad spread of wealth. Spout House in Bilsdale (Plate 26 & Fig 35) contains many relics of the development of the earliest surviving longhouses. It stands on a site which was once occupied by a house with timber walls. When the present stone walls of the house-part were built in the seventeenth century, or perhaps even before, the forehouse (the main living room used for cooking, eating and sitting in) was open to the roof. The roof timbers are smoke-blackened, showing that the family sat round a central hearth. During the seventeenth century a new hearth position was created, backing on to the entrance passage, with an enclosed fire area under a smokehood. The inner room beyond the forehouse was shortened in the eighteenth century. Before this happened the house-part must originally have resembled White Cottage, Pockley, perhaps having a forehouse and two parlours, or a parlour and a dairy. At this time, parlours were used as bedrooms. The eighteenth century alterations to Spout House, which included the insertion of stone mullioned windows brought from elsewhere on the Helmsley estate, also involved creating a chamber in the roof against the new gable end. Such upper rooms became built-in parts of an increasing number of seventeenth century longhouses. They became more uniform in plan, with house-parts always of two rooms, the inner one at times divided into parlour and dairy. Sometimes the inner room had a bedroom over it, and sometimes there was one over the forehouse. Spout House has a house-part and byre-end of different dates.

This reflects one of the advantages of the longhouse, namely that its dual purpose allowed each part to be rebuilt piecemeal when and how required. This alternate rebuilding enabled either part to be made taller or longer with little impact on the other. Domestic accommodation might

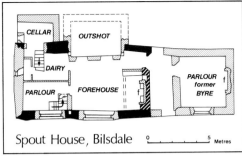

Spout House, Bilsdale

Plate 26 & fig 35 A seventeenth century yeoman's longhouse with its byre later converted to domestic use. The mullioned windows were inserted in the eighteenth century when the house was shortened and a room created in the roof space *(RCHME)*

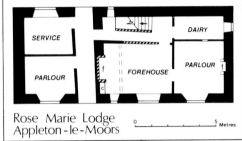

Rose Marie Lodge
Appleton-le-Moors

Plate 27 & Fig 36 An early eighteenth century yeoman's farmhouse *(RCHME)*

extend, by conversion or rebuilding, into the former byre-end.

From the end of the seventeenth and through the eighteenth century, two trends may be observed in longhouses: first the provision of external doors in byre-ends, and secondly the conversion or replacement of byres by domestic rooms. The first removed the nuisance associated with cattle so close to the house, even if it did not get rid of them, and the second responded to the needs for better and more specialised accommodation. At the same time longhouses were alternately rebuilt as fully domestic houses, with two rooms to one side of an entrance or hearth passage and one to the other. Such houses had been purpose-built during the seventeenth century, and this continued in the next two centuries. These later houses are of two storeys, like Rose Marie Lodge, Appleton-le-Moors (Plate 27 & Fig 36). Until the late eighteenth century, on the evidence of probate inventories and surviving buildings, the forehouse was still the centre of domestic life, used for making and eating meals. The parlour beyond it, thanks to the use of first floor rooms as bedrooms, became a family sitting room, and the parlour next to the entrance more of a domestic storage room which was sometimes used for spinning and weaving. This service use paved the way for the adaptation of many of

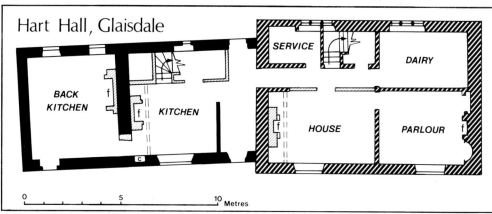

Plate 28 & Fig 37 A longhouse rebuilt in stages, the far wing in 1768 and later, the main block in 1797 *(RCHME)*

these rooms as kitchens from the late eighteenth century onwards, a change which inevitably led to the forehouse, or 'house' as it became known, becoming yet another sitting room. On larger farms it was not uncommon for the room over the kitchen to be a men's room for living-in labourers.

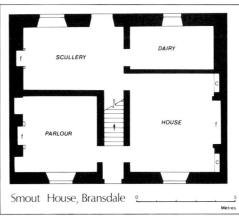

DAIRY

SCULLERY

HOUSE

PARLOUR

Smout House, Bransdale

Metres

Plate 29 & Fig 38 An early nineteenth century central-entry farmhouse *(RCHME)*

The eighteenth century saw yeoman farmers copy their superiors in adopting double-depth and often double-pile plans, and in attempting to create centralised plans, which had previously been adopted by the gentry. In the mid-eighteenth century they were hesitatingly taken up by a few farmers, but were not generally accepted until the end of the century. The former longhouses were difficult to convert to full centralised layout without rebuilding. But attempts were made by inserting doorways between forehouse and parlour, or by rebuilding houses to a pseudo-centralised plan as at Hart Hall, Glaisdale (Plate 28 & Fig 37) and Fryup Hall, Danby. Hart Hall was originally a longhouse, but Fryup Hall is all of one date and has a pair of entrances and staircases. Fryup Hall is not a 'hall' in the sense either of a manor house or country seat, but rather the substantial farmhouse of a well-off freehold farmer in an area with no resident gentry. When advertised for sale in 1846, it was described as on a freehold estate which had been in the family of the present occupier for two centuries; that is, it had been bought by the family at the sale of the manor of Danby, which covered much of Danby and Glaisdale in the north of the region, in 1655 (Chapter 6). The mid-eighteenth century adoption of a double-pile plan is reflected in such freeholder's farmhouses as Red House, Glaisdale of 1748. A later adoption by a tenanted farm has Smout House, Bransdale (Plate 29 & Fig 38) for an example. These later types of farmhouses are easily distinguished from the earlier ones since their squat, symmetrical, box-like appearance contrasts with the longer, frequently lower and more irregular appearance of the earlier ones. The late nineteenth century produced some distinctive farmhouses in the Egton area, where the estate of the principal landowner was in legal trouble, causing farmhouses and cottages to be condemned in 1867–8. A member of the Foster family of Black Dyke Mills bought the estate in 1869, and it was said in 1890 that it had been greatly improved. There were many new buildings, fourteen of them dating between 1872 and

1899, and best described as vernacular revival in style, their details based on houses in the West Riding.

The farmhouses of the seventeenth to nineteenth centuries do not have an even spread in the region. Those of seventeenth century date, which are mostly longhouses, were built in all parts, but many were rebuilt or demolished during later centuries. A number of relatively unaltered and still single-storeyed seventeenth century buildings are to be found in the villages around Helmsley, particularly at Pockley, but also Beadlam, Nawton, Harome and Rievaulx. These villages formed part of the Helmsley estate, where the spirit of improvement, fortunately in some ways, was little felt. Elsewhere the eighteenth and nineteenth centuries saw much rebuilding, reflecting the prosperity of the newly improved farming. In Danby and Glaisdale, where most of the tenants had bought their farms at the sale of 1655, farmhouses were often rebuilt several times as their owners sought better homes. (William Cobbett was only one of the writers who complained in the nineteenth century that farmers were aping their betters. The tendency was caricatured in the 1843 doggerel 'Man, Tally Ho; Miss, piano; Wife, silk and satin; Boy, Greek and Latin'.) In Kildale, as well as carrying out farming improvements, Sir Charles Turner also rebuilt many farmhouses. They are frequently two rooms deep in plan but are traditional in having an end, not a central, entrance. In the nineteenth century, as well as building new enclosure farms, many of the Helmsley estate's farms, particularly in Bilsdale, were rebuilt.

The farmhouses reflect the geology of the region. The fine sandstones of the north were cut into squared blocks even for the earliest of seventeenth century buildings. They were also strong enough to be used for lintels and window mullions, and were capable of taking mouldings. In contrast, the limestones which were dominant in the south-west, and the calcareous sandstones in the south-east, each with their distinctive grey-white and brown-yellow colours, were much less versatile and were mainly suitable just for walling. In these areas, mullioned windows and lintels had usually to be of timber. Brick was little used except on the surrounding plains where it was first used in the mid-eighteenth century for the houses of men of lesser gentry or professional status. It was used for farmhouses from the late eighteenth century, but without substantially displacing natural stone. Pantiles replaced thatch for new building from the mid-eighteenth century, Welsh or Westmorland slate being introduced in the nineteenth century.

COTTAGES

John Tuke wrote in 1800 that the cottages were generally small and low, consisting only of one room, very rarely of two. These unflattering descriptions of the later nineteenth century refer to buildings which have

Plate 30 73-77 West End, Kirkbymoorside. A longhouse subdivided and partly rebuilt as three cottages *(RCHME)*

Plate 31 White Cottage, Beadlam, started as the house part of a longhouse and retains its cross-passage as the entrance. *(RCHME)*

Plate 32 This cottage in the High Street at Snainton also started as the house part of a longhouse. It lost its cross passage and therefore has a new front door

not survived, but there is a good example in the Hutton-le-Hole Folk Museum. The earliest surviving cottages are of late eighteenth century date, but are of a far higher standard than were recorded by these writers.

Cottages were the homes of people holding little or no land who might be labourers, craftsmen, tradesmen or workers in one of the mineral industries. Cottages survive in the towns and villages of the region, as well as in more isolated places. Some are conversions of earlier buildings, others are purpose-built dwellings. Those which result from conversion include many subdivided farmhouses in the towns and villages which, with the movement of farmsteads into the countryside (Chapter 6), were no longer

Fig 39 Cottage plans *(RCHME)*

required for their original purpose. Most of these farmhouses were originally longhouses, and their dual purposes so often reflected in the alternate rebuilding of each part, made subdivision into cottages easy. The house-part could often stand unaltered, only the byre-end requiring subdivision. The hearth-passage might be retained as the entrance to both cottages, or to just one, the other having its own door. Once subdivided, each part could pursue its own separate existence and be rebuilt as required. Helmsley, Kirkbymoorside and Pickering contain the best cottages of this sort and they can be recognised along almost all the principal streets. A good example is 73-77 West End, Kirkbymoorside (Plate 30) where the byre-end was rebuilt as a pair of cottages, leaving the house-part untouched. Pressure of space and population was responsible for these conversions; occasionally in the towns, but more often in the villages where these influences mattered less, the byre-end was simply pulled down. White Cottage, Beadlam (Plate 31) which retains the hearth-passage, and a cottage in the High Street at Snainton (Plate 32) which does not, are examples of this. Other conversions to cottages include a barn in Wombleton and a stable in Nawton.

A wide range of types and sizes of purpose-built cottages was built in the late eighteenth and nineteenth centuries. Erected singly, in pairs and in terraces, some single-fronted, others double-fronted, and either one or two rooms deep, they are all two or three storeys high. Most are unpretentious and are built of stone. The number and use of rooms varies, as the range of different plan forms reveals (Fig 39). The most basic have just a single living room, while others have adjoining pantries, sculleries or dairies. Some better cottages have a separate kitchen and parlour, often

156

Plate 33 Browcotes, Fylingdales. A pair of cottages built in 1769 for workers in the alum quarries *(RCHME)*

Plate 34 Rose Cottage, Danby. A cottage built in 1850 for workers in the local coal mines *(RCHME)*

Plate 35 Hollins Cottages, near Grosmont. A terrace of cottages built shortly before 1850 for ironstone miners *(RCHME)*

combined with a pantry or other service room. The ground floor improvements were reflected on the upper floor where there was more than one bedroom and greater warmth and privacy.

There is some evidence about the builders of these cottages. The Row, Gillamoor, was built as a speculation by John Groves of Riseborough on land bought in 1817, being sold to Lord Feversham in 1833 as five lately-erected cottages. Lord Feversham and his successors built various cottages on their estate, but principally in Helmsley. Here they include the early nineteenth century terrace of 6-10 Pottergate and two substantial terraces, 34-46 High Street, built to plans dated 1853, and 27-51 Bondgate of the later nineteenth century. The last terrace has finer architectural style than 36-46 High Street, but some cottages near the entrance to Duncombe Park are even better, with their Tudor detailing. The North York Moors has no estate village with the unity of that at Harewood, but this does not imply a lack of caring landlords. Marmaduke Langley, formerly Dawnay, who held the Wykeham estate from 1817 to 1851, built twenty-one cottages or terraces between 1832 and 1850. All carry inscribed dates and the initials MBDL and MDL and some are called Lora Cottage, Lora Cottages and Burton Terrace after his mother, Lora Burton, wife of John, 4th Viscount Downe. The buildings are without unnecessary detail. Their simple style contrasts with that of the cottages built in 1858 for the Downe estate at Baldersby, to William Butterfield's design. Baldersby Park became the 7th Viscount's principal seat, and although Wykeham Abbey was left to languish, the estate was not. A church, parsonage, school and school house were built in Wykeham in 1853–4, and the church was enlarged and a school built at Hutton Buscel in 1853–4, all to designs by Butterfield. Of all the houses described, perhaps the most lasting memory of the visitor is of the sturdy farms and cottages. Built of local stone, and roofed with thatch or pantiles, the cottages in particular provide charming settings for climbing flowers, and their walled gardens for the traditional cottage flowers and vegetables.

The mineral industries, often in areas poorly provided with housing, caused the building of many cottages. Alum mining and manufacture, for example, are likely to have prompted the building of a pair of cottages (Plate 33) dated 1769 close to the cliff edge at Fylingdales. The early nineteenth century Clitherbeck Cottage and Rose Cottage of 1850 (Plate 34), both in Danby, are on intakes from Danby Moor where coal had been mined since the mid-eighteenth century (Chapter 8). White Row in Aislaby, of the early nineteenth century, may have been built for quarry-men. A terrace of ten cottages at New Bridge, immediately north of Pickering, complete by 1843, was built by a quarry owner to house his workers. The same man had already speculated in building 87-96 Westgate, Pickering, a terrace of two-storey cottages in 1839–41. Ironstone mining was the boom industry of the nineteenth century (Chapter 8). Grosmont and nearby Hollins in the Esk Valley housed many ironstone miners' families in 1851. Hollins Cottages (Plate 35) are an example of their terraces. Rows of cottages, some now demolished, were built for the miners and other workers in the Rosedale ironstone mines.

8
LANDSCAPES
OF INDUSTRY

INTRODUCTION

MOST visitors to the North York Moors come in summer for holiday relief from the pressures of urban life and, initially at any rate, are unaware that its peaceful pastoral landscape has suffered the turmoil of an industrial past. But much of the land is agriculturally poor and men have turned readily to industry to make a living from it. Increasing familiarity with the area brings an awareness of curious old workings in the valley edges and on the moors, the ragged strangeness of some of the profiles of the sea cliffs and the unnatural geometry of two cone-shaped hills in East Cleveland. Perhaps a connection will be made between these features and the rows of terraced houses to be found, for example, in East Cleveland and in Rosedale. It will soon be discovered that these are the relics of once major industries which have dominated the area until the present century. And every walk through the picturesque dales reveals more of the water mill steadings, threshing barns and horse wheel sheds. Each upland hike across the Cleveland moors will lead to dale edges, scarps or sea cliffs which slice through the near horizontal shales and lay bare a sequence of commercially useful stones. With each visit the landscape takes on a different meaning and raises new questions.

This chapter will provide some of the answers, first to the rural industries of the valleys, and then to the extractive industries based on sandstone, coal, alum, jet and ironstone . . . particularly, perhaps, the ironstone which for a decade from the late 1860s made the Cleveland iron-making district the biggest producer in the world.

CORN MILLING

The North York Moors is essentially a watermilling region because of its well watered valleys. There were windmills in the vale of Cleveland and along the east coast (Fig 41 and Plates 36 & 45) and a few others in Ryedale, but water was preferred wherever it was available, as a more

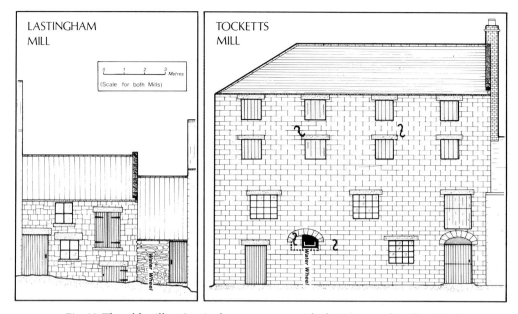

LASTINGHAM
MILL

0   1   2   3
                    Metres
(Scale for both Mills)

TOCKETTS
MILL

Water Wheel

Water Wheel

Fig 40 The old mill at Lastingham contrasts with the 'improved' mill at Tocketts, drawn to the same scale. In addition to the waterwheel and millstones, the Tocketts mill contains much other milling machinery and has ample storage space on the top two floors *(after N. R. Staley, J. K. Harrison)*

manageable source of energy. Today, the water mills of the National Park make a real contribution to the richness of the landscape.

Though only a dozen mills are given in the Domesday Survey, and these all on the borders of the moors, most watermilling sites are in fact very ancient. They were quickly established in early medieval times as settlement penetrated into the dales; at least half of all the 100 or so steadings existed before the collapse of the economy following the Black Death in 1349. However, buildings are less permanent than steadings and the oldest date only from the seventeenth century. The early mills were built by the lords of the manor to service the farming community and for taxing it by taking a percentage of the grain. The miller was a manorial servant. The grain was carried to the mill in panniers on horseback and ground there and then to meal and flour to be taken away on the return journey; the miller had no need to provide storage and he used only the simplest machinery consisting of a waterwheel and single large set of millstones. The buildings which housed them were low-walled with thatched roofs and small windows. In medieval times some were built of wood but from the seventeenth century they were built of local stone, sandstone in the northern moors and smaller limestones to the south. Today's survivors are either slated or pantiled. Very good relics of these humble mills survive at Bransdale (the old mill), Arden, Caydale and Lastingham (Fig 40), and at other sites fragments are fossilised inside later developments.

At the close of the eighteenth century milling began to develop as a result of changes in economic conditions and technical advances. By this time, mills operated on a commercial basis with the miller paying rent for his mill, and making his living by charging at a set rate for the grain which he ground. At the same period, wheat prices climbed rapidly as a result of the French wars. Farmers responded by ploughing higher land and introducing barn threshing machines to avoid the bottleneck of the threshing floor and flail. The flood of grain arrived at the mills in carts rather than panniers and it had to be left at the mill for the miller to process in his own time. The miller needed much more storage space. Ancillary machines such as grain dressers, oat rollers, barley mills and flour screens were introduced. The increasingly complex machinery and the consequently bigger waterwheels demanded that cast iron replaced wood for the more highly stressed parts such as shafts and gearing. Between 1790 and 1850 large numbers of old mills were rebuilt with additional storeys on top, to provide space for storage and machinery, and one or two new ones were set up. These 'improved' mills are easily recognised for the new 2½-, 3- and 4-storey buildings have very handsome, dressed stone façades with regularly spaced doors and windows. Good working examples exist at Tocketts near Guisborough (Fig 40), at Danby (both with major restoration work by South Park Sixth Form College, Middlesbrough) and at Low Mill in Bilsdale, and there are many more untouched exteriors of the same vintage. (See Locations of Old Industrial Sites on pages 223-5).

During the late nineteenth century mills faced increasing competition from roller-milled flour transported from the ports by the new railways,

Plate 36 Windmill at Ugthorpe, photographed in 1965 *(North Yorkshire County Library)*

Plate 37 Bransdale Mill. Built on an early medieval site, the simple mill was expanded into a small industrial complex by William Strickland from 1811 onward. Under restoration by the National Trust, it is one of our most picturesque watermill sites (*Photograph A. Staniforth, NYMNP*)

and from the farm-based stone mills driven by horses and stationary engines. The millers started to diversify. Sometimes they set up smithies, as at High Mill at Farndale and at Raisdale; Yoad Wath mill became a woodworking centre. Estates let additional land to their millers so that many mills have barns, byres and stables; at Kilton there is a fine nineteenth century fold yard. Inevitably, rural milling continued to decline, though the last survivors continued into this century mainly as farm utilities, but with some extra trade during both world wars. By 1969 there was no milling in this area. However, the last fifteen years have seen a considerable revival in interest and, fortunately, the comparative isolation of many of the mills has been their saving. They are now an important part of our building heritage. Particularly fine are the Georgian mill at Ruswarp (built in 1752), the tall stone mill on the Esk at Danby which was built about 1800, and the mid-nineteenth century mills at Robin Hood's Bay and Sinnington. The lovely milling hamlet at Bransdale (Plate 37), being restored by the National Trust, is the highlight of any walk in that valley. The most complete working mill is at Tocketts where the restored machinery and an extensive milling collection is open to the public for four days each week.

The north east of England was one of the earliest windmilling areas in

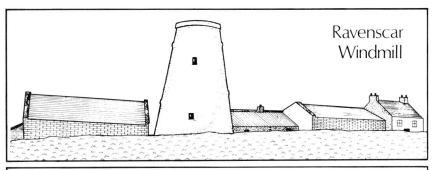

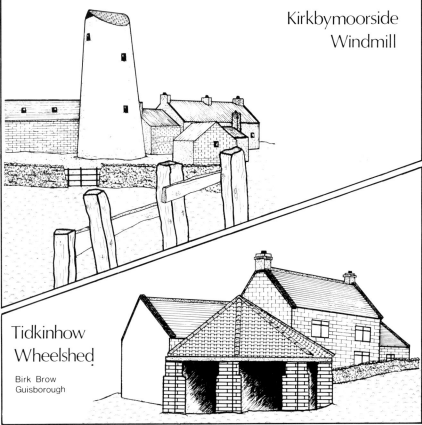

Fig 41 The stone windmill tower at rural Ravenscar and the brick tower in urban Kirkbymoorside are fine features in their own landscapes. The humble horse-wheel sheds are less spectacular and are slowly vanishing from North Yorkshire (*after N. R. Staley, J. K. Harrison*)

Europe and many of the steadings in the Vale of Cleveland have medieval origins. Sadly, however, none of the early post mills has survived and even the later tower mills are now scarce. Tower mills were built from about 1790 onwards and should be seen in the context of the improvements to water mills for the same period which we have already described. At

Yarm, Stockton, Whitby and Scarborough some huge windmills were built at the turn of the century, but in the countryside there was a more gentle progression from the 24 foot high tower at the 1796 Ugthorpe Mill (Plate 36) to the tall mid-nineteenth century structures at Ravenscar and Kirkbymoorside (1838) (Fig 41).

Horse-driven corn grinding mills were also a feature of the area but nothing now survives. On the other hand, there are many square and octagonal wheel sheds which are the relics of horse-driven threshing mills. In North Yorkshire these were always called 'wheel sheds' and never 'gin gans' as in Northumberland. Every large farm in north-east Yorkshire had its wheel shed and no other National Park can claim as many. Horse wheel sheds date from the invention of the first successful threshing machine by the Midlothian millwright, Andrew Meikle, in 1788. The invention took the north east of England and the south east of Scotland by storm, so much so that within 30 years scarcely a wooden threshing floor remained in use in these areas. Elsewhere the spread was either slower or non-existent. The shortage of alternative employment for farm workers in the rural south of England led to deep suspicion of machines which dispensed with the all-important winter threshing and, eventually, in 1830, to the Captain Swing riots in which barns were fired and threshing machines broken up. In north Yorkshire, as we shall see in the remainder of this chapter, industry provided alternative employment and made for more flexible conditions in which it was easier for farmers to mechanise without provoking a sense of grievance. The first threshing mill in the area was set up at Nunnington in about 1790 by E. Cleaver. Hundreds followed. One or two were driven by waterwheels and a few later ones by stationary steam engines but the vast majority were driven by horses walking clockwise (or 'with the sun') inside the wheel shed. The horse turned a heavy overhead wheel from which a horizontal 'tumbler' shaft passed through the barn wall to the thresher itself. The sheds are still reasonably common but only two of the wheels have survived, one at Drummer Hill Farm near Ingleby Greenhow and the other removed from its original site in Urra in Bilsdale to the Rydale Folk Museum at Hutton-le-Hole.

MINERAL INDUSTRIES

The remainder of this chapter will deal with the extraction of commercial stones from the near-horizontal strata of sedimentary rocks; limestone from the Tabular Hills and sandstone, coal, alum, jet and ironstone from the Cleveland moors. Fig 42 shows the underlying geology and explains where the different stones may be looked for. They will be described from the shallowest to the deepest, so that the ironstones are described last. However, before starting on industries connected with these sedimentary

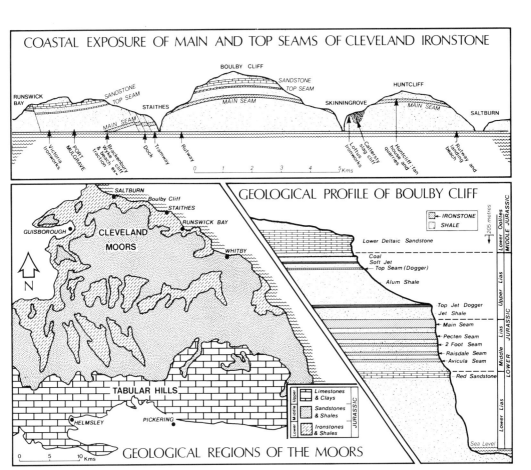

Fig 42 Diagrams of the coastal exposures of the main and top seams of the Cleveland ironstone were available by the early 1850s. Using the two sections and the geological map, all shown above, it is possible to locate all the valuable mineral seams

rocks we must make an important diversion into the quarrying of our only volcanic rock.

Whinstone

A broken line of deep, black quarries gashes WNW to ESE across the North York Moors from Eaglescliffe on the Tees to Blea Hill near Robin Hood's Bay (Fig 43). These workings mark the line of the Cleveland Dyke, a vertical wall of igneous rock intruded into the sedimentary series during the volcanic disturbances, centred on the island of Mull, which took place some 39 million years ago, and described by J. W. Ord as a 'Frolic of nature'. At its thickest, near Great Ayton, the dyke was 25m (82ft) thick, hard enough to become known as 'flint' stone. It would have presented a formidable problem to the quarrymen had it not been severely heat-cracked, though not in the spectacular, hexagonal columns which

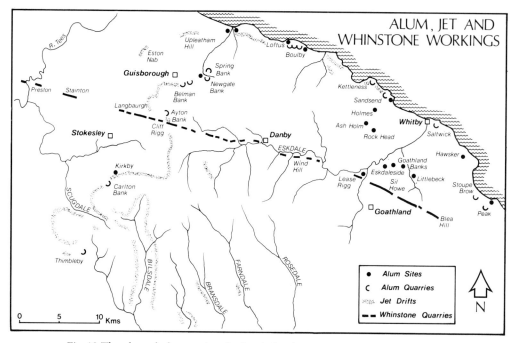

Fig 43 The alum shales overlay the jet shales, but appear together on this small-scale map, running round many sea cliffs and dale sides. Whinstone quarries appear as a discordant gash across the terrain *(after J. K. Harrison)*

can be seen at the Giant's Causeway and the island of Staffa. Exploitation of the dyke began near its western end and advanced slowly eastward. It was worked before 1822 at Eaglescliffe and Great Ayton and 16 quarries were worked near Great Ayton in the mid-1850s but quarrying at Glaisdale and Sil Howe did not start until the 1870s. Work stopped at Sil Howe in 1950 and at the Langbaurgh quarry near Great Ayton in 1964. The stone was produced by a comparatively few quarrymen, and was particularly valuable in an area where there is no other really hard stone. It was used for road chippings and for road setts, locally in Westgate in Guisborough and in large quantities in Leeds. The holes left behind are hazardous; visitors should be very careful when looking at them, because the quarry walls of 'white back' or metamorphosed shale are almost vertical, and there are mine drifts beneath many of the quarry floors.

Limestone

Good limestone occurs in large quantities in the Tabular Hills from Hackness to the Hambletons and in thin, isolated seams under the Cleveland moors. The calcareous sandstone has been widely quarried for building stone, the purer limestone for mortar and hygienic whitewash. The fossil shells of ancient sea creatures were also good for 'sweetening' the land. From the late eighteenth century most local landowners spread lime on their land. Leases for this period for the Ailesbury estate at Swainby include the clause that 20 sacks of lime to the acre had to be spread on newly ploughed land and that only 3 crops could be taken before the process was repeated.

Some of the limestone for this purpose was brought by boat from Norfolk and Northumberland to be burned in small coastal kilns. Some was quarried from small seams found in the Top Seam or Dogger in the Cleveland Hills, for example on the east side of Bilsdale and near Scarth Nick. More important works were at Commondale where the Middlesbrough Pottery built two kilns in the mid-nineteenth century, and at Limekiln Bank near Swainby where fossiliferous 'blue stone' was burned from about 1815. These were relatively minor sources, but there are major quarries on the Tabular Hills. On the southward dip slopes the quarries have flat working floors and faces no more than 10ft high, while on the much steeper northward-facing scarp slopes the quarries are deeper and narrower, many of them now partly hidden by trees. The smallish, pale stones which give such a distinctive charm to the houses of this area came from these quarries. A great deal was also burned to become quicklime. One or two of the small 'field kilns', which were used in the days of the horse-drawn cart, survive on the roadside at Snilesworth Moor. There are many others to the north of the Tabular Hills within carting distance of the moorland collieries which supplied the fuel. However, as transport improved, larger semi-industrial kilns were built. For instance, at Kepwick in 1833 Joshua Crompton built the railway to bring limestone 3½ miles to his kilns at Leake (see Chapter 9). At Cropton the kilns, last fired in the 1960s, are now overgrown, but contain their last abandoned charge of coal and limestone.

Coal
Away from moorland winds in the open quarries, miners burrowed to wrest a living from the earth in conditions which beggar description, for lying immediately below the deltaic sandstone are thin seams of low-grade coal (according to Ord of 'slatey, inferior description . . . unconnected with any important coal band'). The story of the mining of these seams is ignored in national histories of coal mining, but local research is gradually providing a clearer picture. The thousands of pit heads and small waste heaps over a wide area of moorland have left astonishing landscapes to be explored.

Medieval pottery recovered from waste heaps on Blakey Rigg may, perhaps, indicate very early working. The earliest written evidence dates from 1643 for a working on Yearsley Moor to the south west of Gilling; the earliest mention within the National Park dates from 1715 for a colliery on the Feversham estate at Ankness near the south end of Bransdale. For the right to sink three new shafts at Ankness, Matthew Ford of Fadmoor agreed to pay Lord Feversham an annual rental of £100

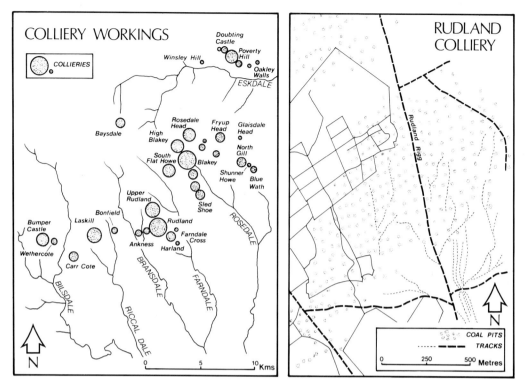

Fig 44 The collieries lie in a broad band from Bilsdale to Eskdale. Each colliery consists of many small pits. The plan of the Rudland colliery shows the regular spacing of pits for pillar-and-bord working, and the many trackways serving them (*after J. K. Harrison*)

and to allow him to collect some 100 tons of coal from the pit heads for his own use. From this venture the industry spread across the Feversham estate moorlands from Bilsdale eastward to Rosedale, with outliers at Baysdale and the heads of Fryupdale and Glaisdale. A second group of pits was sunk to the north of the Esk, mainly on the Danby estate, between Castleton and Danby (Fig 44), with a major concentration in the Clither-beck valley running north from Danby Lodge (now The Moors Centre).

The period of greatest activity in the Feversham collieries was probably in the mid-eighteenth century, and by the end of the century they were in decline. In 1790 a new colliery called the Upper Rudland colliery was opened but the seam was found to be uneven and less satisfactory than that of the earlier and bigger Rudland colliery. At the same period it was noted that at Blakey the seam was 'very near done', at Carr Cote 'Widow Holmes has given up', and at both the Blakey and Sledshoe collieries on Blakey Ridge new pits were being sunk to get coal left behind in earlier workings. Working finally ceased in the 1920s at Rudland and Harland. In contrast, the pits of the smaller Danby colliery are mainly of the late eighteenth and early nineteenth centuries. The first mining agreement

Plate 38 Rudland Rigg colliery. The regularity in the formation of the pits indicates pillar-and-bord working. The disturbance from a recently laid gas pipe line can be seen running alongside the track *(A. L. Pacitto)*

dates from 1749 and in 1753 Lord Downe commissioned a survey of the mining potential by Robert Bewley of York. Expansion was then rapid and reached a peak in value of rental in 1812–13 followed by gradual decline though, as late as the 1890s, queues of farm carts regularly waited at the pit heads at Poverty Hill.

In the Feversham collieries the seams lay at modest depths, 9 to 12m (13 to 40ft) at Rudland for example, but they were very thin, 15 to 20cm (6 to 8in) at Wethercote in Bilsdale and 24cm (9½in) at Rudland Rigg. These conditions did not justify expenditure on heavy gear at a central pit head and, instead, draining was by horizontal adits. The coal was raised up hundreds of small, rectangular shafts by hand, using either a simple 'rowler' (jack-roll) or 'double turngear' (windlass). On Rudland Rigg, where this multi-shaft mining is seen at its best, there are just over 600 pits arranged in lines running roughly ENE to WSW and spaced between 40

169

and 60m apart (Fig 44 and Plate 38). The lines are not straight but they are coherent as though they were laid out by pacing rather than by surveying. In the Danby colliery the seam was better, averaging 43cm (17in) in thickness, but it lay deeper at anything up to 46m (150ft) below the heather. These shafts were bigger, commonly 3m x 2m (10ft x 6½ft) in section, and the winding was done by horse gins (or 'engines'). The pattern of pit heads appears at first glance to be random and the spacing between them is greater, indicating longer underground passages, but there are, in fact, several long rows of pits running up the valley sides and tracing the main drainage adits below. Every shaft had to be cut through the thick bed of sandstone to reach the coal and the sale of the sandstone was probably a vital element in the economy but, much more importantly, it meant that shaft lining was unnecessary for most of the depth. These shafts were not bell pits; they are all linked underground by pillar-and-bord workings and their purpose was to provide ventilation and to reduce the transport problem through the cramped 1m (3ft) high passage underground.

Surface transport was also laborious. In the eighteenth century pannier ponies were used and their tracks ran across typically wet and peaty moorland, their hooves cutting through the heather until each track became a quagmire which was then abandoned in favour of a drier route a few feet away. Over the years the main routeways became wide scars of ribbon tracks braided together and converging only at bridging points over streams. In the nineteenth century carts became more common and roads were built, one or two aptly named 'Coal Road' (as at Harland and at Baysdale) or 'Colliers Road' (as at Carr Cote in Bilsdale). On Rudland Rigg the new road cuts through the middle of the older pannier tracks but follows the same general route south to Gillamoor and Fadmoor.

In the absence of contemporary illustrations we have to imagine the cratered landscape in its hey-day, with the bare waste heaps, the thatched shelters at the shaft tops, the men working round them winding up the coal and the teams of pannier horses waiting to be loaded. The moorland coal was used partly for domestic fuel, but mainly for firing the lime kilns on and near the Tabular Hills. Mining remained primitive to the end (probably on a seasonal basis) and output was always much more limited than in the Great Northern Coalfield of Durham and Northumberland where a new breed of industrialists revolutionised the scale and technology of deep mining.

Alum

The alum industry seems to have attracted a good deal of attention in recent years. Perhaps this is because this, the 'first chemical industry', was a heavily capitalised and highly political operation much more related to modern industry than the other early workings in the area. Perhaps it is because the alum industry was the first to raise the population of East Cleveland, a trend which was to be continued by the ironstone mining industry, in an area which would otherwise have supported a declining agricultural population only. Faced now with industrial decline the East Cleveland community has become more aware of its past as it becomes more anxious about its future.

Long used as a cure-for-all-ailments, for fixing dyes and in the tanning of leather, alum was imported from northern Italy under papal monopoly until the breach between Henry VIII and the Roman church. Alum shales were then explored in various parts of England and the main centre for production eventually proved to be the North York Moors. Thomas Chaloner made the claim that he discovered alum-bearing shales in the scarps to the south of Guisborough between 1598 and 1600, but extraction was first started by John Atherton, of the neighbouring Skelton estate, at Slape Wath in 1604. Two years later Sir Thomas Chaloner, Sir David Foulis and Lord Sheffield of Mulgrave obtained letters patent for a monopoly of alum production and set up a company for working the shale, initially on the Chaloner and Skelton estates. However, there were many difficulties and the industry was taken over by the Crown in 1608, with control passing to Sir Arthur Ingram of Temple Newsam near Leeds. After years of continuing difficulties the industry became profitable by the middle of the century, state control was ended in 1679 and some 16 quarries were opened by 1700.

The alum shales lie below the sandstone and coal seams, the top 31m (100ft) being preferred for quarrying. Suitable shale was available in unlimited quantities but there were practical and economic limitations resulting from the cost of handling the 30 to 100 tons of shale needed for every ton of alum. There were also uncertainties arising from lack of knowledge of the chemistry of the process and the fluctuating price of alum. The sheer size of some of the quarries is almost unbelievable, and the casual observer can be forgiven for seeing them as natural features rather than the results of generations of human muscle power. After quarrying, the loosened shale was heaped with brushwood into clamps, up to 18m (60ft) high, and in order to make the natural salts soluble it was slowly roasted for up to nine months, during which time it changed colour to bright red. John Brewster, in his 'History of Stockton-on-Tees' (1829) mentions the alum works at Carlton as one of the landmarks to be seen from the River Tees, and to this day the evening sun picks out the redness of the great stain below the workings (Plate 39). Near Guisborough the quarries of Rock Hole, Newgate Bank and Belman Bank can be seen from the Whitby road soon after leaving town. But most dramatic are the coastal sites. From the Cleveland Way along the cliff tops north of Boulby Grange there are excellent viewing points of the vast continuous working, almost 3.2km (2 miles) long and up to 61m (200ft) deep, of the Loftus and

Plate 39 Carlton Bank alum and jet workings. The alum quarry and waste tip are on the left, and in the centre right is the horizontal line of jet pits *(NYMNP)*

Boulby quarries. Their vertical sandstone caps, sloped shale faces, and hummocky working floors with the remains of clamps, are so windswept that vegetation has not re-established even after a hundred years (Fig 45). At Ravenscar and Stoupe Brow nature has been more successful, but at Kettleness the 'ness' has been excavated away, leaving another desert. A similarly quarried landscape can be seen to the north east of Sandsend and at Saltwick Nab the shale has been burned red to make a startling contrast with the dull colours of the surrounding cliffs.

Subsequent stages in alum making are less conspicuous. The roasted shale was first barrowed to the leaching tanks (commonly 10 to 20m long and 5m wide and arranged side-by-side in groups of up to twelve with paved barrow ways between them) for a series of washing operations, after which the dissolved salts were retained and the leached shale dumped. Relics of these tanks survive at both Boulby works (Fig 45) where years of dedicated excavations have revealed something of their extent. Later operations were carried out in the alum houses, most of which were sited at some distance from the quarries, the liquor being run to them through culverts. Little remains on the ground except for the warehouse section of the alum house at Boulby (now a dwelling) and extensive foundations of the Peak alum house, now excavated to reveal many interesting features.

172

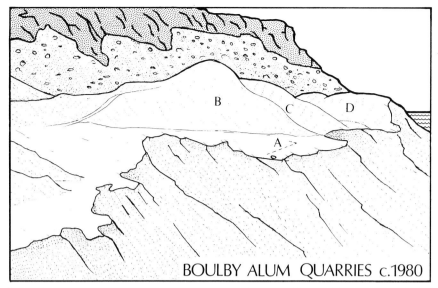

BOULBY ALUM QUARRIES c.1980

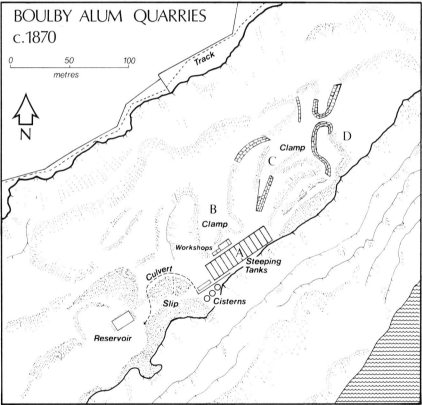

BOULBY ALUM QUARRIES
c.1870

Fig 45 A view of Boulby Alum Quarries from the cliff edge to the south east. The sketch plan shows the steeping pits and clamps for processing the shale, on the quarry floor (*after N. R. Staley. J. K. Harrison*)

173

Roman cement

Roman cement was a hydraulic cement which would set under water and was, therefore, much sought after for building sea walls and piers. In 1766 James Parker of Kent patented a method of making hydraulic cement from nodules found in the clays of the London Basin. Similar nodules were found in North Yorkshire where, in 1811, Lord Normanby established the Mulgrave Cement Works at East Row in Sandsend. Other works were set up at the Ravenscar and the Loftus alum works and, in the late 1850s, at the Victoria Iron and Cement Works at Wreckhills near Runswick Bay. These works used the hard, rounded nodules (called 'doggers' by the quarrymen) which were found in the alum shale in the proportion of 1 ton to every 70 tons of shale. The doggers were easily separated from the shales and, indeed, at Sandsend doggers which had fallen from the cliffs were picked off the beaches to be carried to the works in fishing cobles. There they were calcined in kilns and crushed to powder under millstones or rollers. There is a kiln at Ravenscar alongside the inclined railway from the Peak alum house to the foreshore, and by remarkably good fortune, the complete plant of kiln, mill and warehouse has survived at Sandsend, a survival unique in this country.

Jet

Whitby jet is now a popular antique but few collectors know the remarkable disturbance of the moors for such small quantities of valuable stone. Almost continuous lines of waste skirt the valleys of Bilsdale and Scugdale and are prominent in the scarps behind Swainby, Kildale, Great Ayton and Guisborough, modifying the natural hill slopes and disrupting the vegetation.

Like coal, jet is fossilised wood, but hard enough to take a polish for ornaments. It is found in more or less flattened 'planks' scattered among the shales, several planks sometimes being found together. It was every jet miner's dream to make his fortune by finding such a 'seam'. In fact, there are two types of jet. 'Soft' jet is found with the coal seams on top of the main dogger (see Fig 42) but its extraction has not caused major disturbance. 'Hard' jet is found in shales some 9m (30ft) thick laid down around 100 million years ago in a layer of clayey limestone (Top Jet Dogger) and now overlain by the alum shales.

Though fine jet objects are found on prehistoric sites, the earliest references to jet working in Whitby date from 1394. 'Jeators' were recorded at Skinningrove and Newholm-cum-Dunsley in 1614, these early workers almost certainly working on pieces picked up from the beaches. Jet can be carved by hand with files, knives and drills but it was not until shortly after 1800 that these simple techniques were supplemented by mechanical cutting, turning and polishing. There were two jet shops in Whitby using these new techniques in 1820 and seven in 1850. In 1851 jet ornaments were popularised at the Great Exhibition in Hyde Park, so much so that in 1856 some £2000 worth of jet was worked in Whitby. This figure increased rapidly until by the early 1870s annual output was worth £90,000 and some 1400 people were employed in mining and manufacture. This was the peak period. Cheap Spanish jet soon became available, and fashion is a fickle master. The number of people employed fell to less than 300 in 1884 and by 1890 mining was almost at an end.

Whereas the manufacture of jet-ware was concentrated in one town, the mining was very widely scattered and took place wherever the jet shales cropped out conveniently and where agreements could be made with the landowners. The date of the earliest mining is unknown but large-scale mining did not start until the 1860s following the completion of the railway down the Esk Valley. Expansion was accelerated by the long depression of the iron industry starting in 1873 which caused many redundant ironstone miners to try their hands. The valley of Scugdale near Swainby had no jet mining in 1850, but there were 39 miners working the valley sides by 1877. What are the signs we should look for? All the drift entrances are now collapsed, but they are easily detected by the V-shaped gashes in the hill slopes, each with its own shale tip made up of the waste which was brought to the surface in wheelbarrows. The heaps are fairly uniform in size since the workings never penetrated beyond shales softened by surface water and they are clearly visible, uncolonised by grass and bracken. Some heaps are very distinctive because they have been fired to bright red colour, an easy operation since jet shales contain oil. Burning converted the soft, crumbly shale into a hard, flakey material suitable for improving the tracks which skirted the valley sides linking the many mine entrances. The smoke from these smouldering heaps was resented at Stokesley in the late nineteenth century. Another nuisance is complained about to the present day. In Bilsdale, on top of Carlton Bank and in the woodlands behind Hutton village near Guisborough, there are groups of deep pits whence farmers occasionally find they must retrieve tractors and beasts. These result from subsidence into the shallow drift mines, particularly at the intersections of the underground passages.

Iron

The mining and working of ironstone from the North York Moors spans the period from the Iron Age to 1964. The stone has been hewn from seven different seams, five of them lying below the alum shales. Only a few iron-making sites date from the pre-Roman Age, the majority being medieval and dating from the period before the Black Death. The ancient method of smelting in this medieval industry was a small-scale process which was carried out at many sites scattered over a large area. In spite of this seemingly haphazard distribution, this was not a random activity of itinerant craftsmen; it was an organised industry started and controlled

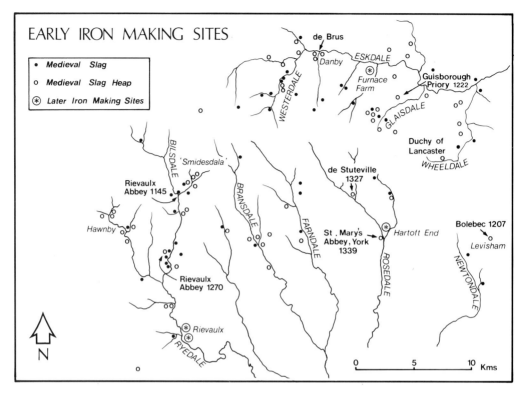

Fig 46 Location of known medieval 'cinder hills', prepared mainly from the extensive list by R. H. Hayes. There are doubtless many others still to be found, but the widespread pattern of the early working is clear *(after J. K. Harrison)*

by lay and monastic landlords, producing metal from which blacksmiths made hand tools and farm implements. The sites of known furnaces, as located by slag remains, are shown in Fig 46, with the names of landowners and dates of historical references where these are known. Particularly important were the workings in the Danby area which were held by the de Brus family, those in Glaisdale belonging to Guisborough Priory and Rievaulx Abbey's furnaces in Bilsdale.

Though the flames and smoke have long since vanished from the dales, there are relics for everyone to discover, particularly the old ironstone mines and the heaps of smelting waste which are often referred to as 'cinder hills'. Among the old mining sites are the pits or 'delves' which survive near Smith's Lane at the Delves near Egton Bridge. The names tell their own story. It is possible, also, that the mysterious row of pits dug into the north face of Roseberry Topping and adjacent scarp slopes may fall into this category. Lying on the slopes below the sandstone cap, these are now somewhat obscured by late nineteenth century workings for both jet and the Main Seam of ironstone, but they are still clearly visible, particularly in snowy conditions. Their purpose had slipped from human memory by the end of the eighteenth century when they were first noticed by antiquarians and described as the relics of 'hundreds of habitations', the remains of a huge prehistoric settlement. Later they were discussed by Canon Atkinson in relation to other groups of similar pits, notably those in Westerdale. These were mentioned in a twelfth century document but not positively identified as ironstone workings until after the geological surveys of the Ordnance Survey. However, although the pits on Roseberry are at a likely level for ironstone nodules they have never been satisfactorily explained, and no medieval smelting remains have been found in the area.

More interesting, perhaps, are the slag remains which have been found in well over 100 sites. By later standards, the process used by men toiling under their thatched shelters was quite simple. Pieces of ironstone were smelted in small clay furnaces with bowl-shaped bases sunk into the ground. Using charcoal as a fuel and a blast of air driven by foot bellows, the temperature of the ironstone was raised until the stony waste was melted and run off as liquid slag. The iron remained as a bright red-hot spongy 'bloom', which was then pulled out of the furnace to be shaped and partially refined by hammering on a stone anvil to drive out remaining slag. The slag heaps left at the furnace sites can appear as a few scattered pieces where heaps have been ploughed out, most sites recorded by Canon Atkinson now being in this category. Or the undisturbed heaps may contain tens of tons of material, which looks like frozen treacle. At Wheeldale Robert Short had a licence to work a forge and make charcoal in 1322, and today the green, sheep-cropped grass on the relics of his waste heap contrasts with the coarse grass and heather of the surrounding valley bottom. At Hagg House in Bilsdale there are the heaps of at least four bloomeries showing that this was part of the area known as Smidesdala ('Smiths' dale') in 1145, an area somewhat larger than the present day 'Smiddales' on the moor above Kyloe Cow Beck. The pattern of large numbers of quite small heaps scattered over a wide area cannot be fully explained by the distribution of ironstone. The main shortage was almost certainly in the other main commodity – charcoal. This was mainly made from timber from coppiced woodlands. Probably smelting on a site would produce between one and two tons of iron per year until the handy supply of wood ran out. Then it would be cleared of portable equipment, mainly the bellows and hand tools, and the furnace secured for further working at a future date. During an excavation at Tarn Hole in Bilsdale, it was found that the bases of the two furnaces had been carefully sealed over with thick pads of raw clay to protect them pending their re-use.

This early, small-scale phase of ironmaking seems to have been abandoned later in the medieval period, probably after the Black Death. When the industry revived it was concentrated in a few permanently

177

housed smithies with stone-built hearths of greater capacity. These new plants were situated where water power could drive the bellows, thus ensuring a strong and steady blast. At a slightly later date, water power was also used for driving mechanical hammers, the first set in this area being constructed at Rievaulx by the French ironmaker Lambert Symar, immediately after the monastery was dissolved. There are substantial relics of ironmaking of this period both at Rievaulx and at Laskill in Bilsdale but research on them is still at early stages.

Eventually, this simple process was superseded by one which was both capital-intensive and capable of much larger-scale production. This two-stage process, the fore-runner of the modern iron and steel industry, started with a blast furnace in which the iron was fully melted and tapped off as a liquid. Some of the resulting 'pig iron' was re-melted in a finery and refined by burning out excess carbon. Probably the first blast furnace in the north of England was built in 1577 close to Rievaulx Abbey. The tailrace of the waterwheel for the bellows and substantial quantities of green, glassy slag can still be seen below the supposed furnace site at Mill House; and there is reddish earth in the gardens above the site where the stone was calcined in heaps before smelting. The finery site was probably near Forge Farm, some distance down the valley, where there are more signs of water courses and slag heaps. Other blast furnace/finery plants were worked at Spiers Bank in Hartoft End (though short-lived) and, probably, at Furnace Farm near Lealholm. However, this first phase of large-scale ironmaking proved to be brief in the face of competition from other areas with more economic iron ore and fuel supplies. The longest-lived of the three blast furnaces, then at Rievaulx, stopped work during the Civil War, in 1647, bringing ironmaking in the moors to a halt for some 200 years.

The amount of ironstone taken from the North York Moors grew quickly from 1800 to 1850 but it was mainly smelted in Tyneside where ironmasters were finding their local ironstone insufficient. From the 1780s some ironstone had been collected from the beaches at Staithes and Robin Hood's Bay for a blast furnace at Chester-le-Street and a little later on a small scale for Lemington on the Tyne. Geological knowledge was then consolidated by a series of surveys in 1828–29. The potential of the thick seams of ironstone exposed in the cliffs began to dawn on north-eastern industrialists and the scramble began. In 1838 Joseph Bewick (senior) took ironstone out of the cliffs at Kettleness and Staithes for smelting at Birtley Ironworks, and in 1840 he recognised the Main Seam at Skinningrove. To understand the hazardous nature of shipping stone from under these formidable cliffs one must know where the ironstone lay in relation to the beaches, and Fig 42 is provided as a field guide. In Huntcliff and Boulby Cliff the Main Seam is high above sea level and, to begin with, the ironstone was simply collected from the beaches where it

Plate 40 Port Mulgrave in 1965. The outer sea wall has now been washed away *(North Yorkshire County Library)*

had fallen. Drift mines were then established. Along the coast at Staithes the seam was at a lower and more workable level, and the village became an early centre for the industry. Further south, in the Port Mulgrave area, the Main Seam dipped below sea level and could only be reached by shaft mining, but the Top Seam was worth taking and was quarried in several places. Also, at other points blocks of stones were prized away from the smaller seams which cropped out in the cliffs and the beaches. No master of a sailing ship could risk being trapped by a north easterly wind under the sea cliffs of north Yorkshire, so activity was seasonal and dependent on close cooperation between collectors and sailors. When conditions were right the wooden ships beached on the few sandy patches between Saltburn and Port Mulgrave, and the stone was brought to them by horse and cart for man-handling into the holds. Samuel Okey described the process at Saltburn in 1847 when he employed local farmers for this work. The carters developed a technique for making their work easier and safer by chopping rutways into the shale of the foreshore to fit the wheels of their carts, and to guide them safely when a returning tide covered the deep crevices in the rocks. These rutways can be found at low tide along

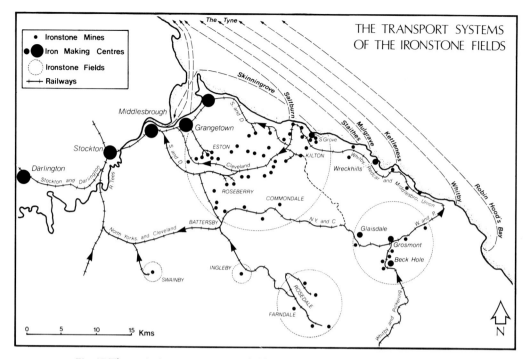

Fig 47 The main ironstone mining fields with the two major transport systems. Early development depended on coastwise shipping, and the large-scale industry from the 1860s depended on the railways leading to the furnaces at Middlesbrough and Stockton (after J. K. Harrison)

the length of the coast but it is only recently that they have been recognised for what they are, by J. S. Owen of Redcar.

The scale of operations soon increased. From the late 1840s stone was drift-mined at Skinningrove to be carried by ship and rail to the Witton Park Ironworks of Bolckow and Vaughan in County Durham. Another ten years saw the development of the Port Mulgrave area mainly by Palmers of Jarrow and of Wreckhills near Runswick Bay by the Leeds-based Victoria Iron and Cement Works Co. These developments still depended on coastwise transport but the rutways were superseded by wagonways whose rectangular sleeper slots can still be found. Steam ships arrived, so that docks had to be cut into the rocks at low-water level to enable these heavier and more expensive vessels to stay afloat during loading. There is an obvious dock lying to the east of Staithes. At other points, safe berths were provided by jetties running out to deep water, or by harbours protected by sea walls. The harbour at Port Mulgrave (Plate 40) survives in part, but elsewhere structures above rock level have been sheared away by the sea, leaving only the post-holes to be found today. The relics of the Wreckhills plant, in particular the calcining kilns, can be found among the tangle of undergrowth and the tumble of loose shale of the landslip which overwhelmed the blast furnaces in 1858 after only two months working. The Heritage Coast has many interesting relics of ironstone working but it was always on a small scale compared with the development of the same seams inland a few years later.

The rapid growth of the industry in the second half of the nineteenth century was a railway-dependent activity. To begin with this was by coincidence rather than design, for although the mining in Eston Nab and Upleatham Hill required the railway from Middlesbrough to Redcar, this was first built as an extension of the Stockton and Darlington Railway to export Durham coal from Redcar. And although the development of the Top Seam at Grosmont and in the Murk Esk Valley depended on the Whitby and Pickering Railway, the ironstone was only discovered as a result of baring of the underlying rock during railway construction. However, from about 1850 the situation began to change. The new town of Middlesbrough became an 'infant Hercules', with industrialists from all parts of the country rushing to place their capital in blast furnaces, puddling plant and rolling mills on the banks of the Tees, and in railways for bringing in the ironstone. The centre for ironmaking in the north east of England moved from the Tyne to the Tees and, as can be seen in Fig 47, a new railway network took over from coastal shipping.

The most important of the ironstone fields, that of northern and eastern Cleveland, was based on the Main Seam. Though of moderate quality (say 33% iron) the stone existed in enormous quantities. It was at its thickest and best in the north in the two outliers of Eston Nab and Upleatham Hill, where the Main Seam lay directly on top of the Pecten Seam to give working faces of up to 5.5m (18ft) deep. In these areas the stone was got by drift mining and the workings were vaultlike. In the area between Brotton and Lingdale the Main Seam was thinner and lay deeper in a shallow basin with its deepest point near the North Skelton Mine. The first shaft mine was sunk at Skelton Park Mine in 1872 and this was followed by some twenty others. The last mine closed, at North Skelton, in 1964. The main relics consist of railways and waste tips. The abandoned track beds of railways abound. In East Cleveland the layer of shale inside the Main Seam was dumped in the large conical tips at Kilton and Liverton Mines. On the other hand, there are few surface buildings left in East Cleveland. There are some remains of winding, pumping, ventilating and servicing buildings, but processing plant such as calcining kilns and blast furnaces have all but disappeared. The most interesting scattered relics can be listed as follows: concrete winding house at Kilton mine, boiler stack at Spa Wood Mine, shaft top with winding pulley at Stang How Mine at Margrove Park, furnace ventilation shafts in the woods near Tocketts Mill, and fan houses at Skelton Shaft Mine, Huntcliff and Lazenby Banks. But of all the eighty or so mines in the North Yorkshire ironstone field the most complete is that at Skelton Park where the range of buildings dating from the 1870s still contain much that was good,

Plate 41 Peaceful Rosedale, with ruins of the ironstone kiln chimney. The deserted railway track runs around the dale side *(A. Staniforth, NYMNP)*

designed by the Bell brothers of Port Clarence Ironworks, perhaps the most architecturally enlightened of all the ironmasters. Skelton Park is now derelict, but at the Loftus drift mine near Skinningrove the Tom Leonard Mining Museum has been established, a welcome sign of returning interest in a once major industry.

The scars of the getting of ironstone are seen most clearly in Rosedale where ironstone, some of which responded to magnets, was found in association with the Top Seam or Dogger. Stone found near Hollins Farm to the south of Rosedale Abbey was first seriously examined in 1853 and from 1856 small amounts were led away southward by horse and cart for trials in various ironworks. Then a lease was taken by George Leeman of the North Eastern Railway Company, Isaac Hartas and Alexander Sherriff with a view to building a railway. The line, with its notorious incline at Ingleby, was opened in March of 1861, the branch along the east side in 1865 and a spur to small workings in Farndale a little later. From a vantage point on the road south of the Lion Inn on Blakey Rigg the track beds of both branches can be seen on both sides of Rosedale. That on the West Side pushed across the moorland, past Sheriff's Pit to calcining kilns and the top of the incline to the quarries in Kitchen's Deposit and Garbutt's Deposit where the magnetic stone was got. The East Side branch followed a man-made terrace to the drift entrances and the two ranges of calcining kilns of the Rosedale and Ferryhill Iron Company. Surviving remains are the drift mines and quarries and the calcining kilns

182

which reduced the weight of the ore prior to its journey to the lowland blast furnaces. In their working days before 1926 these kilns were coated with red oxide dust but they are now mellowed – gauntly impressive reminders of a dead industry, now accepted though not universally liked.

The village of Grosmont, at the meeting of the Esk and the Murk Esk, was an important railway junction and the centre of a third ironstone mining field, based on the fossiliferous Pecten and Avicula seams. Initially, the mining companies here looked to the east for an outlet via the Whitby and Pickering Railway and Whitby harbour. A different solution was required, however, because of the remoteness from the Middlesbrough ironworks, and blast furnaces were built locally so that pig iron rather than ironstone could be shipped out. Blast furnaces were blown in at Beck Hole by William Armitage of Leeds in 1860, at Grosmont by Charles and Thomas Bagnall of Staffordshire in 1863 and at Glaisdale by Firth and Hodgson in 1865. The dream of a second smelting area to rival that of the Tees was ill-founded. The slumps of 1866 and 1873 put paid to many plans and the three ironworks were short-lived because of the limited availability of ironstone and of the freight cost of coal from County Durham. Today there are few relics of either mines or furnaces. At Esk Valley there are two shafts, one with a pump rod in situ, and a fine range of stone-built houses which formerly had workshops in the ground floor. At Beck Hole there is the vitrified base of one of the blast furnaces and, on the opposite side of the stream, disturbances in the woods mark the drift entrances. The most accessible furnace bases are at Grosmont on the upper level of the car park, and a well-known photograph by F. M. Sutcliffe of Whitby takes us back to the days when three blast furnaces worked here amid the smoke and the clamour of the boilers, blowing engines, calcining kilns and railway sidings. That photograph is one of very few surviving illustrations which capture the industrial smelting in the secluded dales.

CONCLUSION

The discordant impact of industry on the ancient rural landscape has frequently been disastrous, and there must be many visitors who view in this light the remaining large-scale industries in the moors. There are still large limestone quarries at Spaunton and Newbridge; the deep Boulby Potash Mine with large ore treatment plant, and the British Steel Corporation works at Skinningrove, where two blast furnaces were blown in during 1874, but which now merely rolls steel made elsewhere. Within the National Park itself, however, there can be few complaints for, although most areas have sustained some industry, the scars are now cloaked with grass and bracken, and where there was the clang and clamour of industry, the curlew and peewit call.

9
COMMUNICATIONS

THE new industries and farming developments of the nineteenth century depended upon rapid transport of heavy loads. Yet, until 1845, in our area speed on land was limited to that of the horse, and at sea to that of the sailing ship. Just to the north, the needs of the coal industry induced the development of the first steam-operated public railway in the world, from the Durham coalfield to Stockton-on-Tees in 1825, and even this started with an element of horse traction. In this chapter the slow progress of the means of transport from earliest times will be contrasted with the rapid changes brought about by the use of steam power in the past 150 years, and of the internal combustion engine in the twentieth century.

EARLY TRAVEL

There is no reason to suppose that trade and travel in Europe from the earliest periods were less extensive than those of the eighteenth century, though they were small in volume. There are many finds from early times to prove the point. Flint was brought from the Yorkshire Wolds in the Mesolithic Period; stone axes from the Lake District in the Neolithic; amber from the Baltic in the Bronze Age. By the end of prehistoric times there were as many people as in the Norman period. It follows that the terrain must then have been criss-crossed by a network of tracks between settlements, and connected with the outside world by frequently used sea and land routes. Many of these continue in use to the present day, but because of the lack of early archaeological and documentary evidence dating of their origins is very difficult.

Our sketchy information on prehistoric routes enables them to be classified into two main kinds – the local tracks and the long-distance roads. For the first we can be confident that some of the distinctive deeply worn hollow-ways which lead to and from nearly all the moorland Bronze Age cairnfields' date from this period. We cannot identify many long-distance routes, mainly because most prehistoric settlements have been destroyed or obscured. However, there are Iron Age settlements on the line of the old road from Guisborough to Westerdale, and houses of

184

the same period on each side of the road from Roxby (Hinderwell) across the moors to Danby Beacon. Both these roads were probably long-distance routes of the Iron Age, and there would have been others like them.

Indeed the system of trackways seems to have been so adequate to the needs of the area that the Romans saw no need to improve it substantially. Their major contribution was to build a military road from near the Malton fort via Cawthorn Camps to the Lease Rigg fort above the Esk. Even this proved superfluous and was abandoned for military purposes in about AD120. The only method of communication to survive from the later Roman period is the chain of signal stations along the coast, evidence of the importance of sea transport at that time.

Knowledge of roads and tracks of the six post-Roman centuries is also rather speculative. Sea travel to the Baltic and the European mainland was of considerable importance. There must also have been local tracks between the many settlements with Saxon and Scandinavian names. For example, the present A170 road running along the foot of the Tabular Hills between Helmsley and Scarborough links no fewer than twelve Saxon -*ton* place-names. There was travel between the Dark Age monasteries of Whitby, Hackness and Lastingham; an ancient road, called 'Lang Gate' on one stretch, following the top of the limestone scarp between these last two places may well have originated at this time. Some of the through-routes must have been rather ill-defined if we are to believe the story that William the Conquerer got lost on a snowy night in the tracks at the head of Bilsdale. The local tale is that 'Billy Norman kep' hissen warm wi' swearin''.

MEDIEVAL AND LATER COMMUNICATIONS

It is only in the period after 1066 that surviving documents, particularly monastic charters, enable a more definite account to be given of travel and transport. The tremendous programme of building churches, monasteries and castles must have involved much movement of men and materials. As just one example, if one drives south through Bilsdale on the B1257 today, the modern road climbs Newgate Bank out of the dale – a major ascent, yet the car never needs to drop below third gear; this skilful piece of engineering was the work of Rievaulx monks who needed to haul massive blocks of stone from the Bilsdale West Side quarries to the Abbey.

Sea routes

Seaborne trade continued to be of the first importance, especially for the eastern half of the moors. This is a dangerous coast for sailing vessels with little shelter in a storm. Thousands of ships have been wrecked over the centuries and countless sailors lost. The construction of piers at Whitby, the only good inlet on the coast, was essential to protect the harbour from northerly and easterly gales. The piers were probably first built in the fourteenth century, but from time to time fell into disrepair. They were repeatedly strengthened and extended, notably early in the eighteenth, nineteenth and twentieth centuries. The safe harbour enabled Whitby to become a major wool exporter in the Middle Ages. After that, the port engaged successively in the import of coal for the alum trade from 1615 to 1857, developing into the east coast collier trade, ship-building, whaling from 1753 to 1837, the carriage of building stone, ironstone, and lime imports from Sunderland, in the nineteenth century. Seaborne trade was much more important than overland carriage, before the coming of the railways; hence the old saying in the town that 'The only road to Whitby is the sea'.

Long-distance land routes

Transport over long distances on land evolved, however, as trade grew in the Middle Ages. The most important influence was the wool trade; contemporary sources show that some 70,000 fleeces were produced annually on the North York Moors by the end of the thirteenth century. As well as the sea route from Whitby, wool was carried overland through Malton and Clifton, near York, and thence by ship to continental markets.

By now documentary evidence enables us to define some of the routes (Fig 48). The lie of the land enabled most roads to develop in a north-south direction, using the tops of the ridges. The most westerly is the Hambleton Street running above the western escarpment from Scarth Nick at Swainby to Oldstead, part of an ancient, probably late prehistoric or Roman, route from Yarm to York. By 1209 it was called the 'main road to Cleveland', and in 1246 it was described as a 'via regalis' or Royal Road. Royal protection of roads started in the Saxon period, and was continued and expanded into the thirteenth century; later it became less important. A few miles to the east of Hambleton Street the road which connected Rievaulx and Byland Abbeys across Scawton Moor must date to the latter's foundation in 1177, as do the branches to its granges around Old Byland. Other north-south routes are the 'magna via' coming from Cleveland across Roppa Edge to Helmsley, and 'Thurkilsti' down Bransdale Rigg to Welburn. Both are mentioned in Walter Espec's second land-grant to Rievaulx in 1145. A similar road ran down Rudland Rigg; it is still an unsurfaced track, probably not much different from the medieval condition of the main roads. The road running north along Blakey Rigg forked at Ralph Cross. The eastern branch went via Castleton to White Cross and hence to Birk Brow, three miles east of Guisborough. A walk along the stretch north of White Cross gives a good impression of medieval travel, for it has the characteristic spread of the rutted tracks, and is followed by the best exposed stone pannierway called the 'Quakers Causeway' (Fig 49). The other branch through Hob Hole to Percy Rigg

Plate 42 A pannier-way above Lealholm, leading toward Stonegate. It was cleared in 1987 *(Photograph P. W. Sutor, NYMNP)*

and Guisborough (Ernaldsty), most likely prehistoric in origin, is well documented in the foundation charter of Guisborough Priory (c1120). Further east, the Pickering-Whitby road ran across the moors at York Cross on Sneaton High Moor. A branch turned east to run via Lilla Howe to Robin Hood's Bay. There it met the most easterly of the north-south roads running between Teesmouth and Scarborough, which is not much documented and was evidently a poor one. None of the numerous journeys from Scarborough to Durham made by Kings of England in the thirteenth century went this way. They all took the old road through Hackness, Lilla Howe, and York Cross to Egton, called 'Staincrossgate' in an 1133 document. The moorland stone crosses are most numerous near the important intersection at York Cross (Fig 48).

East-west roads, always the most difficult, are confined to the northern and southern fringes of the high moors. To the south the road from Thirsk to Helmsley and Scarborough (A170) was called 'Sperragate' in medieval documents. To the north Ladgate (A174) ran from Catterick through Cleveland to Marske; it by-passes Yarm and other old villages, a hint of its pre-medieval origin. The lower moors to the north of the Esk were easier to negotiate east-west than the high moors. One road called Gunnergate ran eastward from Ladgate near Yarm, as far as Guisborough, whence it followed the present A171 to meet the road coming up the moors from Stokesley at White Cross. The Stokesley road west of White Cross, now a rough track, was part of the main Stokesley-Whitby

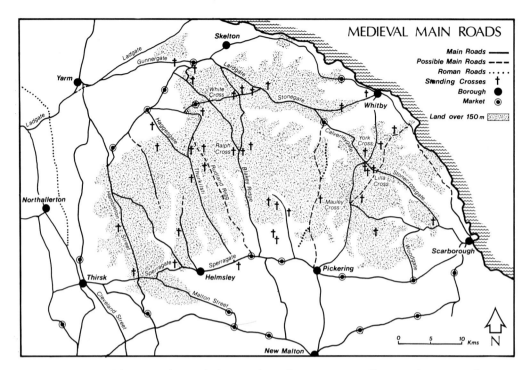

Fig 48 These are the roads known from documentary evidence to have existed in medieval times. Note the close association of the moorland crosses with these roads, and absence of roads in the dale bottoms *(after J. McDonnell)*

road until the last century, and is another good example of a road surviving in its medieval condition. Eastward of White Cross the road ran through Lealholm Rigg, Stonegate and Egton where it continued southeast as 'Calverleygate' to connect with 'Staincrossgate' to Scarborough.

Fig 48 displays the roads which can be proved from documents to be medieval. It shows how much of the present system is based on it, with the exception of the roads which now twist along the dale bottoms. And it illustrates how closely the moorland crosses are related to the medieval roads.

The unsurfaced medieval roads were frequented by horses and pannier-trains, small two-wheeled carts ('coups' or 'cowps'), and in a few cases by four-wheeled ox-wagons. They also served as droveways for livestock. They often have a wide spread of tracks made by their users as they repeatedly avoided the deep ruts by diverting round them. Such multiple tracks are conspicuous on open moorland, as on the ancient road from Roxby to Danby Beacon, and also alongside modern hard-surfaced roads, as on Blakey Rigg.

The mention of Danby Beacon is an apt reminder of the beacon system of communication, or rather telecommunication, successor of the Roman signal stations and precursor of Fylingdales. It was set up in the Armada

188

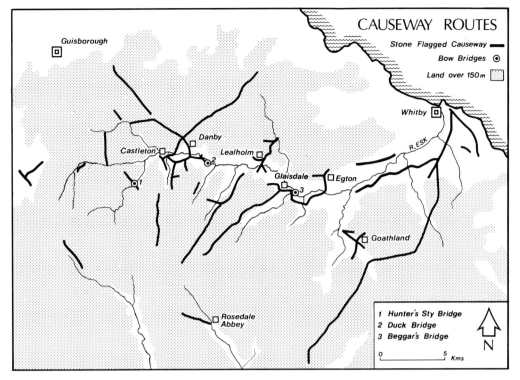

Stone Flagged Causeway ▬
Bow Bridges ◉
Land over 150m ▦

Guisborough

Whitby

R. ESK

Danby

Castleton ◉2

Lealholm

Glaisdale ◉Egton ◉3

Goathland

Rosedale Abbey

1 Hunter's Sty Bridge
2 Duck Bridge
3 Beggar's Bridge

0   5 Kms

N

Fig 49 These are the pannierways which can be clearly seen today. There are many others, more obscure, some of which have still to be traced *(adapted from W. Breakell, Old Pannier Tracks, 1982)*

period and revived during the Napoleonic Wars, to give warning of invasion. Danby and Ampleforth Beacons are the two best known of an elaborate chain of beacon sites usually marked by 'beacon hill' or 'beacon field' names. Both have recently been the site of less alarmist bonfires celebrating the Queen's Jubilee in 1977.

The often miry and occasionally impassable upland roads led to a system of stone-flagged causeways or pannierways created primarily for the use of heavily laden packhorses, particularly on the ill-drained surfaces of the High Moors. Such causeways are common in various parts of England, but most prolific in the Peak District and the North York Moors. A hundred and fifty miles of them have been plotted out on the moors and there are still more remaining unmapped. It is impossible at present to date them. One, near Whitby, is popularly known as the Monks' Path, but others are often attributed to Quakers, smugglers and others. It is reasonable to suppose that monastic houses like Whitby and Rievaulx, which needed to collect and export wool, travel to outlying granges, and in the case of Rievaulx bring fish from its sea-fishery at Tees-mouth, probably pioneered the technique. They had the resources to execute the work of quarrying and laying the flags. The map (Fig 49)

189

Plate 43 Beggar's Bridge, Glaisdale. The height of the bridge is needed because the river can flood dramatically after a downpour *(Tindale's)*

shows that around the eastern Esk Valley they focus on Whitby, while others run south from the central area. It may be that they related originally to the wool trade through the two main collection centres, though wool is a bulky load for a packhorse. They would also have been used for other traffic, such as salt, fish and iron. They continued in use well into the nineteenth century; as late as 1890 dozens of packhorses could be seen resting in Rosedale.

Pannierways connected at river-crossings with the packhorse bridges. Particularly fine and accessible examples of these are Hunter's Sty Bridge in Westerdale, Duck Bridge in Danby, and Beggar's Bridge in Glaisdale (Plate 43). Floods have destroyed practically all medieval bridges in the area, but their successors are usually built on the same alignment and with much the same hump-backed structure. This can be seen at Rievaulx, in both Scawton Bridge, downstream of the abbey, and Bow Bridge upstream.

From about 1700 many of the long-distance roads were used for the transport of lime (Fig 50). A limekiln requires about one ton of coal to calcine four tons of limestone, producing about two tons of lime. It is therefore easiest to build the kiln at the limestone quarry, bring fuel to it, and cart the lime to the user. Many kilns were built on the north side of the Tabular Hills, using coal from nearby moor collieries, and despatching

190

lime to dress the acid soils of the Esk Valley. The trade was conducted by ox-wagons along the medieval north-south routeways. It declined in the nineteenth century owing to competition with lime brought by sea from Sunderland to Whitby, and with limestone shipped from Flamborough Head to kilns at Sandsend and Ruswarp.

A still conspicuous feature of moorland tracks, often crossing feature-less terrain subject to snow and fog, is a wide range of stone waymarkers (Plate 44). Many of the well-known moorland crosses (of which Ralph Cross serves as the National Park emblem) double as boundary markers and guide-posts. Some, like Cockan Cross above Bransdale, have sub-sequently had 'road signs' carved on their shafts to aid the forlorn travel-ler. Other upright stones like the guide-post on the old Thirkilsti track above Bransdale, whose faces have pointed the wayfarer to 'Stoxla' and 'Helmsla' since 1712, are the comparatively recent products of an early eighteenth century campaign to improve guidance countrywide. Some of these posts are perched on top of round barrows – the oldest of all bound-ary and waymarks. The diligent walker in the Urra-Bloworth area may happen upon the crudely carved (and less old than they look) Hand and Face Stones; and there are many more, of all shapes and sizes, to be found

Fig 50 The improved turnpike roads were mainly on the fringes of the moors, leaving the centre with the unsurfaced medieval roads *(after J. McDonnell)*

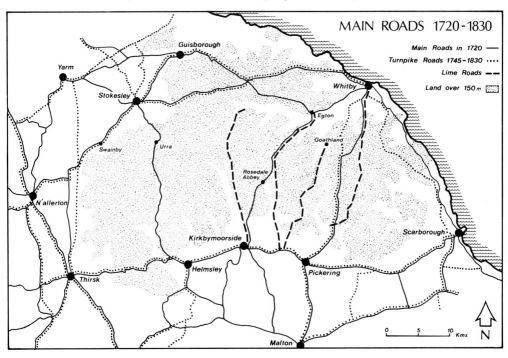

191

scattered along the moorland tracks and trods. All, whatever their age and origin, are sign of our ancestors' good intentions towards the offcomer who travelled hopefully over the ridgeways.

Local tracks

Every medieval village and hamlet had streets and trackways leading through its fields and linking with its neighbouring settlements. We can easily discern these where the village retained its medieval plan into the eighteenth and nineteenth centuries, then to be recorded by map-makers. The main droveway for animals from the village to the 'town moor' is usually obvious, and often still called the 'Outgang'. Trackways to the town fields, sometimes deeply hollowed, are often preserved. There is occasionally a trackway along the dyke which separated the arable from the moor grazing, generally called the 'acredyke' in North Yorkshire. A good example is the right-of-way along the Meredyke (so named in a fourteenth century survey and meaning 'boundary dyke') at Middleton (Fig 27) and similar rights of way are found in the neighbouring villages. Monastic documents also give much information on village trackways since they are often boundaries to the lands described in the charters. By this means we know the names of the tracks leading from Snainton northwards towards Troutsdale (Chapter 5). We can be sure that many of the villages retain their medieval streets and the most important of their field tracks to the present day.

Another conspicuous short-distance track is the turf-road. The cutting of peat and turf for fuel from the moors was a prized right in and after the

Middle Ages. The favoured vehicle for this traffic was the horse-drawn sled, which could survive battering on rocky trackways down the moor-side. Many hollow-ways originated in this way. Good examples can be seen at Skiplam Rigg and Boonhill Commons on the Tabular Hills, and on Trennet Spur near Chop Gate in Bilsdale. Further east a group of sledding roads converges on Saltersgate Bridge on the A169.

THE NINETEENTH CENTURY ROADS AND RAILWAYS

At the dawn of the railway era, communications were not much improved from their condition in the Middle Ages. When Canon Atkinson took up his appointment as vicar of Danby in 1845 he rode horseback from Scarborough to Whitby, where he found no lodging house or hotel. On the following day he continued to Danby along a rough moorland road, where he did not see a soul, until at Stonegate Gill he witnessed the amazing sight of twenty horses and oxen hauling a stone-laden wagon up the steep bank. Such feats with four-wheeled wagons may remind us of the earlier efforts of the Rievaulx masons to bring stone up Newgate Bank from Bilsdale. J. T. Sewell, in his 1922 study of moorland roads south and south-west of Whitby, also recalls how, in the later eighteenth and early nineteenth centuries, the empty wood wagons returning to Nawton and Helmsley after delivering oak timber at the Whitby shipyards took the moor roads from Sil Howe above Goathland straight to Simon Howe Rigg and Mauley Cross 'in order to escape the turnpike dues along the main roads'. They could scarcely have done so when laden on the return journey; the scope for the use of heavy wagons on moorland roads was severely limited until the coming of the petrol engine.

The area contained no navigable rivers or canals; a scheme for a canal from Pickering to Ruswarp was abandoned in 1831. It is true that several roads had been turnpiked (improved by finance from private 'turnpike' trusts) by Canon Atkinson's time, but these were mainly on the fringes of the area (Fig 50), leaving the heart of the moors with its medieval track-ways. The present A19 road along the western fringe was turnpiked in 1752, the road along the southern edge (A170) in 1750–70, and the Helmsley to York via Oswaldkirk between 1768 and 1803. Whitby was linked to Pickering by a largely new road begun in 1764, and to Scar-borough and Guisborough (via Lythe) by turnpiking the old roads at about the same period. There was a coach service between Whitby and York from 1788 and between Scarborough and York from 1793; fearful journeys by all accounts. This was the state of transport until the mid-nineteenth century. Perhaps the wretched roads induced Sir George Cayley, squire of Brompton, to invent, build and fly the first man-carrying glider in 1853. Sir George's coachman, however, conscripted as the pilot, resigned the job, stating a preference for driving over flying.

The emergence of the railway from local horse-hauled mineral lines to the steam-powered form is usually dated from the opening of the Stockton and Darlington Railway in 1825. This line, just to the north of our area, was the first public railway to use steam power; its prime purpose was to haul Durham coal to tidewater, and horses supplemented steam traction in its earliest years. Within our area, horse power survived a little longer. The first line was built in 1833 from the hills above Kepwick to take limestone to kilns at Leake on the A19 turnpike. It was a downhill run, with horses hauling across the low ground. The quarry, the remains of the track and its bridges, can be seen on a walk through and above Kepwick village. At the scarp top on the Hambleton Street there was an inn called Limekiln House, one of a series along the old drovers' road. It was a stance for cattle on their long march south from Scotland, and used by drovers and quarrymen alike. Droving continued until about 1840, and the site can still be seen on the east side of Hambleton Street.

The second line, the Whitby and Pickering Railway, which opened throughout in 1836, also used primitive methods, for its trains were horse-hauled until 1847. It surmounted the difficult ground between Beck Hole and Goathland by a rope-worked incline with an average gradient of 1 in 15. Its origins, however, were not in mineral traffic but in the desire of Whitby's citizens for an effective landward link. They chose as their engineer none other than George Stephenson, the 'Father of Railways'.

By the 1840s, the limitations of the primitive Whitby and Pickering railway were obvious, and moves were made both to link it to the emerging national railway network and to upgrade its facilities. In 1845, the company was taken over by the York and North Midland Railway, part of the empire of George Hudson, 'The Railway King'. The latter company's York to Scarborough route was opened in 1845, and linked to Pickering by a line from Rillington in the same year. In the ensuing two years, the line to Whitby was rapidly upgraded to permit working throughout by steam-hauled trains. The rope-worked incline remained until 1865 when the present 'deviation' route through Goathland was completed by the North Eastern Railway, allowing steam locomotives to work trains uninterrupted from Whitby to Pickering.

One of Hudson's main objectives in acquiring the Whitby and Pickering was to revive the fortunes of Whitby, then at a low ebb. Hudson bought land on the West Cliff to build hotels and guest-houses, the first major promotion of its tourist industry. Plate 45, a lithograph of this period, shows the turning point when steam replaced wind power. The windmill and the sailing ships represent the old order; the new railway station, the hotels and the steamship the shape of things to come. It is a dramatic scene, showing Whitby, and with it the whole region, changing from the power sources of the medieval world.

The Whitby and Pickering Railway is still very much alive. The route

Plate 45 Whitby in 1850. The age of wind power gives place to the age of steam. Notice George Hudson's new hotels on the West Cliff *(David & Charles)*

south of Grosmont was closed in 1965, but it was re-opened to Pickering in 1973 as the North Yorkshire Moors Railway, and steam trains still snake through the remote recesses of Newtondale. The original route via the incline from Grosmont to Goathland is a signed footpath, the Historic Railway Trail. At Grosmont itself, the tunnel which once carried the horse-worked railway south of the village is now threaded by the footpath to the railway's locomotive works, its diminutive scale contrasting strongly with the parallel main railway tunnel.

Elsewhere in the Moors, the railway network grew rapidly in the middle years of the nineteenth century (Fig 51). There were two prime stimuli for this growth. In the north it was the rise of ironstone mining, whose history is recalled in Chapter 8. Most notable of the ironstone lines was that built to serve the Rosedale mines, and opened between 1858 and 1865. From Battersby, it reached the highland moorland by the rope-worked Ingleby incline, almost a mile long and with gradients as steep as 1 in 5. It then ran for ten miles, hugging the contours high above the sides of Farndale and Rosedale to Rosedale West, and with a four-mile branch from Blakey Junction to Rosedale East. In the peak year of 1873, over half a million tons of ironstone were produced from the Rosedale mines. It was hauled over these isolated lines to the incline top by locomotives which could have only the most infrequent absences from the line for overhaul. The line was finally closed in 1928 and the last locomotives were lowered down the incline in 1929. Sixty years later, however, virtually the whole course of the trackbed is still intact, and from Blakey

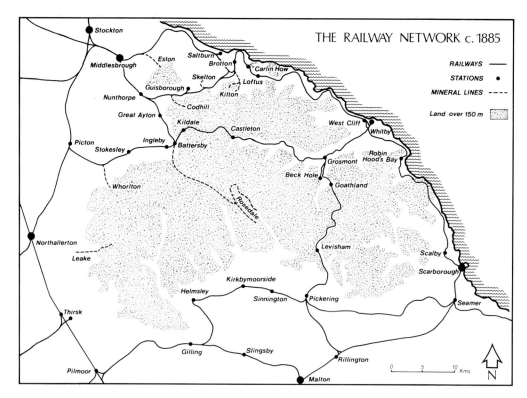

Fig 51 This represents the fullest extent of railway development

Ridge makes a readily accessible and splendid near-level walking route, with incomparable vistas of Farndale and Rosedale.

Away from ironstone working, the railways were built to serve the more general transport needs of the moors communities. The detailed history of these lines has been fully chronicled elsewhere, but by 1885 (Fig 51) few places of consequence in our area were unserved by the railway. Whitby was the focus of no less than four routes – to Pickering; along the Esk Valley to Glaisdale and Castleton (completed 1865); north along the coast to Loftus and Middlesbrough (completed 1883); and south to Scarborough (completed 1885). Though several had been developed by local, independent companies, all were worked in 1885 by the benevolent monopoly of the North Eastern Railway, formed by amalgamation in 1854. Its distinctive styles of buildings and of engineering works still stamp their character on many parts of the Moors.

The railways had a great impact on the landscape and on the people. They made raw scars, which time has now softened, but must have appeared horrific to an age unaccustomed to such massive works. Many of the stations, bridges and viaducts, however, were not only of distinctive design but built of local stone and generally blended well with, and in some cases even enhanced, the landscape. But the railways also enabled

196

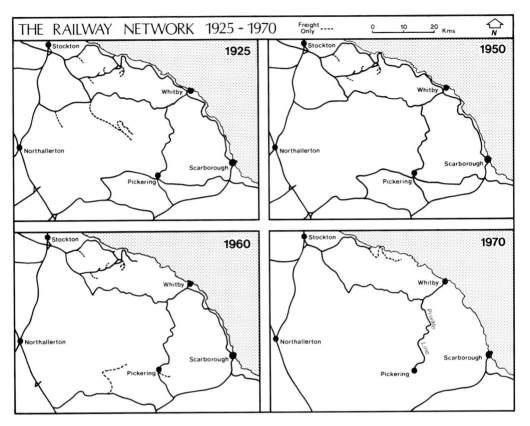

THE RAILWAY NETWORK 1925 - 1970   Freight Only ----   0 10 20 Kms   N

1925

1950

1960

1970

Stockton
Whitby
Northallerton
Pickering
Scarborough

private Line

Fig 52 The railway system survived complete until 1950, apart from the closure of the Rosedale line in 1928. Now only four lines are operating

mass-produced building materials, such as Fletton bricks and Welsh slates, to be brought cheaply into the area, to supplant local materials. They deeply influenced trade, enabling the import of industrial and domestic coal, and the export of fresh farm produce to the towns. And they made access to market towns and holiday resorts easy for all classes of society. In many cases the transport systems and roads in rural areas were adjusted to focus on the railway stations.

Economic and technological change meant that the full railway network lasted little more than 40 years (Fig 52). In the 1920s, the ironstone lines faded as production dropped. In the post-war years, more general purpose routes succumbed to the internal combustion engine. The coast line north of Whitby, always difficult to maintain, was closed in 1958, and in the harsher realism of the Beeching era, the lines south to Scarborough and to Pickering followed in 1965. The last of these survives in preservation, but the coast lines can now only be enjoyed on foot. Much of the trackbed of the Scarborough line is a footpath in local authority ownership: the section from Ravenscar to Robin Hood's Bay is a particular pleasure to walk, with its sweeping views of the bay. North of Whitby, the line which clung to the cliff beyond Sandsend is now a part of the Cleveland Way, though the tunnels through to Kettleness are long abandoned.

The surviving lines are the coastal route from Middlesbrough to Saltburn, mainly used by commuters, shoppers and day-trippers to the coast; from Middlesbrough to Whitby, a delightful run through the Esk Valley serving its scattered communities, and also promoted for its tourist value; the enthusiast-preserved Pickering-Grosmont line, an unforgettable steam-hauled journey through the heart of the Moors; and the freight line to Carlin How and Boulby, serving the British Steel and Boulby Potash works.

THE TWENTIETH CENTURY

Until the Second World War, many of the old moorland roads remained unsurfaced save for periodic dressings with rubble limestone or, quite often, iron slag from old workings; the motor car was still largely a middle-class luxury. From the 1950s, mass motoring became the main means of travel, with lorries taking over freight including farm animals and produce. Several previously unmade roads, like the beautiful moorland link between Hawnby and Osmotherley, owe their improvement to the requirements of Milk Marketing Board tankers. The internal combustion engine again revolutionised farm and village life, and increased the volume of tourist trade many fold. An echo of the Roman signal stations and the Elizabethan warning beacons, telecommunications have produced another great change in employment and social amenities, as well as in the appearance of villages and the landscape. The geography and elevation of the hills have determined their suitability for radar, relay, listening stations and the like. The mast at Bilsdale has replaced the Rosedale ironstone kiln chimney as a symbol of contemporary technology. At Fylingdales today the speed of a missile is of more immediate interest than that of the 1788 diligence from Whitby to York which trundled past the site.

10
MODERN TIMES

DESPITE the changes in British society brought by the Industrial Revolution, the appearance of the countryside changed but slowly. The landscape of the Moors early in the twentieth century was different in detail and degree rather than in form from the landscape of the early nineteenth century. The main change was the introduction of railways and heavy industry, particularly in Eskdale and Rosedale. To be sure, there had been some enclosure and improvements in farming techniques, but the basic farming systems had not changed. The pattern of moorland, dale agriculture, daleside woodland, compact villages and scattered farmsteads also seemed immutable.

The ensuing decades have witnessed changes on an unprecedented scale. Fortunately, there are accurate records of most of them including photographs, films and even personal memories. Not that all rural matters have been carefully recorded. Less is known about the ownership and occupation of land today than is given for its time in the Domesday Survey. There still is no accurate field survey of wildlife and not until 1975 was there an attempt to count the visitors to the Moors.

THE LANDSCAPE IN 1900

The landscape at the turn of the century comprised five main elements. First and foremost was the moorland which covered about half the area. It was being run partly for grouse shooting, a relatively new system of estate management, and partly for grazing by sheep and cattle. As is shown in Chapters 2 and 6, some of the moors had been cultivated in the Bronze Age and as recently as the Napoleonic wars, but the moorland vegetation and general absence of enclosure gave, and continue to give, the basic character to this dominating feature of the landscape. Much of the moorland has been undisturbed since prehistoric times and it bequeaths us a fossilised record of the activities of its early settlers and farmers.

In the dales, the second main element, the enclosures had modified the medieval farming and settlement pattern which still provided the main structure of the landscape. Woodland cover was very sparse; only a few daleside oak woods had survived and most trees were found in hedgerows or in small copses. Most villages and hamlets at this time exhibited the sturdy vernacular with neat buildings of stone and pantile. The scattered farms were often rebuilt but designed in similar materials and styles. On the Hambleton and Tabular Hills, the earliest and most fertile agricultural land of the Moors, the enclosure movement had laid out new or widened roads, larger farms and more regular shaped fields of convenient size for cultivation. Tree cover was sparse on the plateaux surfaces but there were remnants of woodland clinging to the steep slopes of intervening dales. The villages on the lower back slopes retained their medieval form but were larger than those in the dales, reflecting their greater agricultural wealth.

The coastal plain too had been much affected by late enclosure, with improved farming methods increasingly successful on the heavy boulder clay. The need for local food supplies, particularly of milk, meat and eggs, in the nearby industrial towns provided a much needed boost for farmers in this area. The small enclosed farms could diversify to meet the need and this gave rise to a mixed type of arable and pastoral farming, well suited to exploit changes in the demands of the market. Along the coast, the nineteenth century had seen the development of fishing industries at Staithes, Runswick Bay and Robin Hood's Bay, adding to the well-established fishing ports of Scarborough and Whitby.

The fifth element in our early twentieth century landscape was heavy industry with its railways and workers' housing. This was a dominant feature in Eskdale and Rosedale but there were mines, quarries and industrial works scattered over the whole area. The nearby Cleveland industrial towns had grown rapidly in the later decades of the nineteenth century to exploit the iron ore. They were classic 'mushroom' towns of the industrial era.

How did these five components of early twentieth century landscape combine to create a collage of the Moors at the time? What would one of the new breed of tourists arriving by rail at a moorside town and taking to horse and trap, or primitive motor car, have seen in his travels? The dominating presence of the moors framing the horizon would have struck him immediately and left a lasting impression on his mind. Moorland covered all the main ridges and plateau surfaces, often extending down the dale slopes. Only the coastal plain was virtually free from it. There was less bracken than today and much less woodland though some of the dale sides would be clothed in oak and birch woods. Few conifer plantations would be seen and these only small in scale. The farmland would appear as a well tended version of the dale agriculture of today with neat stone walls, well laid hedges and a sprinkling of hedgerow trees and copses. Villages and buildings would give an outward appearance of unspoilt solidity, being mainly built in stone and pantiles. Closer inspection would reveal much squalor, poverty and overcrowding.

The abundance of country people compared with today would be most striking. In Farndale East parish for instance there were over 300 persons in the villages and on the farms compared with only 80 today. Farm workers and other craftsmen would be seen everywhere carrying out their trades except perhaps on the remoter moors. The villages would seem busier with many shops, traders and small service industries. Fellow travellers bent on sightseeing would be a rarity and only at a few railside locations, such as Goathland, would there be any sign of tourist activity. On Sundays, the Moors would seem uncannily quiet compared with today, as the population took its day of rest.

The road surfaces were primitive by today's standards but the network was well established. Our visitor's early motor car would not cope with the steep gradients but could get along some of the moorland ridge roads and along the dale bottoms. The rail network would be at its busiest with frequent trains along the four routes to Whitby and freight on the mineral lines across the moors, as from Rosedale to Ingleby. Industry would feature in many views where it is absent today. Ironstone mining in the Esk Valley and Rosedale with the remains of a large iron smelting works at Grosmont, mining and dock facilities at Port Mulgrave, quarrying for building stone around Aislaby, mining for road stone above Goathland; these activities would present a busy scene of heavy industry where none now exists. On the edge of the moors in Cleveland, recently established towns and mining settlements were in their heyday with rapidly growing, bustling settlements full of immigrant labourers and their families.

During the following years, and particularly after the First World War, this scene changed both radically and rapidly as modern technology evolved on the farm, in the workplace and in the home. We must understand the forces which gave rise to changes in the landscape and the ways in which society has tried to control and shape them.

THE ELEMENTS OF CHANGE

The use of the land
A comparison of the changes in basic land use between 1853 and 1986 shows just how dramatically the scenery of the Moors has altered (Fig 53). Statistics do not tell the whole story of course but the changes are nevertheless quite remarkable. The loss of moorland vegetation is the most significant trend; from 49% of the area of the National Park in 1853 to 40% in 1963 and down to 35% by 1986. The area of farmland increased slowly, but the land under trees expanded rapidly after 1919 when the Forestry Commission was formed. For centuries, the edge of the moorland had fluctuated according to the demand for food, receding in periods of agricultural boom such as the Napoleonic wars when food shortages occurred, only to expand again as the reclaimed land was

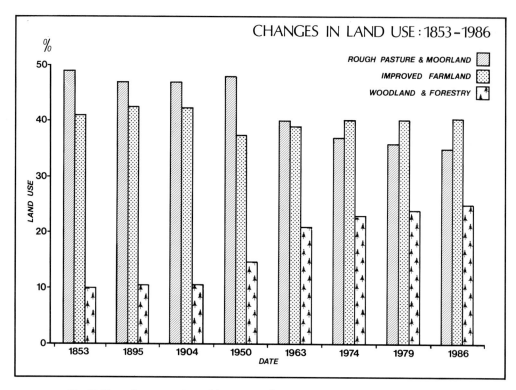

Fig 53 Note the expansion of forestry at the expense of moorland

abandoned in years of depression. This is hardly surprising since the moor edge land can only yield grass and crops with considerable effort and expenditure.

The situation in the twentieth century has been different in three respects. Firstly, the scale of reclamation has been very great, with large areas being broken and cultivated by modern machinery. Secondly, the use of the same machinery combined with new fertilisers and chemicals has enabled the primary moorlands, those which had never been cultivated, to be reclaimed for both forestry and improved farming. The third factor has been the use of the former moorland for commercial coniferous forestry on a large scale by the Forestry Commission, a new state agency. The Commission initially acquired land cheaply in the depression years of the 1920s in the Dalby, Bickley and Hackness areas. Most of the land was moorland, rough grazing and warrens, but some poor quality farmland was also planted. The new plantations were extensive, covering both the plateaux surfaces and the steep dale sides of the Tabular Hills. The chief trees used were various species of pine, particularly lodgepole pine, but douglas fir, larch, spruce and a few hardwoods were also planted. It was an era of rapid expansion and few concessions were made to amenity. The available land was planted up with the most suitable species according to the forestry techniques in fashion. In time, the forest area expanded into Wykeham and Cropton with smaller plantings in the Cleveland and Hambleton Hills. Labour for the new industry was provided on a generous scale with immigrant work gangs which included unemployed Durham miners.

It was several years before the new plantations made a significant impact on the landscape and wildlife of the moors. As the harsh geometrical shapes of the plantations appeared and familiar landscape features were smothered in a dull cloth of dark green conifers, opposition to forestry was voiced by both local people and visitors. It became clear that a better attempt was needed to harmonise the new forests with the old moorland. Opportunities for more enlightened land use were not generally grasped, but there were exceptions. One area which was planned comprehensively for farming, forestry, conservation and recreation was the former Newton House estate near Whitby, which was transferred from the War Department to the Forestry Commission early in the 1960s. An integrated land use plan was prepared using experts from a number of central and local government agencies. The result today is a pleasing mixture of moorland, forestry and farmland with ample opportunities for public visiting.

Nowadays, afforestation and replanting are exercised with great care. Species are selected partly with amenity considerations in mind, the shape of the plantations is expertly contoured and streams are left with margins of hardwoods and unplanted land. Nevertheless, there is a strong body of opinion which considers that the spread of forestry should be more closely controlled by the planning authorities.

During the 1960s, the Forestry Commission became more aware of the demand for public access and recreation in the new forest areas. A variety of facilities were provided including forest drives in Dalby and Newtondale, a caravan site at Spiers Howe in Cropton Forest and a log-cabin complex at Keldy Castle. With more imagination and with encouragement from central government, much more could have been achieved.

The farms of the Moors have changed very considerably during the present century. Mechanisation has not only meant fewer farmworkers but it has led to many changes in the landscape. Hedges, hedgerow trees and small copses have generally declined in number and appearance because of the use of modern cutting equipment and the lack of replanting and day-to-day maintenance. Stone walls have disappeared, sometimes replaced by post and wire fences. In Cold Kirby on the limestone Hambleton Hills, for instance, there are many stone walls and hedges but they declined greatly between 1972 and 1985 (Fig 54).

On the land, the widespread use of fertilisers and chemicals to control weeds and pests has dramatically increased the crops but reduced the variety of wild flowers, birds, animals and insects. The reseeding of

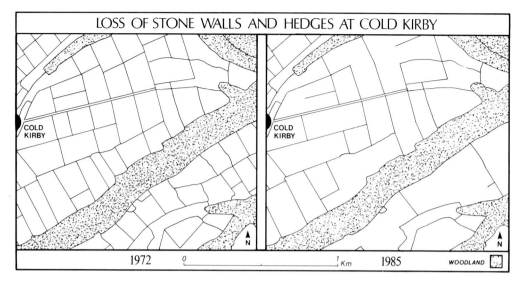

Fig 54 Modern farming has been very destructive of old hedges and walls in the quest for larger crop yields. The loss of them has, in many cases, been detrimental to scenery and wildlife

pastures and the change from haymaking to silage cropping has also led to fewer numbers and varieties of herbs and flowers, and the insect life which depends on them.

New farm machinery began to appear during the late eighteenth and nineteenth centuries. Threshing machines, seed drills and various implements for cultivation gradually became more common and the advent of steam engines to supplement horse power intensified their use. Steam-driven machinery was too heavy and cumbersome for most field cultivations, however, and it was not until the introduction of petrol-driven tractors that the horse was finally supplanted on the farm. This came about gradually from the early decades of the twentieth century until the time of the Second World War, when draught horses were used for some of the lighter tasks only. Thereafter, they disappeared from all but a few farms and, today, they are a rarity. The tractor which replaced them is now so commonplace that it is hard to appreciate that all this has occurred within a lifetime. Together with a few other self-driven machines, such as the combine harvester, the tractor has taken over many of the hard, repetitive manual tasks by using ever more attachments for cultivation and harvesting.

Perhaps the most striking change in the farm landscape, however, has been the erection of farm buildings in new materials, particularly steel, corrugated iron and asbestos. These are now seen on most farm steadings and, with their alien materials and size, frequently strike a discordant note. The most intrusive buildings are used for intensive production of livestock, usually pigs and poultry. Problems of disease, smell and effluent disposal usually demand an isolated location for this peculiarly modern form of farming. Although usually a lowland activity, several such enterprises have developed on higher ground, mainly along the southern margin on the arable land of the Tabular Hills.

Frequent changes in the market make this a high-risk business and the enterprises are usually short-lived. The problems of maintenance and supervision often involve a house for a key worker, thus increasing the impact on the local scene. Much concern exists about the effects on the environment, particularly by pollution, of these units, quite apart from the concern over the welfare of the animals. Given modern mass production methods, however, it is likely that such developments will become more commonplace, as will similar rearing methods such as the winter housing of sheep. This is currently being introduced into the area bringing more buildings of alien materials, including plastic roof coverings.

How has the moorland fared during this period of change? The development of driven grouse shooting during the nineteenth century gave an additional economic and social value to the heather. The visual consequences were not immediately obvious but the demand for higher bags by the Victorian sportsmen led to the introduction of new methods of grouse management. These included the practice of heather burning to give a suitable range of growth for the grouse; providing the birds with grit; the culling of 'vermin'; the building of lines of butts; and the drainage of boggy areas (Chapter 1). The result of this was initially to increase grouse bags quite considerably. After a decline during the First World War, bags increased to reach record levels on many estates during the 1930s, since when they have gradually declined. The reasons for this are not fully understood but disease, climatic change, lack of burning, ineffective vermin control and a decline in the nutrient value of heather on which the grouse depends are all possible contributors. Although the grouse moors are used for rambling by the public, there is little evidence that this has conflicted with grouse management. Public access is, however, a highly contentious issue and was one of the chief factors in the creation of National Parks.

The moors have continued to be used for grazing by sheep and cattle, though the latter are found rarely today. The carrying capacity of the moors averages about one ewe to four acres, well below that of the nearby Pennines. The moor sheep, or 'moor jocks', have a hard existence and lambing rates are notoriously low. About half the moorland area is registered common land where stocking rates are legally quantified. This does not prevent overgrazing of some moors, as the legal limits are sometimes well above the natural capacity of the vegetation to support the stock.

Apart from the loss of moorland to forestry or improved agriculture, or in the two world wars to military training, other changes have taken place during the past four decades. The most obvious is the spread of bracken, a major weed in the northern hemisphere, probably due to the changing, less labour-intensive management of the moors. The erosion of the moors also gives rise to great concern. There are a number of causes: the burning of heather, especially large-scale accidental summer conflagrations; the wear on footpaths by thousands of walkers; and the continual attack of natural forces (Chapter 1).

The concern for the conservation of the remaining moorland during the past few years has led to the creation of a large-scale Moorland Management Programme, coordinated by the National Park Committee but involving many moorland owners, flockmasters, scientists from the Universities, and government agencies. One immediately useful technique is to cut heather by tractor-drawn equipment in some areas instead of burning. A bonus of this process is the baling of the heather cuttings for use in the gardening business.

Farming, forestry and grouse-rearing make up the main land use in the Moors over the modern era. However, other uses have developed more especially after the Second World War. The various tourist and recreational activities have become more important and widespread, to the point where tourism is now the mainstay of the economy. Even so, the majority of the pursuits take place as secondary activities in the primary landscape of farming and forestry. This was also the case with army training which was practised over many thousands of acres during both world wars. The military buildings have for the most part disappeared, but a few pill boxes remain along the coast and occasional shells and bombs, some unexploded, are still unearthed.

Plate 46 Sheep farming *(Photograph Ross Williams, NYMNP)*

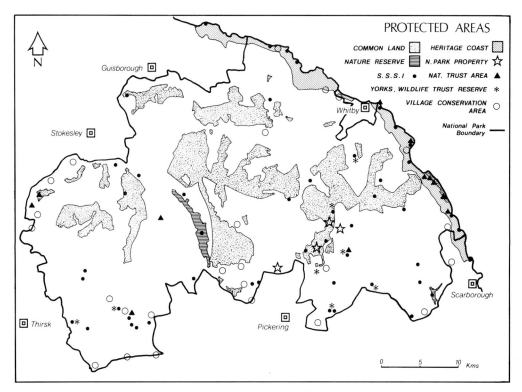

Fig 55 Within the National Park are many other specially designated areas where protection of landscape and wildlife are paramount. In the case of common land this is a by-product of the medieval farming system *(NYMNP)*

A new use of land which has few precedents has become increasingly important. This is the deliberate conservation of a tract of land for its value as a habitat or for its scenic qualities. Nature Reserves, Sites of Special Scientific Interest and Conservation Areas in the villages are all recent attempts to protect the threatened remains of formerly more widespread land uses and management (Fig 55). The Norman hunting forest was, in some ways, a precursor to this attempt to arrest the economic exploitation of land so as to protect certain of its valuable features. With current over-production in farming, it could well become a major factor in the use of the Moors in the future; indeed the designation of the National Park in 1952 can be seen as a first step in this direction.

People and work
The population of the area now covered by the National Park has fallen by about 15% during the present century, while in England and Wales as a whole it grew by over 50%. This overall decline masks wide variations from parish to parish. Generally, the remoter dales and villages of the Moors have seen a considerable loss of people, as much as 60% in Farndale for instance, whilst the peripheral settlements have seen a slight

207

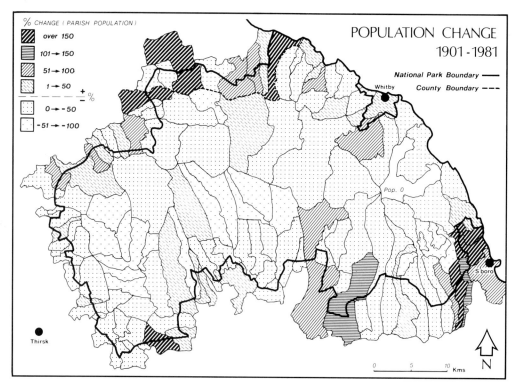

Fig 56 Depopulation is a feature of the remote dales. The fringe of the National Park is a favourite place to live in the twentieth century

increase. In some parishes, this rise has been quite considerable. Taken together, East and West Ayton grew by 160% between 1901 and 1981, reflecting the popularity to commuters of the villages near Scarborough. Likewise villages within easy commuting distance of Teesside, such as Faceby and Swainby, saw high growth rates. Fig 56 shows the pattern of growth and decline over the area since 1901.

The chief reason for the loss is the halving of the agricultural workforce in the last 40 years. In places, this decline has been aggravated by the closing of mines and quarries. Rosedale East and West saw a drop in numbers from 1396 in 1901 to 273 in 1981, mainly the result of closing the ironstone mines. The loss of farm workers has had a bad effect on the landscape of the Moors. The upkeep of traditional enclosed dale landscape with its attendant heather moorland requires careful and constant attention. Tasks such as the repair of stone walls, the laying of hedges, the planting and nurturing of roadside copses and trees, the burning of heather, the drainage of lanes, footpaths and bridleways cannot generally be mechanised. Without the labour to carry out these tasks, the landscape assumes an unkempt, derelict appearance frequently made worse by the use of inappropriate modern materials, such as rusty old bedsteads and wire used to stop up gaps in walls and hedges.

The loss of community services in remote areas has been a cause of continuing concern for several decades. Village shops have disappeared along with post offices and village schools, churches and chapels. During the course of the century the population decline has even affected the supply of modern public services such as public telephone kiosks, which developed gradually over the earlier decades only to decrease again recently because they were insufficiently used. The same is true of bus services and, to make matters worse, their recent decline has coincided with a drastic cut back in rail services. These trends tend to put certain groups in village society, such as the elderly, the unemployed and newly married couples starting a family, at a marked disadvantage to neighbours who can afford a car and other modern conveniences.

Unemployment has been a feature of societies since they were first industrialised; indeed it can be traced back to the privatisation of farming after the Middle Ages. Throughout the nineteenth century, boom followed depression in both manufacturing and the primary industries of mining, quarrying and farming. Work was not always available, but an expanding economy tended to absorb surplus labour, particularly as large numbers were employed in domestic service to the growing wealthy middle class. The relative contraction of the British economy after the First World War, exacerbated by worldwide slumps in demand, created unemployment on a massive scale in the 1920s and 1930s. Although the urban areas were the hardest hit, particularly the northern towns with heavy industries, the availability of cheap food from the Americas and the Empire led to a serious decline in British agriculture, in turn leading to a cutback in the wages and conditions of farm workers. It is remarkable how many small farms, more especially those in the marginal hill farming areas such as the Moors, managed to survive this period of depression. The Second World War ended rural unemployment, and there were serious shortages of labour at a time when maximum production was needed. These conditions persisted for a time after the war, but the gradual rundown in farm labour which had begun earlier in the century gathered pace. The economic base of much of rural Britain changed from one dominated by farming to a reliance on service industries of varying kinds.

Until the 1970s it was usually possible for Moors' residents to find work in nearby towns. Increasingly, this work has been more difficult to obtain and the decline in farm labour has continued. Teesside has become an area of exceptionally high unemployment during the last decade and the coastal towns of Whitby and Scarborough have also witnessed very high levels. Furthermore, much of the available work in the tourist industry is seasonal and notoriously badly paid. In contrast, the Ryedale towns and villages on the southern edge of the Moors and the settlements on the western edge of the Hambleton Hills have not suffered to anything like the same extent. Growth in variety of light industries and service trades has cushioned the fall in farm work so that the Pickering area, for example, has consistently recorded lower unemployment than the regional and national averages.

Added to the young persons' problems of finding work is the high cost of housing. Houses are everywhere in demand and have been throughout the post-war period, a surprising fact when the decline in population and employment is considered. The decrease in the average size of households is a chief reason. Commuting to work is widespread, particularly from the Cleveland fringe of the Park, the area around Scarborough and the edge of the Hambleton Hills. Many villages are popular for retirement, and second homes are also more frequently found than in the countryside generally. Approximately 40% of houses in Robin Hood's Bay and 30% in Runswick Bay were second homes in 1978 against an average for the National Park of 8%. A high incidence of second homes is considered to be a social problem, with intermittent occupation by outsiders, 'offcomers' in the local dialect, who have only a limited stake in a village. Nevertheless, the landscape effects have been beneficial. Many old and decaying properties have been renovated and even whole settlements such as Robin Hood's Bay revitalised.

The loss of young people creates an imbalance in the community with a much higher proportion of the elderly and few persons of working age. In time, this leads to extra demand on public services such as health and social care. There are signs, in 1988, that the decline has slowed down in many areas and a period of greater stability should follow.

Visitors

Visiting the northern hills to view their scenery became fashionable under the influence of the writers and artists of the early nineteenth century Romantic Movement. But tourists had come to the coastal spa towns from the seventeenth century onwards. The building of railways to the coast, combined with the growing wealth of the new industrial managers, led to a marked increase during the nineteenth century and several spa towns developed into resorts. Scarborough and Whitby are the best known on the Yorkshire coast but there were several others.

The demand for coastal property led to a remarkable scheme at the turn of the century. A development company embarked on plans to build a complete new resort to rival that of Scarborough at Ravenscar on a headland overlooking Robin Hood's Bay (Fig 57). A town plan was drawn up with the railway line from Scarborough to Whitby as its focus. Roads and sewers were laid out and plots advertised for sale. A few houses and a group of shops were built before the venture failed and the company went into liquidation. The roads and scattered houses remain, presenting an incongruous and puzzling appearance to the visitor. There were few other

210

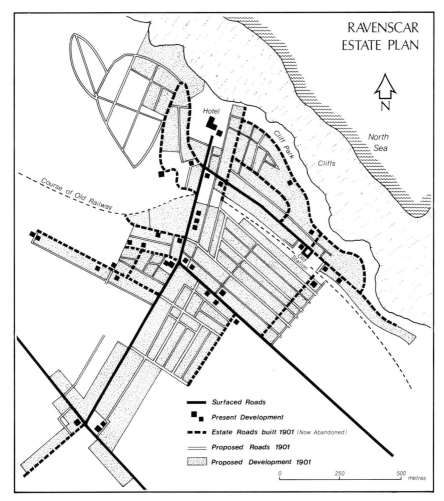

RAVENSCAR
ESTATE PLAN

N

Hotel

Cliff Park

North
Sea

Cliffs

Course of Old Railway

Old Station

Surfaced Roads

■■ **Present Development**

■ ■ ■ **Estate Roads built 1901** (Now Abandoned)

Proposed Roads 1901

Proposed Development 1901

0   250   500
                            metres

Fig 57 The seaside resort which never was. A speculative development of the Edwardian era

attempts to develop resorts in the area but Goathland, hitherto a quiet moorland village, became popular for visits as the rail services through Newtondale developed. A number of hotels and luxury residences were built. Today, they integrate harmoniously with the older village properties although of typical Victorian design. The presence of a large village green is one reason why the attraction of this village remains, even though its character has changed.

During the early part of the century the Moors, in common with some other upland areas, became important for the growing number of ramblers, climbers and cyclists. There was a great boom of such active outdoor recreation in the inter-war period. Clubs and societies were formed in most towns, youth hostels and other forms of accommodation

Plate 47 Goathland on a summer weekend. An example of the 'honeypot' phenomenon (*NYMNP*)

were provided and an ethos of healthy outdoor exercise grew up as an important part of modern life. Though these new attitudes and activities were largely middle-class in their origins, in the north of England many working class people from the industrial towns participated. The importance of this change in lifestyle of the common man cannot be overestimated as it led directly to the creation of the National Parks in the 1949 National Parks & Access to the Countryside Act. Also during the inter-war period, the seeds were sown for the great leisure explosion of the 1950s and 1960s based on the motor car. Car ownership in Britain grew slowly after the First World War to reach a peak in 1939 before the war effort severely reduced the availability of both machines and fuel. It was not until the 1950s that shortages were overcome and there was a rapid rise in car ownership. Many present-day sporting activities had their origins in the early 1900s, including motor bike scrambling and field trials, car rallying, sailing for pleasure and competitive walking.

The car-borne visitors to the Moors, currently some eleven million each year, did not, and do not, spread themselves evenly over the area. From the early days, some villages and features became fashionable as 'beauty spots' and visitors concentrated there. Hutton-le-Hole and Thornton Dale are particular favourites, as is Lealholm in the Esk Valley. Streamside locations have proved to be popular and stream crossing points on moorland roads are a great attraction. Sheepwash, above Osmotherley,

Hob Hole near Westerdale and Forge Valley near Hackness are major attractions for visitors who park, picnic and stroll around the sites or, in many instances, simply view the scenery from their cars.

The roads of the Moors have been steadily improved since the early part of the century. Many have been widened with gradients eased, bends removed and tarmacadam applied. The main roads to Whitby in particular have been transformed from winding moorland tracks to fast arterial roads and traffic speeds are high. One unfortunate consequence is the number of sheep deaths on unfenced sections of road, leading to pleas from the farmers and flockmasters for the roads to be fenced. On the Whitby-Guisborough road only about 2kms (1 mile) of unfenced section remains while the remaining 11kms (6.8 miles) of open road on the Whitby-Pickering road were fenced in 1987-8.

The coastal villages and beaches have long been a draw to visitors. Access to the Moors coastline is not easy and there are few roads in some sections. Congestion is severe at times at the favourite places such as Robin Hood's Bay and Runswick Bay, 'but the steep rocky coast combined with strong planning control prevented the sprawling house

Fig 58 A modern attempt to zone the countryside for planning purposes *(NYMNP)*

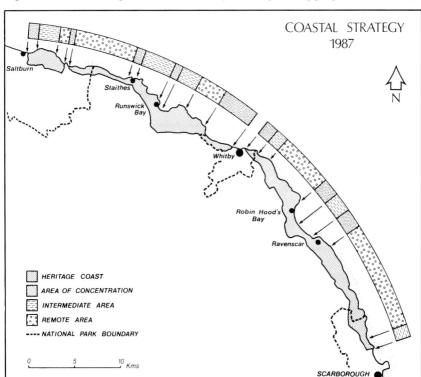

building which occurred on other attractive coasts during the inter-war years. The pressure from tourists has led to a zoning of the coastline so as to concentrate visitors into areas best suited to accommodate them and to protect the wilder and remoter parts (Fig 58). Neither has the area suffered from the proliferation of caravan and chalet sites to the extent of the coastal belt further south around Filey and Bridlington. Nevertheless, there are a number of large permanent sites close to Whitby and Scarborough which can be seen for many miles on the open coastal plateau. Inland, there are fewer sites and they are generally well screened.

The moorland landscape is ideal for walking. The surface is usually dry with springy turf, there are numerous tracks and footpaths and the sequence of panoramic views gives a 'roof of the world' character to the walker. The growth of rambling during the inter-war years was based largely on public transport from nearby towns. It was during this period that the Youth Hostels developed for ramblers to stay overnight. In 1939, there were 13 such hostels in the area. After the Second World War, the car gradually became the main means of transport to the Moors. Rambling grew in popularity but took different forms. Short family strolls across the Moors along the 2000kms (1240 miles) of public footpaths and bridleways became popular whilst, at the other extreme, competitive 'challenge' walking over long distances developed. There are now about 20 such long-distance routes, including the official Cleveland Way designated in 1969.

The most famous footpath is the Lyke Wake Walk. This was created by Bill Cowley of Potto in the early 1950s as a moorland route on which a fit and active walker could cross the Moors in less than twenty-four hours. It is 67kms (42 miles) long and is almost entirely on heather moorland, crossing the main moorland divide, west-east from Osmotherley to Ravenscar. It became so popular during the 1960s and 1970s that a campaign was organised to reduce its use. The erosion along the wetter, peaty sections had become severe and, in places, the route was over 100m wide. The campaign had a good effect initially, but numbers are again creeping up above the tolerable 5,000 per year.

Many other active pursuits have developed. They include rock climbing in the Cleveland Hills, sailing and rowing along the coast, horse riding and pony trekking along the bridlepaths, car rallying in the forests. In recent decades, sports such as hang gliding and orienteering have become popular. These are in addition to the traditional field sports of hunting, fishing and shooting which continue to flourish.

The tourist boom has been a salvation for the local economy as employment in farming has declined. The provision of accommodation, refreshments and souvenirs for visitors is now such a common feature that it is easy to forget that it is of very recent origin. Guest houses, cafés and similar facilities developed during the inter-war years, especially in the Esk

Valley, but expanded greatly with the leisure boom of the 1960s. Country inns became fashionable and began to provide snacks and meals. Eating out later became commonplace and the traditional inns and public houses have captured much of this lucrative trade. The strict planning policies which have been applied since the late 1930s have prevented unsightly sporadic tourist development and advertisements. This control has also prevented the development of large-scale tourist facilities, though many small caravan sites and a few larger ones have been allowed. One major tourist development, however, has been promoted and is widely appreciated. When the former Pickering to Whitby line was closed in 1965 as part of the Beeching Plan to modernise the railways, moves were made almost immediately to secure its retention for historic and recreational purposes. A group of enthusiasts banded together and a small section was reopened in 1968. Support was obtained from the National Park Authority and other bodies and eventually the whole line from Pickering to Grosmont was reopened as a tourist railway. It now carries over 300,000 passengers yearly, mainly by steam trains, and there are plans to link it to Whitby using the British Rail Esk Valley Line. This latter line itself, increasingly uneconomic to maintain, has become the focus of a project to encourage railway use by visitors. The stations have been improved, walks and trails established from them and linked to the service timetable.

It is the Moors landscape and its features, however, which remain the chief attraction for visitors. The abbeys and castles, villages, viewpoints and sandy beaches provide the focal points for the visitors against the backcloth of moorland. Only recently has the value of this landscape been truly appreciated in economic as well as in cultural and social terms.

Modern industry and technology

Technological development has been at the root of landscape change since prehistoric times. The introduction of agriculture brought radical though slow changes to the landscape of the Moors. The rate of industrial change in the twentieth century has been very high and has touched every aspect of landscape. With the decline of the heavy industries of iron ore mining and iron and steel manufacture, together with the related quarrying and railway industries, many dales and hills have lost an industrial element in the landscape that, in visual terms, few would mourn, whatever the social and economic repercussions. The application of new technology to the farming scene, as we have seen, has not enhanced the landscape. Neither has large-scale commercial forestry in its most utilitarian form improved it.

The provision of modern public services such as telephones, electricity and telecommunications has debased the landscape in the many areas in which wires, masts and various intrusive forms of equipment dominate

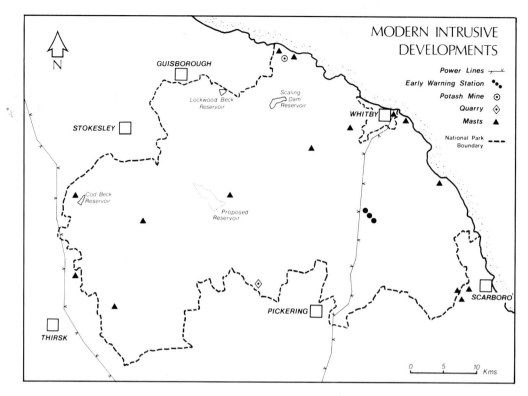

Fig 59 Designation as a National Park has not stopped modern technical developments. The high ground is particularly suitable for telecommunication masts

the views. The proliferation of such structures is depicted in Fig 59. Some
of them can be seen over wide areas and one of them, the Bilsdale TV
mast, can been from all the high ground in the National Park on a clear
day.

The Fylingdales Ballistic Missile Early Warning Station is particularly
intrusive with its large 'golf ball' radomes and gaunt radar dishes. The
reason for its siting in the centre of a moorland landscape is not altogether
clear from the record and there is an impression of compromise and
intrigue in its hasty erection in the National Park in 1962. A redevelop-
ment is proposed which will involve the removal of the golf balls, the
radar dishes and towers and their replacement by a new pyramid-shaped
radar. Ironically, the golf ball radomes are now a well known and even
admired feature of the Moors, as many intrusive developments tend to
become with age. There was much public concern, for instance, when the
Rosedale chimney, a large flue stack on the moors, was demolished in
1972. Whether electricity pylons and radio masts will ever become so
treasured is doubtful but changing taste is not entirely predictable.

Many attempts, frequently successful, have been made over the past
four decades to lessen the impact of wires and poles. Some services have

been buried or re-routed, and sharing arrangements made for masts. It is a constantly shifting situation as the technology evolves. Despite this gradual improvement, the line of pylons and wires across the moors from Pickering to Whitby remains one of the worst eyesores. With the rapid development of micro-wave and other electronic forms of communication, the erection of more masts and unsightly equipment seems inevitable. It is, perhaps, unfortunate that the high ground of the Park is naturally well suited for mast sites.

The tradition of mineral exploitation of the Moors has taken on new forms in recent years. The whole of the coastal plain is underlain by potash salts at great depths. The deposit was found accidentally in the 1930s when trial boring for oil and gas was taking place. The depth of the deposit at a mile below the surface, and the economics of the world market for potash, precluded attempts to extract the salt until the 1960s, when modern methods made it a viable proposition. One mine was approved at Boulby, and developed almost immediately coming into production in 1973. Permission was given for two additional mines, one using a very sophisticated wet-mining or 'solution' process, in the Whitby area, but these did not proceed. When the permission ran out and the companies applied to renew them in 1977, the National Park Committee, after a series of stormy debates, declined and one company pursued their case to appeal, eventually losing. The one permitted mine occupies a large site on the coast and pipes its waste out to sea. It supplies a large part of the country's potash needs and provides local highway authorities with road salt. It employs over 800 people, the single biggest workforce in the Moors. Interestingly, Fylingdales Ballistic Missile Early Warning Station has the next biggest, with over 600 civilian jobs.

The trial boring for natural petroleum in the inter-war years proved successful when small pockets of natural gas were detected, and later exploration led to more discoveries. Whitby was supplied with natural gas for a time from a well near Aislaby, and several wells in the Lockton area provided a major source for the national grid in the 1970s before running dry. Oil and gas drilling rigs have been a familiar sight in the Moors landscape for several years now, although attempts to drill in the remoter areas of Farndale and Westerdale Moor have been forcefully resisted. The large offshore reserves have taken the pressure off the inland sites, but whether this situation will prevail as the North Sea gas runs out remains to be seen.

One ephemeral nuisance which frequently shatters the peace of a moorland walk or picnic is low flying aircraft. The Moors are within the NATO training zone and the National Park is a favourite venue for practising low flying runs along its narrow valleys running north–south from the main moorland ridge. Bilsdale, Farndale and Rosedale are particularly badly affected.

CONTROLLING CHANGE

Town and country planning

Control over building development and related land use was brought in early in the Moors. 'Planning', as it is now universally termed, arose initially as a by-product of Victorian attempts to provide hygienic housing conditions for the urban masses of the new industrial towns. The great rash of uncontrolled housing sprawl in the inter-war years ushered in the first compulsory controls, first by restricting ribbon development along roads and later by more comprehensive controls over all building. Under the provisions of the 1932 Town and Country Planning Act, local authorities were enabled to draw up planning 'schemes' which laid down in considerable detail the restrictions over building development.

The authorities in the North Riding were among the first to take advantage of this new, and in many ways revolutionary, method of public control over private development. The district authorities combined with the County Council to enable schemes to be prepared over a wide area and a specialist planning officer was appointed as early as 1934. Although rudimentary and somewhat inflexible in their operation, these early schemes did much to prevent sporadic housing and other development which already was beginning to appear, particularly in the Esk Valley. Today's generation owes a considerable debt to the dedication and foresight of the North Riding authorities. The unsightly sprawl and substandard development which characterises so many towns and villages, is remarkably absent in the Moors and surrounding area.

With the advent of war, building and other development virtually ceased unless needed for essential military purposes; and there was strict control during and immediately after the war to safeguard materials. However, there was much discussion about the form of post-war planning, and an all-party consensus was virtually achieved on the needs for public direction of the post-war landscape. A wave of new legislation followed victory and a socialist government introduced a new system of town and country planning which has formed the basis of planning control, not only in this country, but in most developed and many undeveloped countries. Like most successful innovations, the new system was basically very simple. Building and changes in land use were subjected to a simple test of definition. If they passed this test, they were deemed to constitute 'development' and put into a classified system. Development generally required the approval of the planning authority unless it fell within classes of 'permitted development'. Thus many minor changes and small building operations were excluded from control. Also expressly excluded was control over most of farming and forestry operations, although there were provisions for preserving trees and, later, valuable ecological sites. Since the 1940s, the system has developed into an accepted and valued part of public service though there are differences of perception and emphasis across the political parties.

So far as the landscape of the Moors is concerned, the main problems have stemmed from the lack of control over farming and forestry, which have been the main agents in changing the landscape. It is not surprising that recent legislation has aimed at bringing in some controls and incentives to retain the character of the Moors and other valued landscapes. The farming lobby has been a very strong one in post-war Britain and the operation of the EEC policies, particularly the Common Agricultural Policy, has militated against both sensible environmental policies and further controls. Only the growing food surpluses of the last few years have brought the problem into focus and, at the time of writing, a debate is taking place on the future of rural policy. For the first time, controls over farming and forestry management are being proposed by government.

Housing development, which constituted the main item of planning initially, has been strictly controlled in the Moors. The general policy has been to allow a reasonable supply of land for building in accordance with what is known as 'local need', and to concentrate this in and around suitable sites in villages. Sporadic development has been largely prevented and houses in the open countryside have been rarely permitted, except when required for farm management. Housing design, and building design generally, has been closely controlled since the Planning Acts were introduced. The prevailing policy is to emphasise the use of traditional materials, such as stone and pantiles, in a traditional design. Successful examples abound but the Park has not escaped the standardised and often jarring effects of modern bungalows and the introduction of pseudo Georgian windows and doors into older houses. Very few examples of contemporary design are found, and these are generally frowned upon by Planning Committees of lay members. The designs of the seventeenth and eighteenth centuries are universally admired and copied; a sad reflection on both the taste of the public and lack of imagination of present-day architects.

Many other aspects of the landscape have been subjected to a degree of public control in the post-war period. These include trees, historic buildings and archaeological remains. Some success has been achieved in retaining valuable features but much damage has occurred. The character and qualities of the Moors landscape, however, were recognised as needing special attention and this was achieved by the designation of the area as one of the first National Parks in 1952.

The National Park

National Parks had a long gestation period in Britain. There was virtually no natural wilderness left to preserve, and it was clear that a compromise would have to be devised to meet the needs of people eager to pursue outdoor recreation in remote and beautiful places. Nearly all the land surface was privately owned and access to it had long been a contentious issue. The pressure for National Parks grew inexorably during the inter-war period and several reports were prepared by committees and pressure groups. Nothing came of these but a government report was commissioned during the unpromising circumstances of wartime. Written by John Dower, an architect in the Ministry of Works and Planning, it was published in 1945. In it, Dower defined a National Park as:

> an extensive area of beautiful and relatively wild country in which, for the nation's benefit and by appropriate national decision and action, (a) the characteristic landscape beauty is strictly preserved, (b) access and facilities for public open-air enjoyment are amply provided, (c) wildlife and buildings and places of architectural and historic interest are suitably protected, while (d) established farming use is effectively maintained.

Eventually after more discussion, a Bill was passed in 1949 establishing a National Parks Commission with the duty to identify suitable areas for the new Parks. The North York Moors was the fifth Park to be set up out of a total of 10. For the first time in its history, the Moors was declared to be a special landscape worthy of national status and protection.

During the first years after designation, very little was achieved by the new National Park Planning Committee under the firm control of the County Council. A few car parks were provided and in 1964 a new Youth Hostel was built with Park aid in Helmsley. The planning control powers were pursued with more vigour and generally high standards were achieved. In the mid-1960s, specialist staff were taken on and the work programme grew steadily, though miniscule compared with the scale of the problem of conserving the area and the growth in tourist use. In 1974, there was a re-organisation as part of the local government restructuring of the time, and the administration and financing of the Park was greatly strengthened. It became a statutory requirement to prepare a plan for the future management of the Park, and in 1977 the first National Park Plan was published. This was the first comprehensive analysis of the state of the landscape and the measures needed to protect it. It was well received and generally approved by all the many official and voluntary agencies involved in the countryside. A review of the Plan in 1984 detailed the progress and focussed on the future of the moorland area, a subject which had been greatly studied and debated in the preceding years.

Since 1974, much more emphasis has been placed on positive conservation work by way of management agreements with farmers, by making grants through a number of schemes and by direct action by the Park staff. Tree planting, woodland and wildlife management, repairs to walls, gates and stiles, and maintenance of footpaths are some of the wide variety of tasks carried out. Longer-term projects have been achieved for improving the management of the moorland and for conserving and enhancing farm landscapes. The most difficult area has been the resolution of conflicts between farm improvements and conservation. A system of compensation based on management agreements has developed which ensures that the farmer is not out of pocket by forgoing farm improvements. This approach has been greatly criticised and can only be an interim measure, pending clearer government policies for the future of farming. In some instances, usually where the ploughing of moorland has been threatened, the Park Authority has resorted to purchase and direct management. There are now some 1200 ha (2,965 acres) of land in Park ownership in the Levisham area as a result of this policy.

The designation of the National Park can be seen as a fortunate if, perhaps, a somewhat premature event for the Moors landscape. It, more than any other modern change, symbolises the future of the Moors. Or, as Wordsworth said of the Lake District as long ago as 1810, 'persons of pure taste . . . deem the district a sort of national property, in which every man has a right and interest who has an eye to perceive and a heart to enjoy . . .'.

THE FUTURE

A large question mark hangs over the future of the rural areas of Britain. The post-war policy of expanding farm production while protecting the land from development has broken down. The scale of public subsidy and other incentives, combined with rapidly evolving modern methods on the farm, has led to overproduction at prices well above those of the world market in most commodities. This means that, measured by the normal yardsticks for commerce, the Moors farms are not economic, and the country could well manage without them and many others elsewhere. Indeed, some economists argue that there would be considerable benefits to the economy as a whole by re-investing the subsidies in other sectors likely to create more wealth. Current government approach is to recognise the enormity of the social and environmental consequences of the problem but, so far, to take few measures to deal with it. The recently announced 'set aside' scheme for cereal cropped land is one of the first serious attempts to reduce output. Indeed, because of the operation of the Common Agricultural Policy, the crucial decisions will need to be taken in Brussels, not in Westminster. There are few signs that the other EEC countries are willing to tackle the difficult and unpopular decisions needed to rein back production. A financial crisis seems inevitable before the system is changed.

In this situation, one would expect forestry as the other main

221

competitor for land to expand. The difficulty is that it is hard for British forestry to compete with imports, currently running at about 90% of the UK timber needs. There are several reasons for this, but it seems that commercial forestry will only expand on a significant scale if the present very high level of tax relief and grants continues.

The other chief component of the economy of the Moors is tourism. From small beginnings, this has now become the single most important industry and is steadily expanding in its range of services and the generation of jobs. For a tourist industry to flourish, the visitor must be provided with the environment and the facilities he desires. Herein lies a particularly important factor for the future of the Moors landscape. Most people probably prefer the traditional landscape of moors, dale farms and small woodlands to the new landscapes of improved farmland and commercial forestry. Certainly the wildlife conservationists, growing in number and influence, would wish to retain the inherited landscape and its pattern of habitats.

Thus a stage has been reached where choices are available that have no precedent. Should we maintain for environmental and recreational purposes the working landscape inherited from the past? Should we accept major and alien changes for dubious economic reasons? The introduction of more conifers on a large scale would certainly be violently opposed, as would the abandonment of farms and the dereliction that would result, although this could be ameliorated by modest expenditure. Since there is a consensus developing between farmers and conservationists on the maintenance and promotion of the inherited farm landscapes, in upland and lowland areas, this would seem to be the most likely outcome for the future of the Moors.

Our landscape history has described how the needs of successive generations were met. Hunting and fishing for the earliest men; farmland, pasture and woods for later settlers; food and clothing for the Roman army; assimilation of strangers from Roman to Norman times; defence for the Normans; havens for the monks; farm improvements from the eighteenth century; minerals for heavy industry; hospitality and amenity for the visitors; and ever more sophisticated communications. All these survive in some form to the present day, and look likely to stay. None of them, if pursued with reason and compromise, need seriously prejudice any of the others. If the past is any guide to the future, we shall see them all continue and new ones arise, the balance changing according to people's needs and the resources of the region. To fossilise the past is to die; to adapt is to thrive and retain the enjoyment of this sublime landscape.

LOCATIONS OF OLD INDUSTRIAL SITES

Old mills		Sil Howe	NZ 852028
Bransdale	SE 620979	Blea Hill	NZ 899005
Arden	SE 521906		
Caydale	SE 544867	*Lime kilns*	
Lastingham	SE 728905	Commondale	NZ 673103
		Snilesworth	SE 497951
Nineteenth century mills			SE 514941
Tocketts	NZ 627181		SE 528931
Danby	NZ 707083		(All on roadside)
Bilsdale Low Mill	SE 571953	Kepwick	SE 436903
Levisham	SE 835901	Cropton	SE 760868
Farndale High Mill	SE 668970		
Rosedale	SE 724958	*Collieries*	
Kepwick	SE 452905	Ankness	SE 635933
Raisdale	NZ 538005	Baysdale	NZ 621035
Rigg	NZ 910075	Fryup Head	NZ 706020
Yoad Wath	SE 707876	Upper Rudland	SE 650953
Ruswarp	NZ 888090	Rudland	SE 654940
Ramsdale	NZ 925034	Carr Cote	SE 576915
Robin Hood's Bay	NZ 953040	Sledshoe	SE 687978
Kilton	NZ 711190	Weathercote	SE 559929
Sinnington	SE 738841	Winsley Hill	NZ 698088
		Poverty Hill	NZ 723091
Windmills		Oakley Walls	NZ 735085
Ugthorpe	NZ 790115	Jackson's Road	NZ 672006
Ravenscar	NZ 976006	Cockpit Hill	SE 681995
Kirkbymoorside	SE 696864		

All of these are multiple sites and are plotted on Fig 44. Grid references are given for the estimated centre of each group.

Horse mills			
Drummer Hill	NZ 569075		
Urra	NZ 571019		
		Alum quarries	
		Carlton	NZ 520028
Whinstone		Rock Hole	NZ 640160
Cliff Rigg	NZ 574116	Belman Bank	NZ 630147
Langbaurgh	NZ 555122		

Loftus	NZ 740200
Boulby	NZ 754194
Ravenscar	NZ 969016
Stoupe Brow	NZ 959023
Kettleness	NZ 833159
Sandsend	NZ 859134
Saltwick Nab	NZ 914112

Alum and/or cement works

Great Ayton	NZ 589108
Kettleness	NZ 833160
Boulby	NZ 752196
Peak (Ravenscar)	NZ 973021
Wreckhills	NZ 809166
(Runswick Bay)	
Sandsend	NZ 860129

Jet

Bilsdale	SE 552973
Scugdale	SE 523992
Roseberry, Great Ayton	NZ 582127
Gisborough Moor	NZ 591136

These are linear workings extending, in some cases, for a mile or more. They are shown on Fig 43. The Grid references are for one or two interesting points.

Glass

Hutton Common	SE 705883
Rosedale	SE 745932
Hagg House	SE 582972

Early ironworking
Most early works are multiple sites. For a full list consult R.H. Hayes*. A few representative examples are given here but also see Fig 46.

Wheeldale	SE 798991
Tarn Hole	SE 591978
Egton Bridge	NZ 785046
(The Delves)	
Roseberry Topping	NZ 580128
(extensive workings around	
adjacent scarps)	
Hartoft End	SE 752931

Lealholm	NZ 741068
(Furnace Farm)	
Rievaulx	SE 575851
(site of blast furnace)	

Nineteenth century ironstone mines
For a complete list of Cleveland Ironstone Mines see S.K. Chapman, Gazetteer of Cleveland Ironstone Mines, Langbaurgh Museums, Research Report No 1.

Brackenberry Wyke	NZ 796182
(workings in beach shales)	
Port Mulgrave	NZ 799177
(relics of harbour)	
Wreckhills	NZ 809166
Eston Nab	
(extensive workings under the Nab)	
Upleatham	
(the whole outlier is undermined)	
Skelton Park	NZ 644181
Loftus	NZ 712192
(Tom Leonard Museum)	
Kilton	NZ 694169
(winding house)	
Liverton	NZ 708178
(shale heap)	
Cattersty	NZ 707205
(slag cliff)	
Spa Wood	NZ 637157
(boiler stack)	
Margrove Park	NZ 653155
(shaft head)	
Tocketts	NZ 621183
(furnace shaft)	
Lazenby Banks	NZ 581189
(fan house)	
Warren Moor	NZ 625088
(Leven Vale mine)	
Lounsdale	NZ 614105
(Cornish pumping house)	
Esk Valley	NZ 822044
Rosedale	SE 705986
(East Side mine)	
Rosedale	SE 729945
(Garbutts deposit)	

Rosedale (Sheriff's pit)	SE 697962	Wreckhills	NZ 809166
		Calcining kilns	
Iron smelting		Swainby	NZ 485007
Skinningrove	NZ 709198	Wreckhills	NZ 809166
Grosmont	NZ 827053	Rosedale East	SE 705988
Glaisdale	NZ 780056		SE 705981
Beck Hole	NZ 818024	Rosedale West	SE 721948

*Hayes, R.H. 1978 Early Iron working sites in North East Yorkshire. *Journal of the Historical Metallurgy Society Vol. 12, No. 1, 18-26.*

BIBLIOGRAPHY

This is not a definitive reference list, but a guide for further reading.

Books covering wide time-spans

Atkinson, J. C. *Forty Years in a Moorland Parish* (London, Macmillan, 1891)

Carstairs, I. *The North York Moors National Park* (Published jointly by Webb and Bower, Michael Joseph and the Countryside Commission, 1987)

Elgee, F. *Early Man in North-east Yorkshire* (Gloucester, Bellows, 1930)

Hoskins, W. G. *The Making of the English Landscape* (Hodder and Stoughton, 1955)

McDonnell, J. (ed) *A History of Helmsley, Rievaulx and District* (York, Stonegate Press, 1963)

Raistrick, A. (ed) *National Park Guide (No. 4). North York Moors National Park* (London, HMSO, 1966)

Chapter 1

Eyre, S. R. and Palmer, J. *The Face of North-East Yorkshire* (Clapham, Yorkshire, Dalesman Press, 1973)

Gimingham, C. H. *An Introduction to Heathland Ecology* (Oliver and Boyd, 1975)

Rackham, O. *The History of the Countryside* (London, J. M. Dent, 1986)

Spratt, D. A. (ed) *The Prehistoric and Roman Archaeology of North-East Yorkshire. British Archaeological Report No. 104* Chapter 1 by J. E. Hemingway and Chapter 2 by I. G. Simmons (Oxford, British Archaeological Reports, 1982)

Chapter 2

Spratt, D. A. (ed) *loc. cit.* Chapters 3-6 (British Archaeological Reports, 1982)

Chapter 3

Spratt, D. A. (ed) *loc. cit.* Chapter 7 by B. R. Hartley and D. A. Spratt (British Archaeological Reports, 1982)

Hayes, R. H. and Rutter, J. G. *Wade's Causeway* (Scarborough and District Archaeological Society Research Report No. 4, 1964)

Chapter 4

Gelling, M. *Place-Names in the Landscape* (London, Dent, 1984)

Hall, R. A. (ed) *Viking Age York and the North* CBA Report 27 (London, Council for British Archaeology, 1978)

Smith, A. H. *The Place-Names of the North Riding of Yorkshire* (Cambridge, English Place-Name Society, 1928 reprinted 1969)

Chapter 5
Faull, M. L. and Stimson, M. (eds) *Domesday Book, Yorkshire Parts 1 and 2* (Chichester, Phillimore, 1986)
Hall, D. *Medieval Fields* (Shire Publications, 1982)
Roberts, B. K. *The Making of the English Village* (Longman, 1987)

Chapter 6
English, B. *Yorkshire Enclosure Awards* (University of Hull, 1985)
Hartley, M. and Ingilby, J. *Life in the moorlands of North East Yorkshire* (Dent, 1972)
Marshall, W. *The rural economy of Yorkshire* (London, 1788)
Tuke, J. *General view of the agriculture of the North Riding of Yorkshire* (London, 1800)

Chapter 7
Harrison, B. J. D. and Hutton, B. *Vernacular Houses in North Yorkshire and Cleveland* (Edinburgh, John Donald, 1984)
Hayes, R. H. and Rutter, J. G. *Cruck-framed Buildings in Ryedale and Eskdale* (Scarborough and District Archaeological Society Research Report No. 8, 1972)
Pevsner, N. *The Buildings of England, Yorkshire The North Riding* (Penguin, 1966 reprinted 1985)
Royal Commission on the Historical Monuments of England. *Houses of the North York Moors* (HMSO, 1987)

Chapter 8
Hempstead, C. A. (ed) *Cleveland Iron and Steel. Background and 19th century history* (British Steel Corporation, 1979)

Chapter 9
Breakell, W. *Old Pannier Tracks* North York Moors National Park (1987)
Hoole, K. *Regional History of Railways of Great Britain, Volume 4: the North East* (David & Charles, Second Edition 1974)
Sewell, J. T. *Account of some medieval roads crossing the moors south and south-west of Whitby* (Whitby, Horne & Son, 1923)
Tomlinson, W. W. *The North-Eastern Railway* (Newcastle, Andrew Reid, 1914. Reprinted David & Charles, 1987)

Chapter 10
Patmore, J. A. *Recreation and Resources* (Oxford, Basil Blackwell, 1983)
Lacey, W. S. (ed) *Britain's National Parks* (Leicester, Windward, 1984)

INDEX

Ainthorpe, fields, 97; Low
  Bramble Carr, 97;
  population fluctuation, 135
Airy Hill (Whitby),
  place-name, 61, 95
Airy Holme (Great Ayton),
  place-name, 95
Aislaby, 103, 146, 158, 146–7
Aldborough, 51
Alder Carr, etc 55
Allerston, 41, 96, 111, 76, 146,
  131
Ampleforth, 33, 78, 80
Anglian Period, 55–65;
  archaeological finds, 62;
  carvings 64–5; cemeteries 61;
  Christianity, 62–5; houses,
  63; industries, 63;
  monasteries, 62–5; place-
  names, 55–61
Anglo-Saxon Chronicle, 65
Ankess, colliery, 167, 223
Appleton-le-Moors, 85;
  common, survival of, 139;
  place-name, 62; plan, 84–5;
  Rose Marie Lodge, 151
Arden, Hall, 142, 144;
  grassland, 24, 25; mill,
  medieval, 160, 223; priory,
  109, 142
Atkinson, J.C. (Canon), 31,
  136, 177, 193
Augustinians, 108
Ayton, East and West,
  place-name, 61; population,
  208

Barnby, 98; colonisation, 103
Barton-le-Street, carvings,
  Norman church, 112;
  Domesday entry, 75–6
Baxby, Domesday entry, 77
Baysdale, Abbey, 56, 109,
  rebuilt 142; colliery, 168, 223
Beadlam, longhouse, 154; villa,
  Roman, 51; White Cottage,
  155
Beck Hole, iron working, 136,
  183, 225; railway incline, 194
Bede, 61, 64
Belman Bank, alum quarry,
  223

Benedictines, 106
Bernicia, 62
Bickley, assarting, 105;
  forestry, 202
Bilsdale, 8, 98–9; Akitt, 98;
  Birch Wood, 23; Broadfield
  Farm, 98; Chop Gate, 98;
  collieries, 169, 223;
  colonisation, 98; cotes,
  owned by Rievaulx, 110;
  enclosures, 16; Garfit Farm,
  98; granges, 110; intakes, 25;
  iron working, 177; jet
  working, 174, 224; mill, 223;
  rebuilding, 19th century, 154;
  Seave Green, 98–9; Spout
  House, 150–1; Stonehouse
  Cote, 98; TV mast, 198, 216
Birdforth Wapentake, 77
Blackamore, 12, 34; Helmsley
  Blackmoor, 132
Blakey Ridge, colliery, 167;
  railway, 196
Blandsby, Domesday entry, 75;
  timber felling (1651), 119
Boosbeck, assarting, 103;
  Holywell Farm, 103
Boltby, 38; Hillfort, 43
Borrowby, colonisation, 103
Boulby, alum mining, 140,
  172–3, 224; cement works,
  224; cliff, 11; ironstone seam
  in, 178; potash mine, 183,
  217
Brankenberry Wyke, ironstone
  mine, 224
Bransdale, 130; colliery
  (Ankess), 167; Lodge, 146;
  new mill, 162; old mill 160,
  223; Smout House, 153;
  watercourse, 129
Brigantes, 46, 51
Brocka Beck, 55
Brompton, Domesday entry,
  76; High Hall, 142; Low
  Hall, 142
Bronze Age, amber, 184;
  barrows, 31–33; cairnfields,
  26, 29, 33–36, 184;
  territories, 36–41
Brotton, ironstone mining, 181
Bumpar Castle, 146

Burnolfscales (Guisborough),
  95
Byland Abbey, 107–110

Carlton, 84; alum quarries,
  171-2, 223; jet workings,
  172, 175; plan, 84
Carthusians, 106
Carucates, definition, 75
Castles, Danby, 141; Helmsley,
  141; Norman, 78–9;
  Pickering, 141. See motte and
  bailey Castles
Castle Howard, 134, 141
Castleton, 136; hamlet (17th
  century), 134; motte and
  bailey, 74; silk mill, 136;
  Three Howes Rigg (round
  barrows), 31
Cattersty, ironstone mining,
  224
Caydale, mill, medieval, 160
Cawthorn Roman Fort, 48–51;
  fields, 51; place-name, 56
Caydale, mill, medieval, 223
Chaloner, family, 132, 171
charcoal burning, 120
Christianity, Anglian, 62–65;
  medieval, 106–112; post-
  medieval, 138, 201; Viking,
  66–71
Cistercians, 106–110
Cleveland, place-name, 56
Cleveland Way, 43, 214
Cloughton, field pattern, 94
Cold Kirby, 38; fields, 26;
  stone walls, loss of 202–3
Cold Moor, 98
Coldman Hargos
  (Guisborough), 95
Commondale, limekilns, 167,
  223; place-name, 66
Coxwold, 78; Church, 111–2;
  Domesday entry, 77–8;
  Enclosure, 115
Cringle Moor, 98
Cropton, Banks Wood, 21;
  Caravan site, Spiers Howe,
  203; forest, 203; Keldy
  Castle, 146, 203; limekilns,
  167, 223; motte and bailey,
  74, 79; Sutherland Lodge, 146

Crunkly Gill, 20; Domesday entry, 96

Dalby, forest, 202–3
Dale Town, Domesday entry, 95, 100; strip lynchets, 95–6
Danby, Ainthorpe Green, 97; Castle, 141; Clitherbeck colliery, 168–70; Clitherbeck cottages, 158; D. Dale reclamation, 119; enclosure, 116; fields, ancient, 26; fields, enclosed, 102; Fryup Hall, 153; High Moor, 26, 94; Iron workings, 176; D. Lodge, 146; Low Bramble Carr, 97; medieval fields, 97; mill, 161, 223; moor, 97; Oakley Walls, colliery, 223; place-name, 66; population drift, 135; Poverty Hill, colliery, 169, 223; Rose Cottage, 157–8; settlement pattern, 134; Suwardholm, 97; Winsley Hill, colliery, 223
Dawnay family, 146, 158
Deira, 62
Derwent, River, 14
Domesday Book, 66, 72–8, 160, 199
Douthwaite, sub-manor, independent, 119; place-name, 56
Duncombe Park, 131, 141, 144–5; House, 144–5; temples, 131, 138
Dunsley, 20, 48

Ebberston, 30, 40, 96; barrows, long, 30; Church House, 142; Domesday entry, 76; Ebberston Hall, 142; Ebberston Lodge (now Hall), 145; Oxmoor Dykes, 39; parish, creation of, 111; rabbit warren (Scamridge), 131; Scramridge Dykes, 39, 93
Egton, farmhouses (19th century), 153; Grange Head, 105; Hall Grange, 105; High Moor, 4; Lodge Hill, 105; Mauley tenants, 104; Park Dyke, 105; village drift, 135. *See* Newbiggin
Egton Bridge, iron mining pits, 176, 224
Ellerburn, Church (11th century), 69; Domesday entry, 76; Ellerburn Bank Nature Reserve, flora, 25; Vicarage (Old Ellers), 147; Viking brooch, 68; Viking sculpture, 69
Ellerby, colonisation, 103; woods, 20
Ellermire, place-name, 55

Ellerker, place-name, 55
Environmentally Sensitive Areas, 207
Esk Dale, 6, 7, 8, 97; cairnfields, 33; cereal crops, 139; churches, 138; cottages, industrial, 158; fields, 26; 27; granges, 109; Hollins Cottages, 157–8; jet working, 175; Mauley estate, 104–5; medieval settlements, 97–8; railway, 196; tourist amenities, 214; vaccaries, 105
Esk Valley, ironstone mine, 183, 224
Eston Hills, barrows, round, 32; hillfort, 42–3; ironstone mining, 181, 224

Faceby, population, 20th century, 208
Fadmoor, watercourse, 124, 129
Farmanby, Domesday entry, 76
Farndale, colliery, Sledshoe, 168, 223; colonisation, 101; Ellers House, 104; fields, 26; gas drilling resisted, 217; mill, 162, 223; place-name, 56; population in 20th century, 201, 207; serfs, 101
Fen Bogs, peat bog, 14, 15
Feversham, Lord, 129, 140, 157, 167
Forge valley, monastic cell, 63; tourists, 213
Fryup Dale, de Brus estate, 105; collieries, 168–70, 223; in Danby parish, 134; population fluctuation, 135; reclamation, 119
Fyling, place-name, 61
Fylingdales, Ballistic Missile Early Warning Station, 216; Bay tree, 148; Browcotes, 157–8; Fyling Hall, 148–9; cottages, industrial (1769), 158; Moor, 14, 94; Prospect House, 148; Thorpe Hall, 144; whinstone quarry at Blea Hill, 165
Fylingthorpe, Enclosure, 115

Gillamoor, watercourse, 124, 129
Gilling East, place-name, 61
Girrick, colonisation, 103
Glaisdale, 14, 98; collieries, 168; in Danby parish, 134; Hart Hall, 152–3; ironstone working, 176; ironworks, 183, 225; Moor; fires, 19; peat bogs, 15; population changes, 135; Red House, 153; whinstone quarries, 166

Goathland, 14, 96, 98, 102; Abbot's House, 120; colonisation, 101–3; railway incline, 194; settlement history, 101–3; tourists, 201, 212; West Beck, 16
Goldsborough, Camp, Roman (?), 49; Signal Station, Roman, 54
Great Ayton, Airy Holme, 95; barrow, long, 30; cement works, 224; church (Norman), 42; enclosure (Iron Age), 42; jetworking, 174; whitstone quarry, 165–6, 223
Great Broughton, ploughing, illicit (1629), 120–1
Great Edstone, church, 11th century, 70; Vicarage, 147–8
Grosmont, cottages, industrial, 157–8; ironstone mining, 81, 183; ironworks, 183, 225; railway, 195; settlement, 19th century, 98
Guisborough, alum quarries, 171; boundaries, 132; Burnolfscales, 95; church (perpendicular), 112; Coldman Hargos, 95; forests, 27; jet working, 171, 224; priory, 108; road to Westerdale (Iron Age?), 184, 186

Hackness, cross, Anglian, 63; enclosure, 116; forestry, 202; Hackness Hills, 4; hall, 142, replaced, 146; Monastic cells, 63; tourists at Forge Valley, 213
Hambleton, forestry, 203; place-name, 56; racecourse, 138
Hambleton Street, 186, 194; barrow, long, 30
Hangton Hill Farm, Domesday entry, 97
Harland Moor, colliery, 168, 170
Harome, houses, 17th century, 154; place-name, 56
Hartoft, assarting, 103; High Hamer, colonisation, 119; iron working 178, 224
Harwood Dale, peat bog, 15
Hawnby, boundaries, 36–7; fields, 25; grassland, 24; intakes, 25; Saxon burial, 62; Spring Wood, 23; Vicarage, 147
Hawsker Hall, 146, High Hawsker, settlement plan, 98
Hayburn Wyke, woodlands, 20
Helmsley, 140; Archaeological Society, 129; Bridge House,

148; 19 Bridge Street, 158; Castle, 77–8, 99, 151–2; enclosure, 115; fields, 26; Helmsley Blackmoor, place-name, 131; mote and bailey, 78; parish, 115; population, 133; Rectory House, 142; Ryedale House, 148; Survey (1642), 120; Viking sculpture, 69; Youth Hostel, 220

Henderskelfe, village destroyed, 134

Hilton, Church, Norman, 112

Hinderwell, 113, 115, 140

Hole of Horcum, 13

Hovingham, Church, 11th century, 70–1; Villa, Roman, 51

Huntcliff, ironstone mine, 181; ironstone seam, 178; signal station, Roman, 54

Husthwaite, parish, creation of, 110

Hutton Buscel, field pattern, 93–4

Hutton-le-Hole, 117; Douthwaite Dale, 119; enclosure, 118–9; glass working, 224; Lund House Farm, 118–9; place-name, 119; plan, 84; Ryedale Folk Museum, Anglian carving, cottage, 154; longhouse, 150, Viking cross shaft, 70, wheel shed, 164; tourists, 212; Westfield Farm, 26

Hutton Mulgrave, colonisation, 103; Mauley estate, 104; settlement plan, 98

Hutton Village (near Guisborough), jet workings, 175

Ice Age, 13–14

Ingleby Greenhow, church, 111; wheel shed (Drummer Hill), 164, 223

Iron Age, 42–4, 184

Keldholme, place-name, 56; priory, 101, 107

Kempswithin, reclamation, 121–2, 139

Kepwick, barrow, long, 30; flora, grassland, 25; limekilns, 167, 223; limestone quarry, 167; mill, 223; railway, mineral, 194

Kettleness, alum mine, 172, 224; cement works, 224; ironstone mining, 178

Kilburn, fields, 26; parish, creation of, 110

Kildale, improvement

agricultural, 123; enclosure, 114; farmhouses rebuilt, 154; Hall, 147; ironstone mines, Lounsdale, Warren Moor, 224; jet working, 174; motte and bailey castle, 74; peat bog, West House, 15; Percy Rigg Iron Age Houses, 42; Vaccary, Lounsdale, 105; Viking burial, 67

Kilton, castle, norman, 74; ironstone mine, 181; mill, 223

Kingthorpe, Domesday entry, 76; House, 146

Kirkbymoorside, Buckingham House, 142–3; fields, 26; hedgebreakers, 139; High Hall, 142–3; Low Hall, 148; Petch House, 148; population, 133; roman fields, 51; Viking sculpture, 69; Vivers Hall, 142; watercourse, 124, 129; 73–77 West end, 155–6; windmill, 164, 223

Kirbymisperton, field names, 86

Kirkdale, church, 11th century, 70–1, 111; forest, 27; monastery, Anglian, 64–5; sculpture, Viking, 68; sundial, 11th century, 70–71

Kirkleavington, sculpture, Viking, 69

Kirkleatham, 137

Langdale, assarting, 103; reclamation, 119

Laskill, colliery, Carr Cote, 168, 223; iron working, 178; place-name, 95; reclamation, 119

Lastingham, burial, Viking, 67; church, 108, 112; mill, medieval, 160, 223; monastery, Saxon, 64; monks, Benedictine, 108; place-name, 61

Lazenby, ironstone mine, 181, 224

Leake, limekilns, 167; village drift, 135

Lealholm, ironworking, 178, 224; place-name, 56; tourists, 212

Lease rigg, Mauley estate, 104; place-name, 56; Roman fort, 47–51

Levisham, 101; church, 11th century, 70; Domesday entry, 76; place-name, 55; mill, 223; moor, 19; purchase of by National Park, 221

Lindisfarne, 62–3

Lingdale, colonisation, 103; ironstone mining, 181

Liverton, church, norman carving, 112; colonisation, 103; ironstone mining, 140, 181, 224

Locker Low Moor, fields, ancient, 26

Lockton, place-name, 55

Loftus, alum quarries, 171, 224; cement works, 174; ironstone mine, 182, 224; Tom Leonard Mining Museum, 182

Lyke Wake Walk, 15, 19, 42, 214

Lythe, monastic cell, Anglian (?), 64; Mauley tenants, 104; sculpture, Viking, 68; townships in, 79, 81

Malton, church, norman, 112; fort, Roman, 46–52; priory, 74, 90; wool trade, 186

Malton Cote, 91–3, 110

Manners family, Earls of Rutland, 142

Margrove park, ironstone mine, Stanghowe, 181, 224

Mauley family estates, 104–5

May Moss, peat bog, 15

Mesolithic period, 29–30

Mickleby, colonisation, 103

Mickledales, place-name, 61

Middlesborough, iron industry, 181

Middleton, 85, 118; church, Anglian fabric in, 65; church, 11th century, 70; Domesday entry, 76; enclosure, 116; field pattern, 129; Hall, 146; Meredyke, 42, 192; place-names, 55, 62; Saintoft Grange improvements, 123; sculpture, Viking, 67–9; strip fields, 87

Moorsholm, 103, 134

Morton Grange, 87

Mount Grace Priory, 107

Mowbray, Vale of, 4; iron age settlement, 44

Mulgrave Castle, 104; castle, norman, 78

National Park, 219–21

Nawton, houses 17th century, 154; Tower (shooting lodge), 146

Neolithic period, 30–31

Nettle Dale, 88

Newbiggin, Hall, 143–4, 146

Newburgh Priory, 108–9

Newbridge, Limestone quarry, 194

Newgate Bank, 185

Newholm, jet-working, 174

Newton Dale, 14, 20, 39;

forest drive, 203; railway, 195, 198; trees, decayed, 119

Newton Mulgrave, settlement plan, 98

Newton on Rawcliffe, Domesday entry, 75; pond, 124

Normanby, colonisation, 103; place-name, 66; settlement plan, 98

Nunnington, threshing mill, 164

Old Byland, boundary, 39; church, Anglo-Saxon, 112; church, Norman, 112; Domesday entry, 112; fields, 26

Old Malton, church, 112; roman fort nearby, 47

Ord, J.W., 31, 134, 165

Ormesby, grange, 109

Orm Gamalson, 71

Osgodby, Byland Abbey purchase, 110

Osmotherley, Lyke Wake Walk starts, 15, 213, 214

Oswaldkirk, cross, 66, 69

Oulston, villa, roman, 51

Ousegill Head, forest, 16

Outgang, 192

Oxford Clay, 12–13

Pannierways, 189–90; packhorse bridges, 190; Danby, Duck Bridge, 190; Glaisdale, Beggars Bridge, 200; Rievaulx, rebuilding, 190; Westerdale, Hunters Sty Bridge, 190

Peak, alum mines, 172; cement kiln, 174

Pickering, 14; church, cruciform, norman, 112; cottages, 156–8; Domesday entry, 75–7; motte and bailey, 78; parliamentary survey (1651), 119; place-name, 61; strip fields, 90, 96; Viking sculpture, 69; Vicarage, 147; woodland, destruction, 119; woodland, medieval, 96

Pickering, Forest of, 96, 114, 96, 114; Norden survey (1619), 120

Pickering Vale of, 11, 13, 14, 20, 29, 38, 39, 44, 46, 51, 54

Pockley, place-name, 61; shrinkage, post-medieval, 134; watercourse, moorland, 129; White Cottage, 150

Population, Ayton, East and West, 208; Castleton, growth in, 136; explosion caused by ironstone indusry, 141;

Farndale, 207; fluctuation in vilages, 136, 207–8; Helmsley, 133; post-medieval, 133–5; prehistoric, 28; twentieth century, 207–8; Whitby, 135

Port Mulgrave, Ironstone, export of, 179; ironstone mining, 179–80; harbour, 180, 224

Raisdale, 98; enclosure, 116; Hall Garth Farm. 98; Little Raisdale, 98; mill, 162, 223

Ramsdale, mill, 223

Ravenscar, alum quarries, 172, 224; Beast cliff, 20; cement works, 174, 224; Lyke Wake Walk, 8; resort, abortive development, 210–1; windmill, 163–4, 223

recreation, outdoor, 211–5

Redcar, Durham coal, export of, 181; submerged land offshore, 14

Riccaldale, forest, modern, 27

Ridings, 79

Rievaulx, Abbey, 101, 106–10; dissolution of, 113, 116, 141; acquired by Earls of Rutland, 141; iron working, 178, 224; houses, 17th century, 154; Moor, 13; road, for stone haulage, 185, terraces; 145

Rigg, mill 223

Riseborough, Hall, 142

Robin Hood's Bay, 13; cemetery, Saxon, 61; enclosure, 115; fishing industry, 200; homes, second, 210; ironstone, collection from beach, 178; mill, 162, 223; traffic congestion, 213; whinstone quarry, 165, 223

Romans, 29, 45–54; army, 46–51; forts, 47–51; roads, 45, 47–8, 52; settlements, 51–3, 61; signal stations, 48, 53–4; villas, 51–2

Roppa Edge, watercourse, 129

Roseberry Topping, 71; jet working, 224; pits (ironstone?), 176, 224

Rosedale, chimney demolition, 216; collieries, 168; cottages, industrial, 158; glass working, 224; ironstone mining, 12, 136, 182, 195, 224; kilns, 225; mill, 223; monastery, 109; robbed, 142, moor fires, 19; packhorses in 1890, 190; population in twentieth century, 208

Roxby (near Hinderwell), colonisation, 103; house, romano-british, 61; plan, 98;

remains, Saxon, 61; Ridge Lane, 20; Scaling, 95

Roxby (Thornton Dale), Domesday entry, 76; strip fields, 88

Rudland Rigg, colliery, 168–9, 223

Runswick Bay, cement works, 224; enclosure, 115; fishing industry, 200; homes, second, 210; traffic congestion, 213

Ruswarp, mill, 162, 223

Ryedale, boundaries, prehistoric, 36–7; cairnfields, 33; settlements, medieval, 95

Saltburn, cemetery, Saxon, 61; field pattern, 94; ironstone export, 179

Saltersgate Brow, 13

Salton, church, norman, 112

Saltwick Nab, alum works, 172, 224

Sandsend, alum quarries, 172, 224; cement works, 224

Sawdon, place-name, 56

Scaling, colonisation, 103; place-name, 95

Scamridge, dykes, 39–41; long barrows, 30

Scarborough, castle, norman, 78; church, late norman, 112; sognal station, Roman, 54; 64; Spa, 140; tower mill, 164; tourism, 140, 210; unemployment, 209

Scawton, church, norman, 112; parish, creation of, 110

Scugdale, jet working, 175, 224

Seaton, place-name, 61

Selley Bridge, place-name, 56

Sheepwash, 36, 212

Sil Howe, whinstone quarry, 166, 223

Sinnington, Dawson's Wood, 20; mill, 162, 223; sculpture, Viking, 66, 69; Vicarage, 148

Sites of Special Scientific Interest, 207

Skelton, colonisation , 103; enclosure prevented, 134; ironstone mines, 181–2, 224

Skinningrove, iron works, 183, 225; ironstone mining, 178, 180; jet working, 174

Skiplam, place-name, 56

Slape Wath, alum quarries (1604), 171; alum quarry, Rock Hole, 223

Sleightholme, place-name, 56

Sleights, 14; Carr View, 148; Esk Hall, 146; Vicarage, 147–8

Smiddales, iron working, medieval, 177; place-name, 61

Snainton, 72, 88–94; Cliff Grange, 148; Cockmoor Dykes, 39, 93; cottage, High Street, 155–6; Domesday entry, 76; fields, medieval, 88–94; fields Roman, 51; plan, 86; rabbit warrens, 131; sheep farms, medieval, 91, 93; Thorndyke, 89, 93

Sneaton, parish, creation of, 111

Sneck Yat, 43

Snilesworth, boundaries, prehistoric, 36–7; limekilns, 167, 223

Spa Wood, ironstone mine, 180–1, 224

Spaunton, forest, 119; limestone quarry, 183; Lodge, 146; Oldfield Lane, 26

Sproxton, dykes, 38, 40; Grange, 110

Staithes, dock, 180; enclosure, 115; fishing cobles, 140; fishing industry, growth of, 139, 210; ironstone collection from beaches, 178; ironstone mining, 179

Stanghow, colonisaztion, 103; Kateridden, place-name, 103

Star Carr, 30

Stockland, place-name, 56

Stonegate, stone haulage, 193

Stonegrave, church aisles, norman, 112; church, 11th century, 70; sculpture, Viking, 68

Stoupe Brow, alum quarry, 224

Street House, barrow, long, 30

Studfold Ring, 44

Sutton-under-Whitestonecliffe, Garbutt Wood, 20; place-name, 62; pollard tree, 23

Swainby, cairnfield, Near Moor, 34; ironstone kilns, 225; jet working, 180; limekilns, 167, 223; lime spreading, 166–7; population, 20th century, 208

Swinacle, place-pname, 56

Swinton, place-name, 56, 62

Tarn Hole, iron working, 177, 224

Teesside, market for farm produce, 139

Thirkleby, Domesday entry, 77; parish, creation of, 110

Thirley Coates, place-name, 61

Thirsk, castle, Norman, 82

Thornbrough, place-name, 56

Thornton Dale, Domesday entry, 76, 101; Thornton Hall, 144; tourists, 212; town field, 88; Vicarage (Comber House), 148

Threshing machines, 164

Tocketts, iron works, 181, 224, mill, 160–1, 223; Scalestedes, 95

Tripsdale, ironworking, early, at Hagg House, 224

Troutsdale, place-name, 56

Tuke, John, 121, 139, 154

Turner, Sir Charles, 114, 121–3, 130, 137-8, 146, 154

Ugthorpe, colonisation, 103; Mauley estate, 104; school, 137; windmill, 161, 164 223

Upleatham, ironstone mining, 181, 224

Vicarages, 147–8; Ellerburn, 147; Great Edstone, 48; Hawnby, 147; Pickering, 147; Sinnington, 148; Slieghts, 147; Thornton Dale, 148

Viking period, 65–71; churches, 66–71; iron working 68; jet, 68; landscape, 71; place-names, 65–6; sculpture, 66–71

Wades Causeway, 9, 47–8, 52, 185

Wapentakes, 79

Welburn, grange, 109; Hall, 142, replaced (1891), 146

Welldale, 88

West Ayton, High Hall, 148

Westerdale, enclosure, 114; enclosure, Iron Age at Crown End, 42; iron mining (?) pits, 177; orthostatic field walls, 130; tourists at Hob Hole, 213

Wheeldale, forge, medieval, 177, 244; road, Roman, see Wades Causeway

Whitby, Abbey, 42, 63, 65; dissolution of, 113, 115, 142; Abbey House, 142; Airy Hill, 95; caravan sites, 214; church, 112; fishing, 135; jet, 135; mill, tower, 164; Newton House, 203; Norwegian speakers, 66; pannierways, focus on, 190; piers, 185–6; place-name, 55; railways, 194–8; Roman camp (?), 49; Saxon comb, 62; sea traffic, 186; settlements, medieval, 95; ship building, 135, 193; tombstone, Viking, 68; town crest, 12; whaling, 135, 186; wool trade, 186, 189

Whorlton, castle, norman, 78; church, norman, 78; motte and bailey, 78; vaccary (Scugdale), 105

William the Conqueror, 73, 76, 185

Wilton, Domesday entry, 76; Friar Dyke, 38; parish, creation of, 111

Wreckhills, cement works, 174; ironstone mining, 180, 224; ironworks, 180, 225

Wydale, 88; cote, 93; Hall, 146; place-name, 56

Wykeham, Abbey, 142, alterations, 146, left empty, 163; church, 158; cottages, 158; forestry, 203; Saxon settlement, 61

Yearsley, colliery, 167; Domeday entry, 77

Yedingham, nunnery, 90–1

Yoad Wath, mill, 223

York, 45, 47, 52, 71; Danish conquest (867), 65; Edwin baptised, 62; 1069 massacre, 76; St. Mary's Abbey, 101, 108; wool trade through Clifton, 186

York, Vale of, 39; iron age settlement, 44

Yorkshire Gliding Club, 44

Youth Hostels, 211, building in Helmsley (1964), 220